Writing in Flow

Writing In *Flow*

keys to enhanced creativity

Susan K. Perry, PhD

WRITER'S DIGEST BOOKS
CINCINNATI, OHIO

www.writersdigest.com

Dedication

To my parents,

Daniel and Frances Selden,

in appreciation of their countless
and generous gifts of a lifetime

Visit our Web site at www.writersdigest.com for information on more resources for writers.

To receive a free biweekly E-mail newsletter delivering tips and updates about writing and about Writer's Digest products, send an E-mail with "Subscribe Newsletter" in the body of the message to newsletter-request@writersdigest.com, or register directly at our Web site at www.writersdigest.com.

03 02 01 00 99   5 4 3 2 1

Library of Congress Cataloging-in-Publication Data

Perry, Susan K.
    Writing in flow / by Susan K. Perry.
        p.   cm.
    Includes bibliographical references and index.
    ISBN 0-89879-929-5 (hc. : alk. paper)
    1. Authorship. 2. Creative writing. I. Title.
PN145.P44   1999
808'.02—dc21   99-19820
                                                                    CIP

2292-8294
1/00

Edited by Jack Heffron
Production edited by Bob Beckstead
Interior designed by Wendy Dunning
Cover designed by David Mill
Production coordinated by Kristen D. Heller

Acknowledgments

I want to thank the poets and fiction writers I interviewed for allowing me to quote them in all their endearing and surprising humanity. I owe gratitude to Mihaly Csikszentmihalyi, for his beneficial insights and organizing hints, as well as to the other members of my doctoral committee who helped ensure this was good social science as well as a book of interest to writers: Libby Douvan, Judy Stevens-Long, Jeremy Shapiro, Michele Harway, and my friend and colleague, Jan Jackson.

Sheree Bykofsky, my agent, and Janet Rosen, her associate, get my pleased appreciation for their persistence and warm responsiveness. Grateful acknowledgments go to Jack Heffron, my editor at Writer's Digest Books, and to Richard Hunt, the Marketing Director, both of whose rare x-ray vision saw the promise in my proposal. I also owe thanks to the following for offering questions, suggestions, and other helpful contributions: Frank Barron, Irene Borger, Idelle Davidson, Bruce Dobkin, M.D., David Groves, Melanie Lee Johnston, James Corey Kaufman, Susan Newman, Kathy Sena, Arlene Sobel, Jeff and Joan Stanford and Tina B. Tessina. Doug Dutton of Dutton's Brentwood Books is gratefully recognized, as is Diane Leslie who runs their Book Group with Author series, from which I culled four of my interviewees.

Thanks, too, to all of the following for so generously sharing their musings about flow along with the friendship that means so much to me: Troy Corley, Suzy Jacobs, Jan Johnson, W. K. Scott Meyer, Marilyn Oliver, Jim Valentine, and, above all, members of the Long Beach-based Writers' Bloc, present and past: all the Steves (Reynolds, Barber, Deeble), Patti Couch, Lisa Liken, Jeff Glover, Greg Kamei, Curt Blamey, Rich DiCapua, John and Peggy Knopf, Val Harner, Marguerite Marler, Jane Boyd and Elizabeth King.

Infinite love, of course, goes to my sons, Simon Lakkis and Kevin Lakkis, who continually inspire, delight and challenge me. Finally, thanks beyond words are owed to my husband Stephen Perry, who besides providing me with relevant quotes and acting as test animal for my flow hypotheses, read through the entire manuscript several times, smoothed out some rough spots, let me know when I might be crossing a line (coming from him, I took all such suggestions seriously), and shared with me his deep knowledge of some of the best poets in the country, which made me realize for the first time how and why the poetry section of our home library had gotten so huge. I take full responsibility for all remaining clichés.

About the author

Susan K. Perry, Ph.D., a social psychologist, was educated at UCLA, Pacific Oaks College in Pasadena, and The Fielding Institute in Santa Barbara, where she earned her doctorate in Human Development. She is an instructor at the UCLA Extension Writers' Program and an adjunct in psychology at Woodbury University in Burbank. Her previous books include *Fun Time, Family Time*; *The Twelve-Month Pregnancy* (with Barry Herman, M.D.); and *Playing Smart: A Parent's Guide to Enriching, Offbeat Learning Activities for Ages 4-14*. Dr. Perry has written more than seven hundred articles on psychological and other topics for such publications as the *Los Angeles Times*, *Los Angeles Magazine*, *USA Today*, *Billboard*, *Woman's World*, *Parenting* and many others. A Contributing Editor to *Child*, *L.A. Parent* and *Valley* magazines, she has also published numerous personal essays, book reviews, advice columns, and a sprinkle of poetry.

Among Dr. Perry's awards are the Outstanding Service Article Award from the American Society of Journalists and Authors, and the First Place Award of Excellence for Feature Writing given by the Parenting Publications of America. She has been featured as an expert on television, radio, and in a wide variety of publications, such as *Ladies' Home Journal*, *Daily News*, *Hartford Courant*, *Suburban Journals of St. Louis*, and regularly addresses writers' organizations and classes. She is on the board of the Southern California chapter of the American Society of Journalists and Authors, and is a member of the American Psychological Association's Division of Psychology and the Arts. She lives in Los Angeles with her husband in an old Spanish-tile-roofed house behind a white picket fence and a lush rose garden, where she keeps no pets but is entranced by literary and stuffed bunnies.

Table of contents

Foreword

MIHALY CSIKSZENTMIHALYI

There is much written about writing—the process of creating a poem or a novel is a source of endless fascination, especially to those who have tried their hands at it. There are poems whose theme is the *ars poetica*, there are uncounted fictional and biographical accounts of how hard and how wonderful it is to bring a story out of thin air. Many of these descriptions give vivid insights into the subjective experience of writing. Yet to my knowledge nobody has asked a large number of distinguished authors to describe how they think and what they feel during the creative process, so as to provide a comprehensive and systematic description of the art of writing.

At least not up to this point; for Susan Perry has done the job for us. And what a fascinating job it is. This volume is alive with the distinctive voices of great writers, preserved in the unobtrusive yet scintillating medium of her own writing. Readers who have struggled with verse or prose will recognize the ring of truth in these descriptions. Those who are just curious to know what's involved will have a chance to get a glimpse into the strange world where as yet untold stories gestate.

Creative individuals—painters, sculptors, physicists, musicians . . .— have left many accounts of what goes on in consciousness during the creative process. But writers have the advantage of being able to describe this process in their own medium, in words. This brings their accounts to reflect much closer the actual mental process, so that in reading some of the excerpts Perry quotes one can almost imagine oneself being in the place of the person writing. The dance of images and emotions in the poet's head comes alive so vividly that readers may be excused for believing that it takes place in their own mind.

But Perry's volume is not just a series of exciting glimpses into the creative process. For those who appreciate a more systematic understanding, she has organized her material in terms of a conceptual model—based on the theory of flow—which brings order and meaning to the interview material. The model and Perry's application of it takes the concrete descriptions to a level of generalization that gives them added power. Yet she has been wise to conceal the conceptual apparatus enough so that it never becomes obtrusive. The reader who likes reality straight, without the framing of theory, will barely notice its existence.

To end on a personal note, I must say that in the past twenty-five years I have often thought of the quip attributed to Leonardo da Vinci: "Unfortunate the master who has no apprentices to surpass him." Indeed one feels like a failure if one's work does not stimulate the next generation to do better. Therefore a book like this one, which builds on my writing but takes it into a whole new dimension, is extremely satisfying. But I am sure it will be almost as satisfying to everyone who reads it.

Introduction

FLOW IS A RELATIVELY NEW TERM for an essential and universal human experience. You know you've been in flow when time seems to have disappeared. When you're in flow, you become so deeply immersed in your writing, or whatever activity you're doing, that you forget yourself and your surroundings. You delight in continuing to write even if you get no reward for doing it —monetary or otherwise— and even if no one else cares whether you do it. You feel challenged, stimulated, definitely not bored. Writing in flow, you're often certain you're tapping into some creative part of yourself—or of the universe— that you don't have easy access to when you're not in this altered state. Sports figures call this desired condition being "in the zone."

Many books have been written that claim to offer the one true way to write or, at best, the several true ways to write. Some of these may even be helpful for entering flow. Many concentrate on particular aspects of writing fluency, advising you to "let go," or "write from the heart." I believe that each of these advice books leaves out crucial information. This book differs from others in that it is not based on one person's secrets of success, but rather on the widely varying secrets used by *many* successful writers.

You can also, as I did, read hundreds of interviews and profiles of writers in which some aspects of the creative writing experience are mentioned. Until now no one has systematically collected information or looked for underlying patterns about writing in flow, which is the most likely and enjoyable psychological state from which creative work emerges. One of the age-old questions is "Do we have any control over the muse?" By asking writers how they prepare to write, and also how they believe they enter flow, I sought to discover if those preparations were the keys to flow. What does a creative writer experience in the days, hours or moments just before the shift into flow begins? Is it sudden or is there a slide along a continuum of consciousness? Might there be larger themes that connect the many personalized ways various writers have found to induce flow? How much control can a creative writer have over flow entry and thus, perhaps, over the so-called muse herself?

I investigated poets, short-story writers and novelists for whom writing is a major part of their lives (although not all of them make their living at it), and who, in most cases, enter flow with some frequency too. Participants included both those who publish literary work and writers who write in popular genres such as mystery or science fiction. I studied those who are succeeding in their chosen field. Among them are half a dozen Pulitzer Prize winners, as well as writers who have received American Book Awards, National Book Awards, Pushcart Prizes, Guggenheims, National Endowment for the Arts Awards, MacArthur Fellowships and Nebula and Hugo Awards. Several have appeared on national best-seller lists. Former and current U.S. Poet Laureates participated. Each is producing written work regularly and getting it published regularly also.

While at least one researcher has found that few individuals can easily describe their entry into flow, on the contrary, *my* interviewees *did* talk about it—with delight, at length and, in many instances, with extraordinary insight. And regardless of whether writers are more psychologically astute than other creators, they are certainly more articulate and original in the way they express themselves.

As no two writers are alike and no two person's needs, personalities, personal histories or tendencies are identical, so too, your preferred manner of flow entry may be entirely different from the way others do it. Nevertheless, I have found that all of the methods used by writers have certain aspects in common, certain purposes they fulfill. Once you understand how flow entry happens to contemporary writers struggling with real-life jobs, families, insecurities and fears, you can choose to try several routes and determine for yourself what works for you.

Whether you're a poet, novelist, short-story writer, essayist or creative nonfiction writer—whether you are just starting out or are already an accomplished writer—you will learn ways to enter flow and enjoy writing more.

This book is primarily based on an intensive study I completed for my doctoral dissertation. It also includes material from additional research I performed later. Social scientists, psychologists and other research-minded readers who are interested in how I chose my interviewees and how I arrived at my assertions and conclusions may read the detailed chapter in the Appendix describing how I conducted the research. Chapter one describes the various attitudes writers have about how much control it's possible to have over the creative process. Here you'll also gain a much deeper understanding of what flow is and what the benefits of writing in flow are. Chapter two zeroes in on what the experience of flow is like in writing, with examples of the many metaphors writers use in thinking about the shift into the altered state. This information will help you recognize your flow experiences, which is valuable for increasing them.

Part Two is the core of the book, where you will begin to learn the answer to the question: How can I make the shift into the timeless, totally engaged state of writing in flow? If you're like the vast majority of writers, you maneuver into a writing session with a particular pattern of thought—which some think of, paradoxically, as nonthought—and with the help of a routine. Such routines often include one or more rituals, however brief and unremarkable the rituals may be. I'll share with you what I discovered about what deeper purposes are being served by each of these habits of thinking, routines and rituals. After collecting a vast amount of information from writers, I divided these deeper purposes into five Master Keys. Each Key is based on one or more of the elements of flow that most intimately affect the creative writing process.

The first two Keys, "Have a Reason to Write" and "Think Like a Writer" are part of your whole self and way of relating to the world. They involve aspects of your life that are relevant to the process prior to any particular writing session. The last three are concurrent to the actual writing itself: "Loosen Up," "Focus In" and "Balance Among Opposites." All three of these need to come into play very near the time you begin to write—and throughout the process—if you are to enter flow and stay there for some time during that session.

Each of these Master Keys blends into the next—and back again, in a cyclical system. Thus, for example, I talk about planning in Key One, as part of the motivation and challenge involved in getting started. Planning (or letting go of one's plans) will also be mentioned in Key Three, as part of the loosening-up process, and again in Key Five, where it relates to how "in control" you are while writing. Another example is challenge: it's a motivator, leading you toward greater interest in your work, which helps your focusing-in process, which may also relate back to an increased sense of confidence, and so on.

These Master Keys might be thought of as skills or as capacities or as attitudes—each is needed for the best writing. Five chapters discuss each Key in turn, from having a strong enough reason to write and thinking like a writer, to loosening up, focusing in and balancing among several contradictory opposites. You will discover which of the Master Keys you have most control over, and you will also learn how to affect even those aspects that seem most resistant to change.

In Part Three, we get to the specific techniques writers use to make flow happen. Chapter eight answers the intriguing quantitative questions, such as how long writers write and how much of that time is spent in flow. Here you'll learn that you can be a successful writer whether you work on your novel for a half hour a day or you lose yourself in a trance for three days at a time. Chapter nine details each of the many idiosyncratic ways scribes have found to shift into that lovely state of consciousness in which the work proceeds smoothly. Chapter ten tells how major writers avoid, reframe or cope with writer's block, and how you can learn to flow past such blocks to be a better writer.

Interspersed throughout the chapters are the answers to questions that have come to me from students, friends and others who have heard of my flow research. However unique your life circumstances and writing experiences may be, you'll learn that others have dealt with analogous quandaries. By sharing their problems and a variety of possible solutions with you, I believe you, too, will discover ways to enhance your own creativity and enjoy the benefits of flow.

part one

An Ode to Flow

1 Oh, To Be In Flow Now That April's There

A FEW YEARS AGO, a friend challenged me to write a short story. "I dare you to write fiction," he said. I'd been a professional nonfiction writer for many years, and my first response was, "I don't take dares." My second response, not spoken aloud, was, "Why should I? Anyway, I can't." It had been many years since my last efforts at creative writing: a miserably melodramatic short story or two composed at the cusp of puberty and a folder full of hormone-tortured poems written in high school.

Nevertheless, I found myself thinking about the plot of a certain short story that just might need to be written. Always fascinated by time travel, I imagined a woman with aspects of my history who finds an old watch that, when she winds it, takes her back through the years. Before I'd wake up fully in the morning I would mentally work out the details of the plot. Soon, enough of the action was clear to me that I felt compelled to stop my regular work and begin writing the story.

Then an amazing thing happened to me: time stopped. I was tapping away on the computer, composing, deleting, changing a word or phrase here and there, losing myself in the life of the character who was a lot like me but who was also completely new, until I came to a stopping place. I looked at the clock on my study wall and was shocked to realize that two hours had passed. And I had actually enjoyed every unnoticed moment of that time.

Now, for those who lose themselves in their work regularly, this is hardly worthy of note. To me, though, it was a revelation.

My usual way of working at my writing is more like this: Sensing the clock ticking away the seconds, I struggle to focus. My attention is caught by a small bird on the climbing rosebush outside. I examine the windowsill in case the mating lizards I once glimpsed there have reappeared. I leave a couple of phone messages, then reach out via E-mail for some kind of contact that might be more interesting than what I'm working on. Beyond the computer screen, my eyes light on a shelf crowded with novels I urgently want to be reading, *now*. I promise myself a long lunch break, very soon. Finally, aware of time passing wastefully, I force myself to return to work.

Time, for many of us, whether we're writing or doing something else, is often spent in this sort of distracted manner. We measure the passing of that half-hearted time in seconds and minutes and hours.

Then there are the lucky individuals who, more often than most, find themselves immersed in activities during which time ceases to matter, to register, when they forget themselves and everything else but the task at hand, when the work flows, when *they* are in flow. When I peek into my husband Stephen's writing room next door (if he has forgotten to shut it), it's obvious how single-mindedly focused he is, still in his bathrobe, working on his latest poem, oblivious to the squirrel on the balcony, unconcerned over his lack of breakfast, unaware of whether it is day or night, or, for that matter, what year it is.

Driven by awe and envy, I decided to learn more about this essential difference in our working habits—and to learn how I, and other writers, might more dependably enter flow, in which the best writing often seems to emerge almost effortlessly. This book is the result of that intensive inquiry.

As well as being one of the formal participants in my research study—right down to the official tape-recorded interview with carefully coded and tabulated results—Stephen served also as a kind of especially agreeable and handy lab rat whose behavior I was able to observe closely in the more natural setting of home.

Three kinds of writers

In the writing classes I teach and among my friends and acquaintances, I've found that would-be and novice writers usually come in three kinds. The first includes those who figure that when inspiration strikes, they'll know it, and then, and only then, will they be able to produce the great works of which they dream (or the works that will make them wealthy enough to quit their day jobs).

The second batch of writers are those who plan to get down to writing seriously as soon as they are sufficiently prepared. One friend, for example, intends to write his best-selling novel as soon as he manages to get his memory working sufficiently well to keep all those characters and plot details firmly in mind. Meanwhile he is studying reruns of *The X-Files*, taking notes on each program, struggling to get the convoluted plot clear in his mind, all in hopes, he tells us—perhaps only semifacetiously—of improving his memory. Then there's the young man who plans to get himself a Ph.D. in literature before attempting to write his own fiction. "I first have to know what's come before," he explains.

The third group of writers believes that it's possible to have total control over one's writing output. This view was succinctly epitomized for me by a rather crusty old friend of ours I'll call Bill. A group of our friends, several of whom have written some fiction, were at our home for a party. Most everyone had had a little to drink, some a lot. A flip chart was against one wall of the living room, leftover from the monthly meeting of my doctoral co-students. Stephen got up and performed a completely incomprehensible lecture, complete with meaningless (to all but him) diagrams on the flip chart. The group's good-humored heckling had us all in hysterics.

At that point, because my own glass or two of champagne had taken effect by then, I was itching to take marker in hand and share with my friends what I was studying about writers and flow. The moment I stood at the flip chart and opened my mouth, though, Bill spoke up. "What nonsense! All anyone has to do is plant their butt in the chair and write."

Now, I will concede that "the butt in the chair" theory of writing has some merit. Self-discipline and regularity are essential to many successful writers, as we'll see in later chapters. What's missing from Bill's homespun theory, however, is the *how*. Telling someone to "just do it" is akin to telling someone who's depressed that all she has to do is "think happy thoughts" and happiness and joy will follow. Something is keeping the depressed person from making the very efforts that must be made in order to turn the tide of mood from glum to cheerful, whether that something is chemical, cognitive or a combination of other complex factors. Similarly, when you're not writing but you insist you wish you were, something is getting in the way. At times, the *something* is lack of knowledge about all the many options that are available to make writing happen.

Among more experienced writers, I discovered, there is also a *fourth* group: those who have learned that they do have a certain amount of control over their writing process. A majority of the most productive writers with whom I spoke fit into this group.

Liberating writers from self-imposed constraints and limitations is one of the goals of this book. And once you learn how exquisitely pleasurable writing can be in a flow state—and how to enter such a state more predictably—you're more likely to write more and produce better work.

How flow occurs

Theory states that you enter a flow state when the following requirements are in place:

1. Your activity has clear goals and gives you some sort of feedback;
2. you have the sense that your personal skills are well suited to the challenges of the activity, giving you a sense of potential control;
3. you are intensely focused on what you're doing;
4. you lose awareness of yourself, perhaps feeling part of something larger;
5. your sense of time is altered, with time seeming to slow, stop or become irrelevant; and
6. the experience becomes self-rewarding.

If you're one of those people who can concentrate this intensely, you can enter a state of flow whether you're pursuing a hobby, painting a picture or writing a poem. Flow can occur in any pastime, including athletic activities, during video and computer games, in conversations with friends, while pleasure reading and during sex—each of these activities is self-rewarding and flow-inducing, offering the participant total absorption. When you're intimate with flow, you seem to live life more fully, looking forward both to work you get paid for and to activities more typically thought of as fun. You *want* to be doing exactly what you're doing, regardless of any external considerations. It can feel glorious.

Those for whom being in a flow state is a frequent happening can be found in any field, though it is not unusual to find them pursuing artistic careers. It's not that artists of all kinds cannot be miserable about how their work is progressing, or despairing of ever receiving public rewards. Yet they persist.

Why does flow happen? We *make* it happen when our mind or body is voluntarily stretched to its limit, in the effort to accomplish something difficult or worthwhile. This way of characterizing flow was first set forth by University of Chicago psychologist and researcher Mihaly Csikszentmihalyi, who has been studying the subject for more than two decades. He decided to use the word *flow* for this experience because this is the word that is so often used by individuals themselves. (Sometimes a particular profession will evolve its own word for the state of total involvement; a dancer told me that the altered state in which dancers feel themselves suspended above the floor is known as dancer's "float.")

Csikszentmihalyi explored the intricacies of flow in his popular books *Flow: The Psychology of Optimal Experience* and *Finding Flow: The Psychology of Engagement With Everyday Life*, among others. He and his colleagues found that "every flow activity . . . provided a sense of discovery, a creative feeling of transporting the person into a new reality. It pushed the person to higher levels of performance, and led to previously undreamed-of states of consciousness. In short, it transformed the self by making it more complex."

Just about everyone experiences flow at some time in their lives. The fact is, individuals in a variety of professions, contexts and studies describe flow in remarkably similar terms. For instance, David Crosby, a musician, described it thus:

> It often happens when I'm between waking and sleeping. This motor-mouth mind will kind of shut down, and then BAM! This stuff will start to come, and I'll turn on the light quickly and write, write, write, and play, play, write, and then "Fantastic!" And about that time my other mind is starting to kick back in and say, "David, you're cool! Whoaa buddy!"

While being in flow itself may feel rather neutral, it often taps into positive emotions. That seems to be why many people will persistently pursue activities that have few external rewards. British singer Graham Bell describes this surfeit of feeling as: "A lot of the time I'm singing, it's also like crying; I feel tremendously good, life is just so wonderful,

Q: I'm sure I get into flow when I'm watching TV. Time sure seems to stop. And what about gambling? Or drumming?

A: And what about sleeping? These activities do not provide what are considered true flow experiences because, to enter flow, you have to be doing something that presents enough of a challenge to use your skills so that you feel truly engaged, neither bored nor anxious. Most of the time, television watching isn't demanding enough to qualify as flow. Addictive perhaps, but not challenging. Gambling also can be addictive, but not very hard work. I can pull the nickel slot machine handle for hours, though the altered state I enter is more like being a drugged zombie who just can't stop, rather than feeling that I'm truly using either my mind or body to best advantage. (If, when playing cards, you're busily strategizing, that might be another story.) I have no doubt that a serious drummer, or one who is practicing to be one, can enter flow. *Listening* to drums, like listening to any music, can be more relaxing than demanding, unless you're actively participating, struggling to figure out the composer's intentions. The likelihood of flow rises with the level of challenge.

it's an incredible feeling." A rock climber put it this way: "I feel really high in a way, grateful that I'm up there and not just drudging along in life below."

Classic flow

People experienced flow, of course, long before the term was invented to describe it. Tolstoy, for example, described the attributes of flow perfectly in *Anna Karenina* (first published in book form in 1878). Here he describes the experience of farm-owner Levin as he learns to mow grass with a scythe (we can be reasonably sure he is describing his own experience with flow in writing as well):

"I will swing less with my arm and more with my whole body," he thought, comparing Titus's row, which looked as if it had been cut with a line, with his own unevenly and irregularly scattered grass. . . .

He thought of nothing, wished for nothing, but not to be left behind the peasants, and to do his work as well as possible. He heard nothing but the swish of scythes, and saw before him Titus's upright figure moving away, the crescent-shaped curve of the cut grass, the grass and flower heads slowly and rhythmically falling before the blade of his scythe, and ahead of him the end of the row. . . .

Levin lost all sense of time, and could not have told whether it was late or early now. A change began to come over his work, which gave him immense satisfaction. In the midst of his toil there were moments during which he forgot what he was doing, and it came easy to him, and at those same moments his row was almost as smooth and well cut as Titus's. But as soon as he recollected what he was doing, and began trying to do better, he was at once conscious of the difficulty of his task, and the row was badly mown. . . .

More and more often now came those moments of unconsciousness, when it was possible not to think of what one was doing. The scythe cut by itself. These were happy moments.

In this passage, it's easy to see flow in action: Levin realizes what his goal is (to mow as well as Titus) and figures out a way to do the job (using his whole body), sensing that his skills are indeed up to the challenge. He forgets himself and focuses on the job. His feedback comes when he matches the evenness of the other mowers' rows. Time feels altered. Positive emotion and good work accompany the flow state, whereas as soon as self-consciousness returns, the outcome suffers.

To better understand what goes on as your consciousness makes the shift into flow, think of it as somewhat comparable to the shift that takes place from wakefulness to sleep. Sleep researchers, in fact, have long tried to determine what triggers sleep, and it is now generally believed that there is no single point at which sleep appears.

Another way to understand the shift to a flow state is to compare it to the shift to sexual arousal. In both instances, the subjective sense of time is altered; attention is absorbed by the activity; the sense of space shrinks to that necessary for the activity. In both, body perceptions change, causing a desired sex object to appear especially attractive, and, in flow, causing you to forget to eat or rest.

The benefits of writing in flow

While there is no scientific proof that flow necessarily produces top-quality writing, research has found that many writers are convinced they produce much of their best work while they are in such an altered situation. When you're in flow, scenes and images almost seem to concoct themselves. As one writer told me, "I have to keep reminding myself that all I have to do is get into that place and the language will furnish itself."

If you're a fiction writer or poet, or an independent writer of any kind, the overwhelming odds are that it's up to you to get yourself to write. Whatever state of consciousness is most motivating and effective for getting the work done is clearly a useful state to tap into.

Flow is significant to creative people for another reason. Research has found that creators do not learn to increase the ratio of successful "hits" to overall output over a lifetime of work. Keeping in mind that all such generalizations are suspect when it comes to predicting your unique life's outcome, the gist of the theory is this: the more prolific you are overall, the more likelihood of your producing great work. At least if we judge by the historical record of eminent creators, what matters most is to keep producing. If you would create more great works, you must create more. Therefore, entering flow easily and frequently should enable you to write more fluently and prolifically, and thus, potentially, to produce more distinguished and lasting fiction or poetry.

Stopping time

Writing in flow feels good, makes you want to write more often, tends to keep you writing longer. Yet the advantages of learning to enter flow go far beyond producing good writing regularly. Flow has everything to do with the metaphysics of time. Does time move? Do *we* move through it? Psychologists have studied how subjective psychological time differs from clock time and have found that when you're engaged in something, time feels different. A number of philosophers (not to mention mystics), while not protesting the experience we all have of the flow of time, still deny the objective reality of the phenomenon. "Everything *is*." Helga Nowotny, a social thinker, has gone so far as to imagine a variety of uchronias, idealized societies similar to utopias, in which time is manipulated to finally satiate our human "longing for the moment." Novelist Barbara Kingsolver expresses one way of conceiving of this longing:

> I've always had this sort of undercurrent of terror flowing through me when I think about time passing. When I look at a calendar I feel this profound urge not to stop time, but to stick pins in every inch of the way to make sure that it's attached to me, to make sure that I have passed through and will know that I've passed through that passage of

time when it's over, and that it won't have just vanished. And writing is the way I do that.

My own father owns dozens of clocks. He inherited a melancholy strain from his own father regarding time passing, and passed it along to me. But I believe you cannot control time, nor need you mourn its passing. Instead, it can be transcended, if only in your mind. Flow is about stopping the movement of time psychologically. If you live in flow, in the moment, *each* moment, you don't need to live in fear of loss. Each moment is all moments. Believing this, how could we *not* wish to prolong the amount of time we spend in this happily absorbed, time-suspended state?

2 | What Flow in Writing Feels Like

IF FLOW IS SUCH A DESIRABLE STATE to be in when you're trying to produce a novel or poem—and a majority of regularly publishing writers say it is—it's nonetheless a condition, for many writers, that's more often wished for than achieved. A novice writer told me recently, "I sat down with an idea but it just didn't go anywhere." And then he gave up. That seems to be a common experience: a tiny flash of something, a glimmer of inspiration, followed by resounding silence. What next? Where to? The opportunity to enter flow seems to be lost before it gets a chance to begin.

If you want to know *how* to enter flow more easily—or, at least, more regularly—it can be worthwhile to first know precisely what it feels like to make that shift in consciousness. It's not that you must know what's happening for it to happen. Still, if you're not smoothly entering into flow in the majority of your writing sessions, and you'd like to, the more you fathom flow's mysterious undercurrents, the more control you'll eventually gain. Rather than resisting flow entry, you'll be able to facilitate it.

Where flow fits into the creative-writing process

Entering flow may feel differently to you depending on where it occurs during your writing. Flow, in fact, can begin at any point in the entire

15

Q. Does flow guarantee quality? I wrote a short story some time back, and was extremely absorbed in it, very much in a flow state, but after I passed it around to several friends, I found that most everybody felt it was way below my standard of fiction at the time.

A. Writing in a flow state is no guarantee that a particular piece of work will pass critical muster. Once the words are down on paper, you have to go through the same polishing and revising process regardless of whether the work emerged from deep flow or from a more highly conscious aware place. That is, does it meet your own standards? In flow, your critical faculties are put aside, for the most part, to allow for a more spontaneous outpouring. Novelist, memoirist and nonfiction author Mark Salzman, who doesn't enter flow often or regularly when he writes, told me he has found that the material that comes to him in flow is "usually clichéd and oversentimental and I usually have to erase it all." His experience is the exception, however, as many writers say they can take what they get from flow and craft it into better work. Some writers also manage to enter flow again and again while rewriting, a process I've heard called "re-visioning."

creative process. To describe it simply, the four stages of the creative process currently accepted by many creativity researchers are preparation, incubation, illumination and verification. For a writer, this means that after you accomplish your preliminary labor, say, immersing yourself in the research and doing some thinking about your initial ideas, you allow the material to incubate for some length of time. Individuals have come up with their own names for this stage, just as they have for flow. When I speak of it—for instance, when I feel compelled to explain why I'm lying down on my bed in the middle of the day, in the middle of work on a writing assignment—it feels right to say "I'm percolating." And I'm not making excuses: something is happening as I lie there. I know, because suddenly I'll jump up and dash back to the computer with fresh mental energy.

Next, your ideas somehow integrate themselves, often seeming to arrive with sudden inspiration (the "now why didn't I think of that before?" phenomenon). Finally, the verification process is when you look at what you've got so far and determine whether it fits your requirements.

Although, when described this way, the creative process seems to be divided into separate stages, it's much more complex than that, with interrelated, overlapping and repeating parts. One researcher's description seems apt: "The incubation phase flitted around inside the immersion [i.e., preparation] phase like a bubble in a very viscous liquid filling an enclosed container."

Like all writers, of course, you look at flow and the creative process through your own unique psychological lens. Esther M. Friesner describes how she moved among the various stages of the creative process when discussing the origins of her Nebula Award-winning short story:

> There are instances in a writer's life when a certain combination of words touches off a spark that won't blow out. All I know is that "Death and the Librarian" sounded like a good title for *something*, and I was going to have to find out what that something was and write it or be haunted forever. . . . I know where I *get* my ideas, but at times they're something else entirely by the time I finally set them down on paper.

To recap: you can enter a flow state anywhere and anytime: during the preparation/thinking/dreaming/planning stage, the incubation stage when you're consciously doing something else (resting, tidying the drawers, playing racquetball) and waiting for the ideas to gel, the illumination/inspiration stage, or the rewriting and revising stage. Two opposing examples show the variability possible, from flowing during first draft to flowing only during revising:

> I never do any "research" until the first draft is finished; all that matters is to begin with the flow, the story, the narrating. Research material then is like swimming in a straitjacket. (John Fowles)

> You have to . . . clean it up, and that's the most pleasant part of the work. From then on I am able to work much longer hours without the anxiety and tension that accompanies the writing of the first draft. (Mario Vargas Llosa)

Incubation, by the way, can be quite lengthy: novelist John Irving reports that he "procrastinates longer with each book—it can take from eighteen months to two years before writing the first word." Naturally, you can't justify all procrastination as part of the incubating process, as later chapters will explore in more detail.

Q: Is "flow" a new discovery?
A: Flow has doubtless been around since the days of cave paintings, when an early artist might well have been so absorbed that
he forgot to listen for the soft sounds of a leopard approaching.
An example of flow from before our era comes from Virginia
Woolf's classic novel, *To the Lighthouse*. In the following scene,
we listen to the thoughts of painter Lily Briscoe as she struggles
before a blank canvas, and we can see clearly the experience of
flow even though it is nowhere named as such:

> Can't paint, can't write, she murmured monotonously, anxiously
> considering what her plan of attack should be. For the mass
> loomed before her; it protruded; she felt it pressing on her eyeballs.
> Then, as if some juice necessary for the lubrication of her faculties
> were spontaneously squirted, she began precariously dipping
> among the blues and umbers, moving her brush hither and thither,
> but it was now heavier and went slower, as if it had fallen in with
> some rhythm which was dictated to her (she kept looking at the
> hedge, at the canvas) by what she saw, so that while her hand
> quivered with life, this rhythm was strong enough to bear her
> along with it on its current. Certainly she was losing consciousness
> of outer things. And as she lost consciousness of outer things, and
> her name and her personality and her appearance, and whether
> Mr. Carmichael was there or not, her mind kept throwing up
> from its depths, scenes, and names, and sayings, and memories
> and ideas, like a fountain spurting over that glaring, hideously
> difficult white space, while she modelled it with greens and blues.

It seems from passages such as these that many individuals
in the past very likely experienced flow and noticed they were
participating in an altered state. Yet flow has only been spot-
lighted and scientifically examined beginning as recently as three
decades ago.

When time stops

To determine, first of all, whether a writer I was going to interview
had experienced flow, I initially asked whether he or she had had the
experience of time stopping or altering when writing. Although a few
said it was a highly unusual experience for them, almost everyone I
spoke to immediately recognized the phenomenon.

You may find that time becomes essentially irrelevant. When the writing session is over, you may find yourself astonished at how much time has actually gone by. Numerous writers said this is exactly what happens to them. Novelist Phyllis Gebauer exemplifies this experience:

> The most recent time this happened was this morning. I sat down to work on my novel, the first few sentences were awkward, I was aware of trying to decide between this word or that, then, bingo! I was up and running (or rather scrawling on the paper) and the next thing I knew an hour had passed and I hadn't stopped to take a shower or get dressed, and it was—gads—midmorning.

In an essay, poet Peter Davison describes how time spent writing "is measured on a different scale, a different continuum from the rest of the world. Five minutes of pure attention to an emerging poem is longer than a week of clocks and hours."

Q. I get into flow in conversation all the time, so why is it so much less common when I'm writing?

A. You need to ask yourself why you get so engaged in conversation. It may be that you're usually talking about what interests you a lot; you're using a variety of skills to keep the conversation involving for the other person; you get feedback from the other person that your insights or contributions are valuable; and nothing much appears to be at stake, which removes performance anxiety. By recognizing this, you can then do some self-reflection about which of these elements is missing from your writing experience that keeps you from entering flow. For instance, are you writing about what interests you, are your skills adequate, do you have a sense of how well you're doing, and do you feel free to be creative without being judged harshly?

Flow's timelessness, for some of us, is the best part of the experience, highly valued for its own sake. It feels incredible.

> [As I enter this state] words come easily from that reservoir I sometimes believe I have, but never quite know how to tap. This is when time ceases to exist, when all my senses are focused on writing; this is the closest I will ever come to an out-of-body experience, and in the end, it is the possibility of re-creating these moments that keeps me going as a writer. (Faye Moskowitz)

I think it's almost always the case when I feel I'm writing well, that happens. Those kinds of parameters of time, time consciousness, actually are very acute to me. I'm one of those people who can sort of wake up in the morning and know within five minutes what time it is. Yet when I'm working, I won't know how much time is elapsed. . . . Most noticeable to me always is the sense of that sort of realm of timelessness, that for me has a real physical manifestation. That really is becoming part of some pulse, other than yourself. I like that a lot. (David St. John)

> **Q.** What about journalists at daily newspapers who are always on a rush-rush due-an-hour-ago deadline. How can they afford to forget time and enter flow?
> **A.** Journalists may be akin to surgeons who have to be totally aware of the time, yet who can block out every distraction and focus fully on the operation they're performing. Time awareness in such cases is an intimate part of the task, rather than a distraction from it.

Losing—and finding—the self

Your sense of self is altered during flow. You may feel strangely when you come out of your writing room, as though you've been participating in some bizarre ritual, as though your body's been taken over by "something." Possibly you've had the common experience of reading over your own work and seeing it as if for the first time. I came upon a linguistic tag of this split when talking to writers about their flow experiences, as they sometimes shift from first to second person (or vice versa) at particular points. I'd like to say that this shift is emblematic of the split between your everyday self and the self in flow, which is somehow "other." It's true that pronoun shifts occur during conversations about *any* subject, yet I noticed a pattern in *where* the shift occurs in conversations about flow. One poet, for example, switches to "you" just as he begins to speak about the way his mind spins off into an imagining mode. Another poet, Carol Muske, vacillates as she describes what she experiences as she exits flow: "But it's so weird. I feel as if I'm coming back to a shore when I come back to normal consciousness. I feel crippled. My body is crumpled up, this shell that you left behind."

Dutch novelist and poet Cees Nooteboom shifts from "I" to "you" as he talks about how he surprises himself with what he writes:

> With the new book that I'm doing, I know more or less what's going to happen. But the adventure of the writing still remains, of how the formulation will come out. How you will formulate it. And you always are suddenly surprised by what you . . .

Because these pronoun shifts occur precisely as writers describe slipping into or out of flow, it suggests that they may be experiencing a split between their nonflowing self and the self that is in flow. This is perhaps common to any creative writer invested in inventing new selves for the aesthetic pleasure of others.

Metaphors to write by

Flow is such a complex psychological process that it's impossible to describe it fully using straightforward, literal language. In order to augment your chances of spending more time in flow, it can be rewarding to consider how you—and other writers—conceptualize the experience. Most authors spontaneously mention a metaphor, whether "flow" or another one, when discussing the state of consciousness in which the words seem to gush out of them. Even those who say they don't experience time seeming to disappear when they write, agree that something distinct is happening when the work is going well.

Nearly twice as many poets as fiction writers offered metaphors in responding to my questions. Poetry is typically a metaphor-intensive form of writing. Yet when I compared the types of metaphors used by poets and by fiction writers, the differences were surprisingly small. Novelists used phrases like "moving into the movie screen," "peeling layers" and "opening a faucet," and poets used such phrases as "enter the poem," "tapping into a vein," "diving underwater" and "turning on a switch at the end of a hall." Not much real difference there. But poets also more often used such evocative phrases as "becoming part of some pulse," "surfing the wave of transformation" and "feeling my way into the skin of the poem."

A few of those I talked to volunteered numerous metaphors and could have gone on almost endlessly. Short-story writer and essayist Faye Moskowitz referred to the sense of an archaeological dig, a writing journey or path, a "plug that must be expelled so imagination can come forth" and "peeling away the layers to the heart or core." Poet and novelist Carol Muske mentioned a "bursting of the dam," "like rolling downhill," out-of-body travel, and being "on automatic pilot," among other metaphors.

But something else stands out in the vast majority of the metaphors: a sense of active participation in making flow happen.

Moving from here to where

You may best be able to express what the experience of entering flow is like for you with metaphors that include a sense of travel, of having to perform a physical movement through space to get to the place of no time, no self and, perhaps, no rationality. In the usual reality, space and time are thought of as two dissimilar concepts, which then collapse in the state of flow.

Some of the movement metaphors people use are about going down, deeper, inside, under and below. This may be because such images best describe the common sense of moving from ordinary reality to the other, more internal, reality: "I come up for air and go back down" (Charles Harper Webb); "like a place, a country I live in or a house that I enter" (Donald Hall). Faye Moskowitz wrote that she removes one layer of memory at a time, going down deeper and deeper, as though on a dig. "At first," she adds, "I am reasonably sure of what I will be charting, but at a certain depth (I can never predict quite where), I uncover what I could not have predicted and, then, flow begins."

When I asked poet Richard Jones how he deals with the blank page, he described the commonplace things he does, such as washing the dishes and making coffee. While he's doing those, something extraordinary is beginning to happen: "I'm dropping down—down into the unconscious part of myself, the fertile part, the dark part where the poems have been preparing themselves." Ethan Canin thinks of flow as a cave he can't purposely find a way into: "You spend so much of your conscious effort to approach this cave and looking at this dreamy, unapproachable mass of rock and there's no entrances, and you look and push there, and nothing is there, and then you give up and you leave, and on the way out, you see an opening. And that's so often how it starts."

Novelist Aimee Liu spoke of how the work turns suddenly real, that she feels as though she is crossing through the movie screen into the movie itself, no longer watching but participating. And Judith Freeman also describes a physical process:

It seems to me like it is getting a running start or getting a start down the same path. And you start walking into the story first in a kind of pedestrian way, a very conscious way, in which you're aware of sitting there rereading what you've written, rereading what I've written. . . . And then it really is as though you're starting to enter a landscape. And when you get to the point where you finish reading what you've already done, and you begin then to take it further, is the point at which I see myself beginning to descend into a timeless, much more timeless, realm. Which is the realm, in a sense, of pure story, pure imagination. And I can almost visualize it as walking down a series of steps that lead me into some sort of wonderful secret illuminated chamber.

U.S. Poet Laureate Robert Pinsky explains his process thus:

Mixed metaphors, mixed experience, mix, mix, mix. Sometimes I am well into the process of trying before the clay gets warm, sometimes the notes come immediately, sometimes I labor at the wet plaster in desperate hurry, sometimes I navigate that coast and those islands for long, multicolored months or years.

The movement in many of these metaphors demonstrates a sense of agency, activity or willfulness. That is, it's a common experience to feel as if you are pushing through, not only on a metaphorically physical level to another place, but that you are exerting your will to get to that place where the work can happen best. Such expressions imply that you don't have to wait passively, but can instead actively invite the muse to join you at your writing desk.

Water and assorted images

If some watery image works for you when you think about the flow state, it's not surprising, as many writers use and embellish water metaphors for the flow experience. Pulitzer Prize-winning poet Philip Levine, who told me he denies the validity of the flow metaphor, uses the term "periods of dryness" for its opposite. Water imagery, then, may be a dominant one for creativity in this culture. According to Lola Haskins, "It's a little like swimming. You get warm on the bank then you dive in, relax, cool off, get out, get dry, lie around for a while, then dive in again. Unless it's gotten late and chilly. Which happens." Bill Mohr describes his "trancey place" this way: "It was sort of like diving, going underwater. Sort of like instead of scuba diving, it was more like old-fashioned take a deep breath and kick down and come back to the surface." Former U.S. Poet Laureate Mark Strand has a humorous take on the water theme: "Before I enter 'the flow' I must extricate myself from 'the trickle' of small household duties."

Other metaphors make use of language and images from the surrounding culture, such as Elizabeth Hand, who, describing the origin of her Nebula Award-winning science-fiction short story, "Last Summer at Mars Hill," writes, "For me, writing has always resembled childbirth in that afterward, regarding the product with delight (or dismay), I am blessedly without memory of the agonizing process which brought it to life." Steve Reynolds has likened it to looking at those 3-D drawings that you have to stare at for a while to "get." He says he can feel himself slip into flow the same way such pictures change in his head when the image finally becomes clear.

One of Stephen Perry's surreal metaphors shows how extensive descriptions for this time-transcended experience can become:

> I use the metaphor of an old-fashioned operator switching terminal, where you plug things in, plug things out. Well, those are the synapses that you plug into one place, plug into another place. And the conscious mind is the operator that does that. It's a logical sort of sequence. This person wants to be connected with this thing, and so you take both of your hands and you plug. For flow, it's eliminating the operator and becoming the whole system itself. The person is still there, in the sense that the mind is still there, and you're both the operator and the switchboard. But the first image I had was some sort of green bubbly floating hair gel, where all of these wires are free to touch whatever they want, to connect wherever they want to connect. What may be happening in this loosening process is that lightening is connecting everywhere, and it's not schizophrenia and it's not lost, because there's always that collaboration going. Once a connection is made, there is a patterning process that goes along with the connection. It *may* start off as a random connection. And then the mind comes over and forms a relationship pattern and then begins to manipulate it. And the subconscious and the flow state begin sifting through all those and coordinating all of those. And all the snakes of the telephone operating terminal come alive and are hydra-ing, they're splitting off into two different heads, and plugging into two sockets at once, and then there may be another that loops into a whole different kind of socket. So everything absolutely is happening at once.

Your own preferred way of thinking about and describing flow is as unique to you as your writer's imagination. Learn something about your creative process by taking a moment to consider your own sense of what flow is and how you get there.

When flow isn't "flow"

By now it should be apparent that your experience of writing is truly your own. You may resist the term flow, preferring other metaphors that work better for you. If you construct your life around words, the *right* metaphor can be critical. You may find yourself more comfortable with terms that emphasize your own responsibility for what you write. Some writers, like the following, find the term flow an oversimplification of the complexities involved.

> I use the term "fire," as horse racing maniacs use it (I was once one): a horse is said to fire when suddenly it finds all the speed it's capable of. . . . I don't like your phrase "enter the flow," for it suggests that something is going on, perhaps going on outside me, and I suddenly get in touch with this something, this flow. I have never had that sense. (Philip Levine)

> A fluid is far more fluid than we are. To my mind, the metaphor some-how has to acknowledge the friction, the resistance (something beyond the chaotic patterning of weeds that water creates when it hits them). This may seem like a stretch, but what does water do when it hits sandstone, versus schist, versus pebbles. When it hits mud is it always necessarily "cloudy?" I'm sure you see what I mean. Longing is a part of the state of writing if it's part of the writer; finally, "flow state" con-notes "go with the flow" too much to convey the state a writer is in when time gets lost track of. Still, in so many ways it is a seeing term. (Elizabeth Macklin)

> I believe the repetition of the words "flow state, flow," tend to reify a psychic state or set of states which is in fact extremely elusive, subtle, varied and complex. The language of your questions rather implies that getting "into the flow" of work is like popping into and out of a bathtub. It's not that clear and not that simple; to make it clear and simple is to falsify it dangerously. (Ursula K. Le Guin)

Why might so many disparate images come to mind to describe the same thing? First of all, of course, it may not *be* the same thing at all. Flow is experiential, subjective and changeable. Clearly, writers think of flow as being entered in many differing ways. You may experience it as a state to be gotten into by crossing a gate or doorway or line, or by flipping an on/off switch. On the other hand, you may find it feels more like moving along a continuum, somewhat the way light changes during dusk. I have lately begun to think flow may be a process, not of having access to the subconscious, but of having access to one's whole mind. Expanding on that metaphor, then, ordinary consciousness would be a subset of the larger mind, with flow allowing all the walls in the mind to disappear so the writer has access to an Omnimax of consciousness. Along those lines, too, it may be worthwhile to consider that, instead of losing the self in flow, what may be happening is a suffusing of self.

Think of a group of people who are blind from birth feeling all around an elephant . . . or, better yet, a UFO. Each would describe it in divergent ways, and perhaps differently each time, because they would have no concrete referent for the thing itself. Since flow is subjective, individuals tend to conceptualize it depending on their personalities and past experiences. Some of the writers I interviewed had not previously thought about flow and did not even conceptualize it as a discrete experience.

During our conversations, once writers became more conscious of what it meant to be talking about flow, usually years after their first flow experience, it was typically a struggle to find words for it. Perhaps flow is like those compound German words for concepts that are not directly translatable into English.

A professor of religion, in an article about the difficulties of interpreting the conscious mind, said, "To study memory, we analyze the memory of a sea slug. But to probe consciousness, we need to examine the experience of mystics, who experience their own consciousness in its simplest form." Listening as creative writers express their feelings about flow in metaphor is not so far from listening to the voices of mystics.

The physical experience of flow

People are always asking me about the brain chemistry of flow. Unfortunately, very little is known so far. I have to admit that I've wished I could slice open some writers' brains and compare the ones who get into flow virtually instantly with those who need some unlikely combination of mood, inspiration, no-pressure environment and who knows what else for flow to remain in residence for any length of time. Yet we can't literally dissect brains while their owners are in flow, and it's unlikely we could even take less intrusive brain scans, except for that small number who are able to remain fully absorbed in their writing no matter what's being done to them. (Think of the sex researchers who seem to have learned a lot from laboratory experiments that many of us couldn't imagine being able to function "normally" in.) Nevertheless, anecdotal evidence leads me to believe flow can be learned and can change over a lifetime. (See chapter ten.) But *how* your brain changes as you learn to flow more readily doesn't matter for our purposes.

Clearly, though, flow does happen in the brain and temporarily affects the entire body in both obvious and subtle ways. We can safely say the proof of this is the way people feel when they come out of flow. Knowing how flow feels helps you recognize when you've been in it, even when you didn't realize it at the time.

I got varied responses when I asked writers, "Did you notice any physiological changes during flow?" It may be difficult, if not impossible, to notice your body during an altered state in which you're intensely concentrating on the writing itself. Nevertheless, some writers are able to notice physical effects of the state, such as increased thirst or, as Donald Revell mentioned, "heart rate increases and I smile." Stephen Yenser says he has a sense that "there's a lot more muscle involved when I'm writing hard. That there's a lot of physical torque involved." Here's what others described:

> I know I breathe through my mouth, my mouth opens. I tend to gaze rather than look. I can even feel the muscles in my eyes are different. It's not like I'm looking at someone and talking to them. It's the kind of look you'd have in the dark watching a movie. (Frank X. Gaspar)

> I think that what I do that is right when I'm getting in, and right when I'm getting out, is to take a deep breath. Maybe my breath does alter. It sounds very similar to a meditation practice. And there are some ways I compose myself in terms of breath. It centers my body, it anchors my body, it positions my body in a different way in space and time. I probably do that right when I'm going to get out too. Straightening, and taking a deep breath, and getting ready to remove myself from that place, physically and emotionally and mentally and spiritually. (Maurya Simon)

You're not unusual if you're aware of bodily discomfort but manage to ignore the pain for the duration of the flow experience. "I don't care if my shoulders hurt. Which they do. They hurt while I'm in flow," said Octavia E. Butler. David Gerrold said, "I notice that there are times when I haven't noticed that my back hurts, because of a pinched nerve or whatever." And Jonathan Kellerman said, "Occasionally when I've had a very strenuous day of writing, I'm almost short of breath actually. I must have been tensing up, and I have to consciously relax my breathing. It takes a couple of seconds. It's just that feeling of coming out of the hypnoidal state, of leaving one world and entering another."

Q: Why is a day spent doing something creative so exhausting? After a full day, I'm sometimes spent. I love it, but whew!
A: Writing in flow is really intense, exhausting work. Some find it exhilarating as well. It's a personal response. It may also depend on how successful you were at accomplishing what you set out to do in that session. Brain work is quite physical. According to flow theory, you're in it when you're stretched to the limit of your skills and abilities. That can be hard work.

The purely physical can rarely, if ever, be separated from the rest of your experience. It's not surprising, then, that some writers speak about coming out of flow in a contradictory way, meshing their awareness of physiological changes with mental/emotional changes:

Physiological changes? Absolutely: I don't necessarily notice them but they occur. A fiery alertness until it gets to be so late that I collapse inwards and have to quit. A physical charge, a confidence, an ability to seek all the words at once, and to rapidly assimilate the nuances, possible connections, etc. (Marvin Bell)

Physiological changes, of course: not like those of athletics, physical labor, sex, eating, dancing, playing horn, defecating, sleeping, but comparable to them in a commonsense way; each is a special coordination of body and spirit. Poetry is a bodily art: its medium is not words or lines or images or thoughts or ideas or "creativity," but breath, shaped into meaning in the throat and mouth. (Robert Pinsky)

You may not notice anything until your writing session is over, like Alfred Corn, who says, "I don't tend to notice hunger at these times and so have often skipped lunch when I worked straight through a day. I don't seem to notice being tired, either; although when I finally do stop working, I sometimes discover that I actually am tired or feel drained." Carolyn See describes being "a little fuzzy" after writing very hard, and adds, "Sometimes [my partner] John Espey and I will go over to Catalina or something where we'll both work very hard in the morning, and then we'll go out to have lunch, and we're not even talking. We're just like two zombies." Carol Muske says she completely forgets her body when she's in flow, "so that after those six or seven hours of 'lost time,' I will suddenly come to and I'll be hunched over the keyboard. Sometimes I literally start to gasp for air, and I realize I haven't been breathing. My leg's gone to sleep, and I have bad circulation anyway. I'm literally cut off from my body."

But don't expect your reactions to be exactly like anyone else's. While you may end up empty and limp, you might experience the opposite:

> I don't feel totally exhausted and drained. It does feel like a building kind of pressure. I mean it's not negative at all, but I really look forward to then just walking outside the door and walking for maybe an hour, an hour and a half. It's more of a mental pressure, and I don't mean pressure in the sense of tension or stress. If you've had a good writing day, you don't walk away tense or stressed at all. (Gerald DiPego)

Or, like David L. Ulin, you might experience either or both ends of the emotional/physiological spectrum: "Afterwards, I often am sweaty, as if I'd just engaged in some kind of physical exertion, and my mind is both empty and energized." Novelist Judith Freeman explains that she's exhilarated by the feeling of having achieved something worthwhile. "That room is really, in a sense, like a mine where one goes and mines certain things. And I think just like you can feel tired by a day of strenuous work where you've been picking at some little vein, you can also be exhilarated when you actually strike it rich. . . . It might depend on the sense of having gotten closer. Maybe it's a discovery you might not have even imagined when you sat down in the morning."

Susan Taylor Chehak, who experiences quite deep flow, told me that she notices odd changes that carry over from flow to her nonwriting time, changes that might be attributed to some subtle shifts in brain chemistry due to flow that has not totally ended:

> During the times when I'm immersed in a book, when I'm in the thick of it, things happen in the outside world that don't happen at other times. You know, like masses of déjà vu experiences, or feelings of dis-

placement. You know when you're in a place and you suddenly feel like you're not yourself, those kinds of weird experiences. Or looking around and seeing things look strange, or people tend to be saying things that don't make any sense. I've worked all night last night, and today I'm going to go to the grocery store. And things look strange. There's a carryover. Everything's a little off, everything's a little weird.

To return once again to the erotic shift analogy, researcher Davis found a similar postcoital effect: "Everyday reality does not look quite the same after orgasm. For a time it retains a certain phenomenological coloring conferred by the erotic reality that preceded it, though there is some dispute whether the postcoital world seems more dingy or more dazzling than the precoital world."

Interestingly, the looseness that is such a benefit to writing creatively is not necessarily experienced physiologically. Shoulders hunch, back and arm muscles bunch and ache, hunger and thirst are ignored—and when it's all over, you often have a sense of physical exhaustion. For your body's needs not to get in the way of the writing, your body itself is often somewhat shortchanged for a period of time. Yet, along with being almost physically drained, you may feel a sense of excitement upon coming out of flow.

The sexiness of flow

I didn't start out asking novelists and poets snoopy questions about their sex lives. Yet the sexual aspects of flow emerged as an intriguing subtheme. It first came up when a male writer mentioned the subject spontaneously ("Sometimes there are sexual urges"), as he talked about the shift *out* of flow. After that interview, I asked other writers, because of their forthcomingness or the high comfort level of the conversation, if flow had any sexual aspects for them. As I've said before, the more you understand about how flow feels and what its markers are, the more you can take charge of your own experience. If you've been resisting flow entry, or find it somehow unsettling to write in flow, or, conversely, delight in the experience and want to learn all you can about how to increase it, hearing how others react may provide you with some insight into your own physiological reactions.

Understandably, some of the writers who discussed this subject with me asked to remain anonymous. The following male author was quite open and insightful in his description of how his sexuality interacts with his writing:

There are times when the writing can be extremely stimulating and I would be surprised for any writer to not be conscious of it. Because the whole of effective writing is to become trained in the craft of insight and watching your own reactions to your own life and noticing your own experience and you know, it's like you look at a moment and say, "Ooh, there's source material." Though even when you're working you should be noticing your own reactions, partly because that's a gauge to the reactions that the audience are going to be feeling when they read the work. And partly it's insight into how the human animal works. So any writer who looks at you blankly and says, "What's sexual, huh?" I would suspect that person's work is very dispassionate. . . . It's an intellectual high at first, but it becomes a visceral and physical and emotional thing as well. It's a lot like joggers breaking the wall. There's an endorphin rush. . . . It doesn't happen when you sit down to write. It happens after you've been writing for half a day. And suddenly it starts to click in. That's very sexual. I don't know how it is for women, but for men, a man, the longer it takes for a man to achieve climax, the more intense it is. I assume it's the same for women. . . . So that's the issue with writing, is you don't sit down and have an orgasm, you sit down and work at it for four hours and then you have your orgasm.

Q: You're saying that it's orgasmic, rather than that it's arousing?

A: I think everybody's response is unique. And my own feeling is that for me there's one kind of pleasure from writing and another kind of pleasure from having written.

You may find writing to be frankly arousing, like the following male: "Sometimes it's an erotic experience. If I'm writing an erotic scene, it's very erotically charged. I spoke to another writer who told me he'd write, then he'd get up and masturbate. Well, if I wasn't married, I would." Or the following female writer:

After a really good writing session, I feel very sexual. It seems to be related to the fact that I feel good, and that I feel productive, and I feel some sort of arousal. Sometimes after writing, I'll masturbate. Not consistently, but a lot of the time. Not related in the least to what I'm writing. In fact, I may be writing a very depressing scene, and it's just the fact that it's going well.

When you have a scene that is actually flowing, it's happening under your fingers and so forth, this is first-class A-1 addiction. It gives you a tremendous endorphin rush and you feel wonderful. With sex scenes, it varies. Some of them come slowly and are written in little bits and pieces, so you have a sort of generalized feeling of arousal, of course. It doesn't come all at once, so you may go around for two or three days in this state of heightened sexiness, so you may go and bother your husband. (Diana Gabaldon)

⌒⌒

There are two things that happen for me. Much of my material *does* have sexual content, so occasionally that will carry over. You become so much a part of whatever sexual theme you're describing, you're just floating and slurshing in a Salton Sea of sexuality. The other thing is that when you let one emotion out, they *all* come out. And there may be a process of emotional transference, one emotion bleeding into a different emotion. If you get *extremely* excited—just with your heart pounding and a kind of endorphin star-spray from having created something—that kind of response can convert to sexuality. (Stephen Perry)

The following male found the topic captivating enough to be examined from a variety of angles:

Writing gets one going, and the active body can get horny. I don't get horny from writing poetry, even erotic poetry, but then again I usually write late at night and don't quit, if I'm cooking, until utterly fatigued. Also, the state you call "flow" is by definition one in which the writer is taken out of himself, is unaware of the passage of time, for example, and is so far "into" the body part that makes words that he is unaware of his sex organs or, for that matter, aches and pains—except when he descends from the flow for a moment—because he is cold, for example, in a house in which the heat has long since been turned down. . . . There's an enormous amount of sexuality connected to the writing of poetry. I just don't know how to locate it in words for you. Writing is a metabolic activity. And it can take up with erotic content. Also, one can have a muse, even if she comes in the form of a friend at a distance or a waitress at the local diner, and of course she may arrive in the form of a lover or dream girl. People are the real turn-on. One may be writing because there is that one person somewhere to whom one wishes to show a new poem. Literary lust? Well, all that aside, the flow state is essentially mindless and, while the sex act can be either deeply mindful or gorgeously mindless, the writing flow state is, to my mind, not the same thing as the mindless quality of orgiastic sex. . . . Then there's the matter of the sheer inspiration of sexuality—as flattery, as payoff, as the only way to get everything expressed. . . . Finally, it may come down to this: I suspect writers to be as sexual as any group and to be more expressive of it than some other groups (artistic freedom, rebellion, opportunity, fabulous others). Consequently, sexuality has a large role in many writers' lives but not directly within the flow state. . . . Still trying to encapsulate it: writing is physical. Whosoever has the stamina for it at a certain level of intensity also has the abundant energy to be often aroused. When I enter the flow state, and later fall from it by degrees, and see then that I have made something beyond the ordinary, then I am excited by that, no matter how physically tired. That excitement could easily turn into sex if it were available right then. In fact, the excitement arrives as a sort of happiness, and that carries with it a feeling of inner freedom, which is borne upwards by a rising happiness that wants to boil over.

Or you may find aspects of writing and flow to be erotic in a more general way rather than explicitly sexual, like Diane Johnson, who says, "I think there is a definite involvement of the libido at some level, so that you feel a kind of excitement that could also be *like* sexual excitement. I usually feel energized when I finish writing." Or the following:

> I think it is erotic (I'd use the word erotic rather than sexual), erotically engaging to have connected with the unconscious in a way that's gratifying and in a way that you really feel you've achieved something, even as part of the process, even if nothing's going to be saved for the day. And I tend to get happy, feeling that there's a point to being alive. It's that general eroticism. A lot of my work is about spiritual states that I think are fairly dark, so it's not really about the "content" of the work. It's about the process. (Brenda Hillman)

> I think there is always a sexual component. Most of the women I know who are writers talk of it in those terms.
> Q: Are you aware of it when you're writing?
> A: Oh yes, always aware. . . . It's not a kind of directed sexual energy, more of a kind of Zen sexual energy, because it's permeating things with a kind of tranquility also. It's the Zen paradox of energy and tranquility. But it has to be there, that charge, because of the physicality having to be there. And it may just be due to the way in which, chemically, things are being triggered. But it's not object-oriented for one thing. It's not the same sort of sexual energy that happens in a singles bar. I guess things are basically sort of procreative, you're engendering something. It's a rush. (David St. John)

Again and again, sexual analogies are used by writers to express how flow makes them feel, as in Marnell Jameson's comment: "The analogy that comes to mind is sex—a heightening of senses, a rush, no concept of time, a dimming of the external world, an altered state in which

33

creation is the unconscious though central intent." Or Carolyn See, when I asked her about her thought processes as she writes: "I'm not thinking. In a sense, you're better off not thinking about it. Like sex, you don't want to think, oh now we're in foreplay."

Ellery Washington C. (he added the "C" to his name to honor his mother), who is working on his first novel, writes a scene at a time, usually one per day, and when that scene is finished, whether it has taken him half an hour or three hours, he feels a sense of completion for the day. As we were talking about how he gets up to walk around in his apartment or in a coffee shop during his writing process, sometimes with notebook in hand, but always with a sense of kinetic energy building, he suddenly realized how much his description sounded "like sex":

> That building of energy to some sort of point and then you realize you've nailed something. My style is that I write in short parts, very dense, so what happens is in a day I write one of these scenes, even if there are several scenes in a chapter. I don't interrupt a scene, unless some word is screamed, "Your mother is sick," or "The building is on fire," and even then I might hesitate. There's this energy that sort of builds. It's like you're pushing uphill and you're rolling and it's faster and faster and you can feel this energy building and maybe I walk and pace a little bit and mumble to myself.
>
> With sex, the process of the energy of it is the same: you start, and you maybe catch a glimpse of your partner, or you're feeling something inside of yourself that you then project onto your partner, your partner arouses something in yourself, it's usually something small, it's not like they're standing there, or necessarily even naked at the time, or it could be during dinner or something, or there's some hint of something that happens, and from that hint, there is a process where you're actually building toward it, preparing for it, you're teasing a bit, you're setting up things, you're getting everything in place, then there comes that point where things are in place, and when it's moving, where the energy is very kinetic, and it builds to a certain point where there's this incredible energy and then . . . and with the writing it's like that point where it's just like I feel like I've nailed it, I don't know how else to say it . . . There is a cycle for me in it that completes.

And a casual male acquaintance of mine, when I described how I was studying the flow state, said, "Oh, you mean when you're writing and the ejaculation comes?" Apparently, for many people, the shift into and out of flow and the shift into and out of a sexual place have many similarities. (One of the writers who declined to participate in this project wrote, "But it would be tantamount to offering you our orgasms for study.")

I began to wonder if how one enters flow is as idiosyncratic as how one becomes sexually aroused. It is possible that whatever worked the first time, or the first few times, "imprints" so that you adhere to that method for guaranteed success. An apt but disturbing example is that I once interviewed an incest perpetrator, a divorced father, who tried to explain his repeated desire for a child by saying that "if you had a great orgasm with a tree, you'd want to do it again." Similarly, if you wrote your favorite poem while chomping on a Cuban cigar, you might make extraordinary efforts to keep your supply of cigars coming.

Some writers told me they have a hard time getting into their writing when they know they have a shortened amount of time. I (and other people) experience the same thing—in both writing and in sex. I can't or don't want to begin the process of letting go if I know I may be interrupted or if time is limited in any way, regardless of how little time is actually needed for completion. If a part of the consciousness has to remain aware of the time constraint, total surrender isn't free to happen. But it's not the same for all individuals. Some can become immersed in either writing or sex when time is limited. The deadline, or the thrill of possible discovery, is a bonus for some people. Somehow the increased tension adds to the experience for them.

It's also quite possible that when you're in flow, you're achieving some kind of endorphin high such as exercisers experience, which then transmutes into something sexual. Flow, wrote one researcher, "is probably due to natural opiates such as endorphins that flood our bodies when we're under stress. Such opiates induce a euphoric state of intense concentration. They also play a role in sexual arousal."

Comic novelist Tom Robbins once said, "You should spend thirty minutes a day looking at dirty pictures. Or thinking about sex. The purpose of this is to get yourself sexually excited, which builds tremendous amounts of energy, and then carry that into your work. . . . Keep yourself in, not necessarily a frenzied state, but in a state of great intensity. . . . You should always write with an erection. Even if you're a woman."

part two

The Master Keys to Flow Entry in Writing

3 Key One: Have a Reason to Write

IT'S PRETTY EVIDENT. Writers go to the often unrewarded trouble of writing because they want to. A point often missed by novice writers, though, is that by zeroing in on one or more of the *right* reasons—for you—you're more likely to find the one that will help you enter flow and keep writing in spite of frustration and rejection.

You must feel strongly motivated to get fully absorbed in the writing, if flow is to follow. Popular novelist Michael Crichton, for example, demonstrated the intensity of his drive when he described his early writing years: "I wrote a million words a year, much of it awful, and I was not published for years."

People write for the same range of reasons that they do anything else: something outside themselves may be urging them to do it, or they may have some deep, interior sense of the need to do it. John Rechy, whose first novel evolved out of his own early experience of sex and drugs on the streets, said of his motivation, "I wanted to put order to this overwhelming experience." Personally, I've been motivated to write by all the following reasons at various times: for the rewards of being published; for the approval of my peers/public/critics/Daddy/Mommy; for money; for fame; to change the world; because it's a prestigious occupation, a romantic one; because it's an ineffable, mystical experience; to express myself; for catharsis; to relieve pressure; it's fun and feels good; it's a meetable challenge;

because inspiration has suddenly arrived. Fear can motivate too, claims novelist Susan Straight: "I'm always afraid I won't have enough money, or something will happen to my kids. Whenever something scary happens, I write." And then there's Andrew Vachs, whose dozen investigative novels, inspired by his work with abused children as a health-care worker and a lawyer, have sold more than a million copies. Vachs has been quoted as saying of what drives him, "It is rage. Calling it a higher calling is a load of crap."

Often, a combination of motivating factors comes into play. While, on some days, three reasons aren't enough to get you started writing, on others, all it takes is one good pretext. For a woman I overheard at a recent reading, "writing is what gets me out of bed in the morning." For her, the act of writing provides enough benefits that it has itself become a motivator, urging her to leave a comfortable bed for the pleasures of putting words down on paper. Some authors seem to be gifted with a surfeit of motives. For instance, best-selling novelist Amy Tan posed the question "So why do I write?" in an essay, answering herself and her readers this way:

> Because my childhood disturbed me, pained me, made me ask foolish questions. And the questions still echo. . . . I write because oftentimes I can't express myself any other way, and I think I'll explode if I don't find the words. . . . I write for very much the same reasons I read: to startle my mind, to churn my heart, to tingle my spine, to knock the blinders off my eyes and allow me to see beyond the pale. . . . I write because I have been in love with words since I was a child. . . . Writing, for me, is an act of faith, a hope that I will discover what I mean by truth.

Believing might make it so

By knowing something about motivation in general, you can more clearly reflect on your own drives. In the view of purely behaviorist psychology, for instance, people merely respond to stimuli. According to this view, if someone yells at you when you don't write, or praises or pays you when you do write, you will be motivated to write, and you *will* write.

Less mechanistic theories do not deny the connection between stimulus and response, but they also suggest that people choose what to do based on what they *think* the possible outcomes of such behavior will be, whether the outcomes are external or internal. (Consider the powerful placebo effect, in which the body reacts in response to what the mind *believes* is happening, even when this belief is based on an outright lie.)

In other words, you will write today because certain pleasing events (even simply feeling good) will probably follow; or you will procrastinate because you assume nothing bad is likely to happen (feeling guilty is often not enough to provide motivation, at least until the guilt builds to a critical level of discomfort). The difference between these and the strictly behavioral model is mainly a matter of cognition: the reinforcer—the expected result that moves you to act—is not only what *will* happen, but what you *believe* will happen. Psychologist George A. Kelly, for example, suggested that what someone would do when left to his own devices hinged "primarily on what alternatives his personal construction of the situation allowed him to sense." Consider: how many times have you made what turned out to be a poor decision about how to act because, at the time, with the information you had, you expected a particular outcome? And, conversely, have you ever decided not to apply yourself fully to some goal you very much cherished because you believed you could not achieve it?

Let's assume, then, that motivation results largely from belief. How might this relate to achieving ease and flow in writing? When you expect that what you do and what will happen will be unrelated, you will learn to feel and act helplessly, as though you have no control. Therefore, writers who believe they can to some degree control their entry into a flow state may have the edge over those who believe it "just happens." If you wait for inspiration before sitting down to work, you won't write as regularly as if you believed that you can will your best writing to take place. (See chapter seven for a discussion of will versus inspiration.)

The inside story

When you're writing because you want to, because something in the project is pulling you in, and not because it feels like you have to or because something outside yourself is pushing you, by definition you're intrinsically motivated. And, quite possibly, you're in flow. At those times, since you're not focused on your ego, you may be freer to take creative risks leading to novel solutions and insights because the risks don't carry any liability to your ego. In other words, you've got nothing to lose. "Intrinsic motivation acts like a ratchet on the development of personal capacities," explain researchers Csikszentmihalyi and Rathunde. "A person who has experienced flow will want to experience it again. But the only way to do so is by taking on new or greater challenges or by developing more skills."

Thus, it's possible that people are more creative when they are motivated by the enjoyment and challenge of the work itself. Flow, the exhilarating part of creativity, however, is neither automatic nor easily entered into. The optimal conditions for creativity (and thus for flow entry) include a condition of psychological safety from external evaluation. When you feel (and fear) your efforts are going to be judged, you quickly lose the ability to marshal all your mental and emotional resources in the quest for a new way to express yourself. No one wants to fail or look foolish for writing something that others (or you yourself) will judge to be bad, stupid or silly.

I'm often asked for tricks that can be used to silence the internal censor, the one who's always asking, "Is this worthwhile?" or "Who cares?" or "Will this offend someone?" Here are a few starting points: try to determine the source of those internal voices. Were you raised by a critical parent or two, and have you spent much of your life since then trying to gain their approval? Were your early writing efforts uniformly lauded or did someone, a teacher perhaps, focus on what was wrong, not what was potentially of value?

I can still recall a teacher who wrote, "This is not a story," along with a failing grade, when I once risked beginning a short story with the words, "The End." She could have allowed me to try another way of fulfilling the assignment, if the purpose were to see if I could string sentences together in a linear way. Instead, she helped convince me, someone who was already leery of risk-taking, that creative writing carries risks too. It has taken many years of living with a risk-in-writing-is-not-real-risk person to demonstrate to me that I had nothing concrete to lose and everything exciting to gain by taking chances in writing.

Before you can shut up that internal critic, you have to get to know it. A couple of techniques are suggested by Karin Mack and Eric Skjei in *Overcoming Writing Blocks*. Describe your internal critic in words or a sketch. Is it a real person you know? Is it a combination of fright-inducing figures from your past? No matter how portentous your critic may be, you can whittle him down to size by imagining him and his concerns as ridiculous. Such an exercise can help you recognize that your critic is a projection of your own personality, and that you can take control back if you choose to.

Or imagine a dialogue with your internal critic. Argue back when he says you're taking a risk by writing this poem. Tell him you're more competent than he knows, and that, regardless, the way you improve at your craft is to take chances. Give yourself the last word in the debate.

Tell yourself that no one has to see this, that you can decide afterwards whether to show it to anyone. Make a habit of putting your finished work away for a while before looking at it again. Such a practice serves to separate your creative impulse from that nasty critical voice.

Feedback loop

There's something else you need to enter and stay in flow: some kind of feedback. Writing is one of those creative activities that does not offer clear feedback from the outside, at least until you send your poem or story out to an editor (and even then, you won't usually get much more than a "yes" or "no, thanks"). As former high school English teacher Frank McCourt said about the process of writing his Pulitzer Prize-winning memoir, *Angela's Ashes*, "In a way, it was harder than teaching because you're in a room alone and you don't know how you're doing." Intrinsically motivated individuals are better able to provide this feedback for themselves. McCourt said he imagined an audience of adolescents like those in his high school classes who had once been so interested in and responsive to his stories.

Sometimes the inability to match your internal ideal to the feedback you're perceiving in your mind can be highly troubling. Filmmaker Terry Gilliam once told an interviewer how frustrating it always was for him to see his work on the screen, since "the image or picture that I've got in my head is usually better, or more elaborate, than what we can physically do." Yet, as fans of his films can attest, Gilliam's frustration must have motivated him to keep trying to match that imagined ideal as closely as possible.

Some of those who find that sense of frustration inhibiting to their creativity often make a point of beginning the day's work with *nothing* in mind. Then no failure is possible. That may or may not be feasible in your kind of writing, but don't be too certain without giving it a try.

The feedback process is essentially mysterious. In an interview about creative geniuses, Jean Cocteau described the almost mystical nature of this internally devised feedback:

> Why this and not that? Why does the creator say "*C'est ca!*" and stop
> at some point with an immense sense of relief, really postorgasmic,

though the step before may be little different—perhaps better to objective judgment? He stops where he stops, I have come to think, because that's where he will have stopped. He remembers the ending *beforehand* and is glad to have reached it. Geniuses may have a little better memory of the future than most.

Popular novelist Elmore Leonard has been quoted as saying "I say my sentences inside my head until they chime with some kind of tuning fork." Many of the writers I interviewed weren't able to describe *exactly* how they manage to give themselves the requisite feedback. Nora Okja Keller, for instance, said, "Sometimes I have periods where I can hear my own voice as an outsider, but that's very rare. But for the most part, I'm really so insecure." Keller has so far only published one novel, and it is likely her insecurity will lessen over the years. Meanwhile, she belongs to a writing group that meets monthly, consisting of writers who are also good readers. Still, she doesn't show her work to anyone until she has gotten a piece almost done to her satisfaction. "I tried it the other way, where I've shown a couple of readers stuff that I was still working on, that wasn't fully formed yet. It was just disastrous, and I ended up just not doing anything with it."

Sometimes it is a bit less mysterious. For instance, Thomas Elias Weatherly (who uses just "Weatherly" professionally) says he analyzes his poems "using the objective method, like a prosodist, the science of poetry. I sit down and I will make up a bunch of little charts. Sometimes I write it out phonetically, then I separate out the initial sounds in each syllable. Often I do this without writing it down." The sound of words and lines is so crucial to poets that they often find a way to hear what they've written to provide internal feedback for themselves, as Ed Ochester explains: "What I try to do at some point is sound the lines that I'm writing, usually when I'm writing. I can tell often, not always, but often when something is kinda clunky, long or more abstract than I would wish it to be, just by sounding it out. I can hear it when I'm typing it." It's been said that the ear is smarter than the brain.

Novelist Margot Livesey explains that she provides feedback to herself by trying to see as clearly as possible what is going on, and by reading aloud whatever she writes:

> If a character is sitting in a room, or pruning a hedge or fixing a bicycle or sitting on a bus, I try to see that character both internally and externally as clearly as possible. When I write novels, for me everything is in the service of the novel. I might begin writing a scene with three

dozen details of the bus journey, then decide that only two of them really further the novel, and are therefore to my mind what is needed. . . . I think people in their heart of hearts probably know more about their work than they realize. Now with *Criminals*, I actually read every sentence aloud. If I thought the sentence was boring, I changed it or I took it out. If I couldn't stand to read it aloud, then I thought that was information. I didn't allow myself to think it's just because I wrote it or because I've read it before. Because I realized there were some passages I was very happy to read. But I also tried to push through the screen of self-deception and to acknowledge how much I really did know about my own work.

Q. So you really are your best audience?

A. No, I actually have a better audience in my friend Andrea, but I can't get her to read every sentence. If she would totally give up her own work and totally devote herself to mine, that would be the ideal.

When I asked novelist Diane Johnson if she was aware of some part of her mind giving her feedback as she writes, such as saying, "Yes, yes, this is right," she responded that on some level, something is giving you permission to continue in the vein that you've started in. "And so I assume that that's some sort of sense of rightness. Sometimes it doesn't happen and you know that you're going wrong." She says you have to tell the critic to go away while you're writing, but then you can bring him right back in when you're ready for him.

Writing matters

One of the most powerful combinations of motivators is the sheer love of writing and the belief that it matters. "This is the writer's earthly purpose and her cause, which she serves gladly, in any circumstances, with a sense of its utter and transcending importance," writes Kelly Cherry. Ray Bradbury is unequivocally positive (and more colloquial) about why he writes: "Everything I've ever done was done with excitement, because I wanted to do it, because I loved doing it." Novelist James Lee Burke, who switched from writing literary novels to a popular series of crime tales, said in a *Los Angeles Times* interview, "I think what I'm doing is art. I wouldn't work that hard for any other reason. . . . I believe these are the books I was intended to write."

Writing in flow is the way most writers feel they are their best selves. Psychologist and author Ayala Pines told me, "When I sit down at my computer, even just to make some changes on a paper, I feel so much *like myself*. And I forget everything else around me." According to poet

Ralph Angel, "writing, even more than some of the most important relationships in my life, is where I am most in touch with myself." And poet Donald Hall, after his wife Jane died, found writing to be the only comfortable place for him. "For eleven months I have written about no other subject, and it is the only thing I look forward to—the hour or two in the morning, or three, when I can work on poems out of her death, and also a prose narrative that I am writing about her illness and death. . . . I hate a day without work." Also:

> I consider the gift of being absorbed into my work the greatest pleasure and the noblest privilege of my life. (Ursula K. Le Guin)

> I'd say for the past ten years of my life, the writing has always been a gift, a reward, something I get to do, I love to do, I feel like I'm in my own element. I'm the fish finally in water. All the rest of the time, regardless of how good a time I'm having, I'm always slightly out of water. (Frank X. Gaspar)

> We may feel the power of another force, but I believe the power we're feeling is the power of the presence of the total self. We feel like someone else because we are so rarely totally ourselves. (Philip Levine)

> Sometimes I look up in the middle of writing and I think, "I'm happy." (Nancy Kress)

The joy of flow itself can be reason enough to write. It certainly is for Jane Hirshfield: "To offer myself to the condition of concentration is *what* I want to do; it is a pleasure." It's the same for Faye Moskowitz: "This is the closest I will ever come to an out-of-body experience, and in the end, it is the possibility of recreating these moments that keeps me going as a writer." Here is how Lynne Sharon Schwartz explains the compelling nature of flow:

> I've always thought of [flow] as a high, though not drug-induced, rather life-induced. It comes during an utter engagement of the self with whatever the activity is, but that does not begin to do it justice. When I am in it, it seems to me the way life should always be—freed from time and petty daily concerns and all forms of self-consciousness except the very deepest, which is paradoxically a kind of forgetfulness yet profound awareness of self—but alas, that is not possible very often. Many activities can yield me the state you call flow—reading, listening to music,

sex, walking, a wonderful conversation with a friend, but the high I get from writing is the best and lasts the longest, perhaps it is because my total self is doing what it does best and most naturally. I crave that experience probably the way addicts crave their drugs (and for all I know the drug-induced state is similar); I sometimes cannot wait to get to my desk and enter that place where I finally seem fully alive and in harmony with the world.

I asked Robert Olen Butler what kept him going after so many of his earlier novels, stories and plays didn't get published:

I guess the answer to that goes to the heart of why artists do what they do. And that is: you encounter the chaos of moment-to-moment sensual experience that is life on the planet earth, and behind that chaos you have some deep conviction that there is order and meaning. But you do not have any idea what that vision of order is until you create these art objects, which are books. You're driven to understand the world around you in a sensual way, not a rational, analytical, abstract way, but a sensual dreamspace way, and so you must do this thing.

In the same vein, novelist and short story writer T. Coraghessan Boyle writes to counter existential despair (and have fun doing it):

Everything is chaos and we are so small and so meaningless—this world and universe—that we want to be individuals in some way, and art is great because it's an expression of me and me alone. So it's satisfying in that way because it issues some kind of a sense of order in a completely chaotic universe, which is terrifying. An asteroid could fly through the house and crush me now, you know.

At times, the writer's sense of the significance of writing, of its being what he or she was meant to do and must do in order to be fully him- or herself, is combined with a sense of responsibility to readers, to society or to the world:

I only have one responsibility, and I have to shoulder the responsibility for what the poems convey to the rest of the world. And that's a terrible responsibility. It's a very heavy responsibility. . . . If I don't discover who I am and my experience and the truth of who I am, then I have no chance of making an art object that might make contact with another human being who I'll never meet. That's what it's really all about. One has a message, but it's only after the fact. One has something to say only because in discovering the truth of yourself for that brief amount of time, and finding language for it, you might overlap, you might enter into an intersection of the truth of somebody else. And who are we writing for? People we'll never meet in our lives. People who aren't alive, possibly. I think that's the thrill, that's the exhilaration. Even if what you discover is ugly or dark or shameful.

Q: Poetry is psychoanalysis without the . . .

A: Without the analysis. Relinquishing the language and then hearing something there. (Ralph Angel)

I don't know what people think they're trying to do with literary novels, but they're trying to do something. They're trying to change the world, although that's so crazy. That's just delusional. But I recognize that it's crazy. It will be a little dinky change. (Carolyn See)

If you're like some writers, you may never be able to settle once and for all the question of whether or not writing matters in some essential way. You may have to wrestle with it frequently, perhaps on a daily basis, before you can let go into flow. Poet Brenda Hillman told me that a lot of preparing to work involves "getting my sense that there's some point to it. Or not a point, but a 'Why am I bothering?' Getting into a state of enough affirmation of self even to be able to confront whatever it is." When I asked short-story writer Steve Reynolds why he writes, since he says it's so hard, he responded:

Because I can do it. There is a satisfaction of having it done, having somebody else read it. I get a feeling of satisfaction because I can craft it. I can't build things out of wood worth a shit. But this, I'm able to do. So that's my only struggle: how worthwhile is it to be a writer? Because writing isn't totally necessary for survival, but it's necessary for civilization to advance beyond survival. Because if a meteor is coming, you are going to die. Most people don't start off a day thinking, what if I die today, what will I have regretted that I didn't do? Most people just totally put it out of their minds. So in that sense, a meteor *is* coming.

Nonetheless, an awareness of *too much* importance can get in the way of releasing into flow. For instance, years before I met Stephen, he had tried to write while surviving on unemployment checks, having given himself a certain length of time to succeed. Yet he couldn't write. "If something's too important to me," he says, "I can't do it." The chapter on writer's block will deal with this possibility again later.

Mystery, surprise and challenge

Mystery and surprise come up repeatedly in descriptions of the creative process. The challenge that is so integral to flow is often supplied by these elements. Sometimes you'll know the ending of a work before you write the first word, but if there are no unknowns along the way, you may not find yourself interested enough to finish. The mystery may also be how you recognize you're on the trail of something worth pursuing, that hasn't been expressed before in quite the way you're trying to write it.

Though you need to increase the challenge of an activity to maintain your interest in it over time, when the challenge becomes too great for your skills, anxiety is the result. Then flow is broken. Yet, although exploring and trying out new activities in a search for novelty may cause anxiety, curiosity to see what will happen can be more motivating than the anxiety is inhibiting. Anne Lamott, whose nonfiction books brought her much widespread positive critical and popular attention, finds it harder to write her novels. "It's like spinning plates, or walking a tightrope," she says, but she adds that it's also exhilarating. Jonathan Kent, the artistic director of the Almeida Theater in London, explaining why the Almeida was embarking on a particularly ambitious year, is quoted as saying, "What you have to do is constantly set yourself a new challenge. In a way, you always have to terrify yourself."

About a third of the writers I interviewed, evenly divided between the poets and fiction writers, mentioned something to do with "mystery." Poet Billy Collins, for instance, said, "I begin to feel like an obsessive puzzle-solver." Science-fiction author David Gerrold spoke of a book he had written totally in flow: "I had no idea where it was going. I was aiming somewhere else." Novelist Judith Freeman says, "I do actually write stories so I, too, can discover what's going to happen to these people." David St. John, a poet, has no interest in knowing what he's going to write: "For me, it's the worst possible sign. For me, the pleasure of writing is discovering what I have left to say in some way I've never said it." Or:

> There was a period last spring when I had a poem that didn't work for me and, ironically, I didn't throw it away. Usually I would throw it away. But because I let myself finish it, it had retained some kind of mystery for me, and I trusted that. (Ralph Angel)

> The "flow state" occurs, in my experience, when I'm working well, which means surprising myself, and probably occurs (in the best of instances) just after I've startled myself by writing something that wasn't available to me before the poem began. (Stephen Dunn)

When I'm in flow, all of a sudden I'm going somewhere and I have no idea where. No idea, none. I never write a poem with an agenda. . . . I mean, why do that? (Richard Jones)

If mystery can be so meaningful, what might this mean about the virtues (or not) of planning ahead? Few of the novelists and poets I interviewed talked specifically about planning their writing, and those who mentioned outlines often admitted that their work never ended up following the outline completely. This doesn't mean that *not* planning *at all* is the best or only way to write. Perhaps, though, whatever planning you do ought to remain fairly loose (unless you're tied into strict plotting by the demands of your genre), and ought to take place some time prior to the actual writing. That way the constraints of the plan itself aren't in the forefront of your consciousness as you settle in to work. Having a general goal isn't inimical to flow, so long as the goal contains a bit of mysterious challenge. The most liberating, challenging goals are to complete a poem, compose a story arc that satisfies, or come up with a line or an image that breathes on the page.

When the challenge in your project isn't motivating enough, you can set yourself a new challenge. Some writers do this in concrete ways. Poet and college teacher Maurya Simon, for example, explains why she gives herself "assignments": "To grow, to push myself, to keep myself interested, to keep myself engaged with what I'm doing." David Gerrold says his lesser books are all experiments: "One was written in present tense, one was written with no passive tenses at all, no forms of the verb to be, one was written with a kind of metric prose that had its own lyrical rhythm, and those were all the books where the story wasn't as important as the exercise. So that way when I go back to the book that's important, those muscles have been trained and they just click in when necessary." Similarly:

I might be interested in investigating, not exactly a different genre, but I may see certain things that I'm really interested in trying, whether that might be combining, say, some surreal elements into a very real story. I have now a real attraction to a lightness of language and subject matter. Because the last novel had a great weightiness to it. What you're asking is a fairly large question: What do we learn from what we've already written, how are we inspired to imagine the next piece of writing? All kinds of things come into that and, for me, I want to expand my range. I want to try new things. (Judith Freeman)

During the writing of her first novel, when Diana Gabaldon realized that the previous three scenes with people talking were between two people, she said to herself, "Well, you know, you don't want to have too much of this, this might be monotonous." She knew that writing scenes with multiple speakers is difficult technically. So she decided to write a mob scene. She says she asked herself, "Can it be done at all and is it something I want to do?" Of course, she accomplished what she set out to do. Another way she challenges herself is to write difficult emotional scenes, those scenes that you dread having to live through, or scenes requiring the technical difficulty of getting a very raw emotion down on paper. She says she puts those off for several days, either working up her nerve or just letting her subconscious dwell on it. "But usually when you do sit down to write that sort of scene," she adds, "the writing itself goes fairly well. It's just the emotion accompanying it that is difficult." Although all such challenges have to be, finally, totally integral to the story, at times Gabaldon says she'll try something just to see if she can, such as "a triple-nested flashback."

Beating boredom

Writers, no less than anyone else, are susceptible to boredom. When a writer feels the need to beat boredom, he or she often tries to achieve new writing feats. "After a while, you're doing it automatically, and it's false. It gets boring," says Octavia E. Butler. "And if you challenge yourself a bit, sometimes it helps." Bill Mohr told me he has "a tremendously low boredom threshold" and that this is the source of his creative drive. "It's not because I'm brilliant or smart, but because I'm looking for something," adds Mohr. The way Stephen explains it to me is that

> all you have to do is rub two sticks together. The surprise is a surprise, though always metaphorical and always combinational. If you add new things to the combination, then inevitably you complexify. Randomness is extremely important. I have to surprise myself. Open a book at random and if you're in a semiflow state, not quite there, you can start blurring the edges of those facts and see what marshes up against those facts. Sometimes just simply free associating begins the whole process. . . . If I'm bored, and I see it as more avoiding boredom than setting challenges, I want to do something different. I'd never written in forms before, so I tried. Once you get into the flow state, the form disappears.

A few writers found—and, in some perverse way, appreciated—challenge in whatever came their way. This tends to indicate an intrinsically motivated personality who can adjust to environmental obstacles and turn them into positives. For instance, Cees Nooteboom said he even found "disturbance a challenge," because it was always difficult after an interruption to recall what words would have come next. Sometimes switching tools, such as trying to write a story in longhand with a fountain pen, when you're used to the computer, can be done "on the level of an experiment," noted Judith Freeman.

Some writers are not aware of how they set these challenges for themselves, even when they speak of clearly self-challenging behaviors. Indeed, the very act of writing itself can be experienced as a vicarious and safe way of complexifying one's life, a safe way of playing with novelty and, perhaps, with danger. In this way, the challenge is so integral to the activity that it goes unnoticed as a separate element.

In order to make flow possible, you have to find a way to keep your interest high. Mystery enhances flow by increasing complexity, bringing forth a sense of the new. Wanting to get to the end of the story is apparently a powerful motivator for the human mind, even when it's the mind itself that's creating the story. Alice McDermott, The National Book Award-winning author of the popular novels *At Weddings and Wakes* and *Charming Billy*, said, "I don't see the point in writing a story I already know. I need to be as curious as I want my reader to be, or I'll lose interest."

Novelist Harriet Doerr, who does not want to be characterized as entering flow except on a rare basis, is one of those who nevertheless writes because of the rewarding nature of discovery. "It's like going to the shrink," she said in a recent address. "You suddenly put something on the page and it surprises you. I guess that's why I write."

Is the mind half full? and other reasons writers write

Consider the concept of fullness. Sometimes an overflowing mind is just what it takes to get a cascade of words onto the paper. As poet Marvin Bell said, "I only write when the pot boils over. But I have learned how to turn up the heat." Writers don't always know how they "fill up," but they do know that, when they're "full," it's time to write.

Time spent *not writing* is one way to increase a sense of urgency: "Keep from writing the book as long as you can, make yourself *not* begin, store it up," wrote John Irving. Thomas Wolfe wrote, "I actually felt that I had a great river thrusting for release inside of me and that I had to find a channel into which its flood-like power could pour."

Or Isabel Allende: "Books don't happen in my mind, they happen somewhere in my belly. It's like a long elephant pregnancy that can last two years. And then, when I'm ready to give birth, I sit down. I wait for January 8, which is my special date, and then, that day, I begin the book that has been growing inside me." Urgency can also arrive suddenly, as it did for novelist Ursula Hegi, describing in a *Los Angeles Times* interview how she came to write *Stones from the River*: "Gordon and I were driving from Portland to Spokane, and it was dark, and he was playing Beethoven's Fifth on the stereo, and I had one idea about Trudi Montag. I started writing in the dark on a yellow lined pad, and I filled most of it. We could feel her presence in the car with us." In such examples, the connection between urgency, fullness and inspiration become apparent.

Nora Okja Keller, author of *Comfort Woman*, a novel about the Korean women who were kept as slaves by the Japanese during World War II, heard a former comfort woman give a talk. At the time, Keller was also pregnant with her first child. She explains:

> It was like that story somehow penetrated me to such a degree that I started dreaming about comfort women, a lot of vivid images with no real story line. One night I got up after dreaming and started taking down notes. The images weren't from the talk, and they were kind of entwined with my pregnancy, I guess, in that I saw images of infants as well. Also war images, but not necessarily connected to the talk I heard. But I realized that I needed to write it down to kind of exorcize it from my body.
>
> This has happened before. Sometimes I start becoming obsessed by a story or I start hearing it in my head, and then I sit down and write. It's always a battle to sit down in front of the computer. It almost feels like the story is to the point where it's overwhelming me. Where I have to write it down so it will leave me alone.

Keller mentioned later on that she felt almost as though she became, in a way, a channel for the women shamans in her novel. "There's just this story coming out, or this voice. That's the best part about writing. It's such an incredible release."

A playwright with whom I spoke, Willard Simms, told me that he would sometimes have to put down what was "dictating itself" to him. "If I stopped it, it was like what I call artistic constipation. I would feel bloated."

Susan Taylor Chehak says that her first drafts are messy and not in complete sentences, because she types them quickly to keep up with "what's going on." She fears losing something, not getting it all, "because it just seems to be coming out and coming really fast and I know exactly, and the words are there, I just have to get it on paper or on the screen."

Phoebe Conn, romance novelist, feels similarly when she is busy and can't work for a couple of days: "I can just really feel my characters waiting. They get impatient. Sort of like if you can visualize actors standing on the stage waiting for the director to come in or the script to arrive. Where are you, we've been waiting, kind of thing. . . . For me, I really feel the characters are just anxious to get to work."

Another perfectly fine reason to write is because it's fun. You don't necessarily need to feel that what you're doing is deeply meaningful. If you can find a way to tap into the fun aspects of your work, flow will almost inevitably follow. Some writers tend to emphasize the good feelings as a principal motivator to begin or to keep going. Phyllis Gebauer, for example, said, "Thought processes beforehand and after sitting down: Yippee! Now I can work on my book, get out of here, 'play' with my people."

Another reason to write is a sense of duty, whether to oneself, to one's goals or to one's art. For example, Cees Nooteboom says that what gets him started is wanting to write: "It's a form of *devoir*, that's a sense of duty, and also knowing that if you let it slip, say oh well, after the weekend, or something like that, that is not good." Asked if he means that he would feel guilty, he responds, "No, no guilt. It has to do with the arithmetic that I follow. It's the idea that you must finish the thing. And I have this idea that you have to do a certain amount of words a day. I'm not curious enough to double the words."

Of course, a sense of obligation to stick to your preset goals can be combined with fun as a motivator. David Gerrold describes his elaborate system of helping himself stay productive:

> On a working day—this is very interesting because I have a spreadsheet I use to tally how many hours a day—so about every fifteen minutes I do a word count and put in the word count and what it does is it lets me know I'm averaging about twelve words a minute and earning so much per hour, but also predicts the date the book will be done.
> Q: So this is all a very motivating thing, I guess.
> A: Well, yeah, because also every day there's a target of about two thousand words so I want to see if I can hit the target every day. Now

if I don't hit it, so what, but you know if I play for "let's see how high I can make my cumulative average," then . . . There are days when I hit 150 percent or 200 percent. Once I hit 250 percent, because I was really carried away. And that's pretty good. I can take the next day off if I want to. And the next day I hit 150 percent. Because what happens is I find a really juicy part of the story and I just sail through it.

When deadlines help

Researchers have found again and again that work feels like play when you're motivated intrinsically, that an intense involvement in an activity for its own sake, with little or no thought of future rewards, leads to positive feelings, persistence, creativity and flow. It's also been found, however, that when extrinsic rewards or motivators, such as competition or the pressure of being evaluated, are thrown into the mix, the desire to do the thing for its own sake may be undermined. All rewards, even verbal feedback ("Good writing!") or something as simple as a pat on the back, provide information regarding competence. That is, when someone tells you how well they think you're doing, they mean to give you information about how well you're doing. Obviously. But such remarks and rewards often tend to have a controlling aspect, and *that* is perceived by some individuals as something crucial. It shifts the focus, the locus of causality—the "who's in charge, who's the boss of me, who's the judge here?"—from internal to external. (Poet Lucille Clifton once said, "If someone gives you permission, they can take it away. I give *myself* permission.") This shift, in turn, tends to reduce your inner urge to do the thing for its own sake, at least in the long run. One psychologist writes of the "laxative principle of motivation": "People who always take laxatives become dependent on them—they can't push for themselves." Similarly, those individuals who have incorporated parental "pushings" and societal standards may eventually push themselves, as if from the outside, with similar unfortunate effects on their feelings of autonomy.

Some writers, of course, are able to ignore deadlines when they become unrealistic (to the writer's mind). Says Diana Gabaldon, "Let's put it this way: we have deadlines in my contracts because there's a space for them. I've never met one. They get the book when I'm finished with it. They scream and tear their hair a lot. . . . But I have a much higher loyalty to my book than I do to any of them." (Remember, Gabaldon's a best-selling author and has earned a certain freedom.)

What does this have to do with flow entry? When you're writing *only* as a means to an end (to shut up the voice in your head, to please someone else, to meet a deadline obligation, to pay the rent, to win an award), you're typically less intensely absorbed by and engaged in the task itself, which in turn, reduces the likelihood of entering flow. The good news is that extrinsic motivators may *combine* with intrinsic ones to make flow even more likely, so long as the extrinsic push doesn't come to feel like an effort at control by someone else. That feeling of being controlled by another person or by outside forces may make a difference in your work in both broad and subtle ways, always depending on your response to the sense that you are being manipulated toward ends other than your own. For example, say you are harboring the thought that your editor—whoever gave you the deadline—has marketing and sales considerations in mind rather than quality. If you feel pushed to hurry, you might either shortchange the work or you might resist meeting the deadline in an effort to hold fast to your internal ideal for it.

If your deadline feels as though it would be unreasonable or unreachable unless you sacrificed either your sanity or the quality of the work, then you may, as mystery author Sue Grafton once did, decide to speak up:

> I don't have a formal deadline anymore. I used to do a book a year, and I would turn in the manuscript September 1 or thereabouts. At a certain point the promotional work began taking a larger and larger bite out of my schedule. So suddenly, I could do the book a year, if it was just about the writing, but to stop and do phone interviews, to do the tour, print interviews, I was getting more tense and more stressed, and for me that's the opposite of flow. When I got to *"K" Is for Killer*, I had thought *"K Was for Kidnap*," and pursued that for four months, couldn't make the story work, dumped it, started again and all of a sudden I started having a book, instead of September 1, it was December 1. Holt scrambled around and got the book out. But you start getting hasty, you skip things. So at that point I told them it was killing me. I know how I am, I will hit my mark, I will hit my deadline, and one day I'll wake up and think, screw this, I won't ever write another word of it. If you want to keep me going, you better make it possible. It seems to take me ten months no matter when I start. I just keep them informed as to where I am. . . . I think it's such a drain to have that sense of someone hovering.

Deadlines, certainly, can be experienced as turning writing into a mere means to an end. Yet, plenty of writers find them of value in keeping themselves on track. When you don't have an imposed deadline, consider setting yourself mini-deadlines. Deadlines are also a way of setting standards to measure yourself against, which fulfills the writer's need for immediate feedback. That way you know when you're approaching mastery and you can sense your own efficiency increasing. Surely, sometimes you do your best, most flowing work when you're on a tight deadline and you know it's vital work by which you will indeed be judged. Facing a deadline, your perfectionism steps (or is forced) aside so that you are able to meet the goal. When you have a limited time to produce your work, you may find it focuses you, as Marvin Bell has said:

> Do I procrastinate? Yes, I delay until something has begun, and the right energy seems available. And sometimes I wait for a deadline to come closer, knowing it will force me to stay with the writing. There are inner deadlines I can only sense (the pot simmers) and outer deadlines I can put on the calendar. Both kinds release adrenalin.

Stephen and I and several of our writer friends have for many years now called ourselves the Writers' Bloc, an informal group not to be confused with other "official" groups by the same or similar names (as it happens, this name was only arrived at through a great deal of compromise—at one point, a few of the members wanted to call us "The Dregs," but I vociferously protested that such a low-self-esteem-promoting name could be self-fulfilling). Anyway, every month or so we get together at someone's house or a local coffee house, and share what we've written on a particular theme (though there are no rules and if someone writes on another theme, that's fine too). Those group deadlines have been extremely motivating to several of us. At one point when one key member lived in another state, we tried another scenario that we carried out by mail: we called it "The Challenge." We took turns challenging one or more group members to produce and send around copies of a story or poem.

Nevertheless, if the upcoming judgment somehow becomes paramount in your mind, then you're not only less likely to persist in flow, but psychic paralysis can set in. A noteworthy point about the whole group deadline dynamic I've just discussed is that we have never judged nor even critiqued each other; the whole point is to motivate and support one another.

Q. Does setting goals, i.e., a certain number of pages per day, or determining one day is for writing, one for ideas and concepts only, etc., make writing easier?

A. The best answer to this question is, "Try it." Be scientific about it, if you can. Set yourself a goal of two pages a day, or five hundred words, for example, and stick to your schedule for two weeks. Then count your output. Don't neglect to figure in your stress levels and how you feel about yourself as a writer at the end of the two weeks (if that matters to you—it doesn't to everyone). Then try it another way, either going back to your usual way, whatever that is, or a new way, such as setting aside Tuesdays and Thursdays, or the weekend, for planning and out-lining only, or for research, or for revising. Setting goals and structuring your writing life does work very well for many writers, making it seem like more of a job for which you then feel responsible. Others, of course, figure "What's the point of being a writer if I'm going to treat myself like a factory worker or corporate drone?" I'm one of these. I delight in the flexibility my full-time writing job affords me, and by now, I've come to trust myself to work fairly regularly. Sometimes all I have to do is consider alternative careers I might have chosen—that sends me scurrying back to my computer.

Also, what works best for you this year may not be what most enhances your productivity next year. Sometimes it seems I work best when I have absolutely nothing else to do that day—no appointments, no phone calls expected, no grocery shopping that must be completed before we can eat. At other times, knowing I have to be somewhere at 5 P.M. seems to focus my attention extremely well, and I get a great deal accomplished.

There may also be a personal difference among writers: some are more prey to the deadly, motivation-killing aspects of deadlines and being judged from the outside. If you allow such thoughts—thoughts of being judged—to take hold, you lose your confidence in your own abilities. Some writers, too, have become their own harshest judges, having incorporated critical voices from their own pasts and families of origin.

Your reward or mine?

Some theorists dispute the conclusion that intrinsic motivation is more significant in fostering creative work than extrinsic motivation. For example, novelists such as Twain and Dickens published their great works in monthly serials. On the other hand, it's possible that those who are eminent in and knowledgeable about a domain have developed means of dealing with the potentially negative effects of extrinsic rewards. Experienced writers are often able to transform their task by either concentrating on some previously overlooked portion of the environment or of the writing, or by varying into the way they write. People need to find some internal rewards for uninteresting tasks even when they feel constrained to do them. The distinction between *extrinsic* and *intrinsic* motivation may then blur.

Finally, attitudes toward deadlines and pressure from the outside world vary as widely as the novels and poems created. For example, Jack Kerouac said "you force yourself to sit at the typewriter . . . and get it over with as fast as you can" when the rent is due, but Christopher Isherwood expressed an opposing view when he said, "[I'd get unstuck by] never allowing myself to get frantic. Repeating to myself, 'There's no deadline; it'll be finished when it's finished.'" Donald Hall has exemplified both aspects of motivation. Clearly, he loves to write and is highly intrinsically motivated: "When I finished reading and correcting and grading and commenting on seventy-five student essay-questions about a Ben Jonson or a Tom Clark poem, *then*—as a reward— I could get to work." And yet Hall is also aware that he is driven by additional barely conscious hopes and values:

Absorbedness is the paradise of work, but what is its provenance or etiology? Surely it is an ecstasy of transport, of loss of ego; but it is also something less transcendent: To work is to please the powerful masters who are parents—who are family, who are church, who are custom or culture. Not to work is to violate the contract or to disobey the injunction, and to displease the dispensers of supper and love, of praise's reward.

Some writers are quite frank that they often write due to more extrinsic than intrinsic motivation: "Paying the bills" (Octavia E. Butler); "I also started earning money right away with my writing, so then when you start earning money, I mean I had to earn money, I had to support myself and my kids" (Carolyn See); "I'm not being

Q. Will I work better if I plan a reward for the end of the work session, such as a great lunch, a long walk, a TV program or allowing myself to read a good book?

A. Such external incentives may help you beat back your own resistance to starting the writing. It happens to depend on your personal constitution. Some people tend to rebel when someone tries to manipulate them into doing something they don't want to do, and some carry it even further by rebelling against *themselves*. It's so much better, in the long run, to find incentives in the work itself. What would make it fun for you? Could one of your characters be a real joker? How about having an event happen in your story or poem that fulfills a wish of your own? Can you find a way to challenge yourself within the confines of the project? If you find that you need to reward yourself every single time you write, you are probably not getting into flow. Flow is its own reward.

Think of it this way: there's nothing wrong with working out a pleasantly balanced life. First you write, than you have a leisurely lunch while you read a chapter of a good novel. By making the writing habitual, the lunch and reading time aren't so much rewards as normal parts of the day you come to expect.

facetious when I say that the necessity to get there is that for twenty years writing is the sole way I earn a dollar. And I get into that state or I don't pay the rent. So I don't look at it as very metaphysical. I look at it as a job" (Michael Ventura).

Of course, some of those who mention the lure of money also combine that with a deep intrinsic drive. Take magazine editor Martin J. Smith, who describes in a *Los Angeles Times* interview how he wrote his debut novel, *Time Release*: "I decided to commit to two years of sleep deprivation. I bought myself a good alarm clock. I'm up at 4 and writing until 6 or 6:30, then getting the kids up and starting the day." Explaining why he taped his advance check to his computer, he says, "You need every motivation you can get." But he adds, "Book writing is the best-paying hobby I've ever had."

Reasons to write, then, can be compelling and multiple, accumulating and interlocking in particular ways for each writer.

Turning Key One

To help you put the ideas in this chapter into practice in your own writing life, here are some questions and suggestions to think about.

1. Reflect on why you want to write. List all the reasons that come to mind. Do this for writing in general and for any project with which you may be having difficulty getting engaged. Which of these reasons are particularly relevant to you? Sometimes bringing to consciousness why you want to do something makes it easier to concentrate on what it takes to accomplish it.

2. In most instances, what actually causes you to sit down to write? What do you think will happen if you start a poem, finish a story, work on your novel? What might happen if you don't? Consider whether the results you expect are strong enough to motivate you to write. Expected results might include the delight of your eventual readers, praise from a respected editor, a check in the mail or the sheer relief of completing a long-term project. Might there be other benefits to settling in to write, such as a sense of using your talents or a chance to play around with characters or words?

3. Do you sometimes feel you can't do your most creative work because you're going to be judged? If so, try to determine why that judgment is more significant to you than your own goals. Do the people you imagine to be judging you honestly have the power to determine the worth of what you write? Are you certain they are more qualified than you are to say what's good and what isn't, particularly in the draft stage, or worse, before you've even committed it to paper!

4. Do you have a hard time remaining convinced that what you do matters? Reread one or more of the books that have moved you in the past. Think about the possibility of affecting others with your own work, of provoking emotion, giving pleasure, changing the world in a tiny way.

5. To intensify your motivation, find ways to increase the novelty and challenge of your writing projects. Give yourself assignments; not artificial exercises, but new ways to approach the work you want to do. Try a new genre or a new form. Write from some other point of view. Begin a story in a way you've never done before.

Q. I have the hardest time writing at home. Everything distracts me. Yet I come up with all kinds of reasons why I can't write anywhere else either. Am I kidding myself about my desire to write?

A. You have to get to know yourself. There's no way around it. I had a conversation not long ago with Nigel, a documentary filmmaker. When I mentioned my interest in flow, he told me it was extremely hard for him to write at home. He thought his difficulty might be related to the way his home office was arranged: his desk is in the living room, facing a window. Nigel's back, then, is to the rest of the room and the door, an arrangement he dislikes but for which he can imagine no feasible alternative. He can write more easily in crowded coffee shops, he says, but even then he stops every fifteen minutes to look around and refresh and restimulate himself with the conversations and bustle around him. If he does enter flow at those times, it is a disappointingly fleeting and staccato experience. At home, he has found he can focus better when he wears stereo headphones directing loud music into his ears. It seemed plain, at first, that distractibility was his actual problem, and that what he needed to do was figure out a way to have a totally nondistracting environment or keep using the headphones.

Next he told me that when he is in an office working on a paying freelance assignment, he is able to produce without overwhelming strain. It seems the structure, the paycheck and the deadline all help him achieve the desired focus. I began to wonder if focus was the issue, or whether it was the strength of his motivation to write that was keeping him from the screenwriting. I asked him if he ever enters flow when working on his own. "Absolutely," he said, his entire demeanor changing, the way a person's tone changes when describing an adored child or a new love object. "When I'm editing a project, I can work for ten hours straight on nothing but coffee, without eating and without noticing the time at all." For this creator, it appears, the editing process is when time stops. Our conversation ended with Nigel musing, "Maybe I shouldn't be writing original scripts at all. Perhaps I ought to get someone else to do that part and concentrate on editing."

Start at the end. Forget about the goal and find the fun. If you typically write with an outline, try not to. Or begin writing without an ending in mind. If you never write with a plan, see what happens if you plan ahead.

6. Try letting an idea build up in your mind until you absolutely have to write it all out. Try *not* taking the pressure off yourself by jotting down brief notes. Rather, each time you have an idea for a note, continue to write until the whole series of thoughts has spun itself out. Do not talk about your ideas for a project until you are far along in the writing of it, if then.

7. Do you have a persistent problem with procrastination? Consider how deadlines can work to increase your daily motivation. If you find they help you concentrate, without necessarily making you feel less creative, set yourself realistic deadlines. Make lists or charts, or set aside a special calendar for your writing tasks. Get something in the mail every Friday, or the first of every month, even if it's only to a writing friend for feedback. Break each writing project into a batch of very small tasks and set reasonable deadlines for these. The idea is not to feel guilty when you miss a deadline by a few days, but to better fine-tune your writing process. Eventually you'll learn to set more and more feasible deadlines for yourself, and to stick to them. If you're competitive, see if you can beat your own deadlines or write more words over a day or week or month or year than you did the previous period of time.

8. Serve as your own career coach. Think about how you might motivate yourself on an ongoing basis by determining your writing goals and setting up action steps to achieve them. First define success for yourself. Will you feel you have achieved your aims when you can impress someone in particular, are writing regularly, selling regularly, have written a best-seller, have one piece of work completed that you are totally pleased with? Which of these are feasible, and which ones do you want to work toward whether or not you can be assured of reaching them? Determine dates for assessing where you are in your plan, perhaps rethinking your goals.

4 Key Two: Think Like a Writer

HOW YOU THINK IS SUCH AN INTEGRAL PART of your personality that I wouldn't be surprised if some of you questioned the premise of this chapter. After all, many people believe, like Popeye, that "I yam what I yam." Whether native temperament can be changed or not (you aren't exactly the same person you were ten years ago, are you?), you *can* strengthen and bring to the forefront of your personality those aspects that will contribute to making your writing life more gratifying.

Attitudes, in fact, are most assuredly under your control. And attitudes directly lead to how you act on a day-to-day basis. You can *decide* to approach your work, as well as other parts of your life, with an attitude of greater openness. You can *choose* to work at becoming more absorbed in your writing, difficult as that might be, if it matters enough to you. You can *learn* the skills that go into being a more resilient person, and eventually these skills will translate into having greater confidence in yourself as a writer. Once you move these attitudes in the direction of "thinking like a writer," it won't matter what score you might have gotten on a personality test years ago, or what you might once have thought were the limits of your temperament.

I'm not suggesting you can achieve commercial success and receive all the worldly acclaim you'd like or perhaps deserve, merely by deciding to or believing you can. But if you are so inclined, you can change your attitudes in such a way that you will become a more productive writer, a writer who is more comfortable and self-assured about the creative process itself. In other words, a writer who can flow.

In my research, even though I didn't give anyone standardized personality tests or attempt to turn our interviews into personal, analytic sessions, I did come away from my conversations with writers filled with ideas about how a good writer thinks. Furthermore, in my subsequent readings and conversations with top psychologists in the field of creativity research, I confirmed that my ideas make good sense.

This line of thinking began for me when I first noticed tantalizing connections between the writers' personalities and the way they experience flow. For example, one of the first writers I ever interviewed was a longtime friend, so I was able to see that his flow pattern is consistent with his personality, in that he lives in an especially self-reflective and conscious manner. He tends to work hard to maintain control and autonomy in his life, and he chooses to begin writing and enter flow (and thus, give up some control) only when he has finally determined that the other parts of his life are "just right." Another writer I know tends to blur boundaries in many areas of his life, and so his ability to enter flow and write creatively is no surprise. Yet another has exhibited some rebellious traits, and therefore when he told me he most intensely enjoys writing when he is "supposed" to be doing something else, it seemed a natural extension of his personality. You can't help but get a tiny hint of the personality propelling a writer who says, when asked, that the vertical lines in his preferred notebooks not only don't bother him, but rather, they help him, "because the writing turns out neat." When you work with what comes naturally to you rather than struggling against it—whether it's your preference for an uncluttered workspace or your tendency to do the opposite when those little voices in your head suggest that you ought to be answering those letters rather than writing a poem—you can apply your energy to what matters most to you.

Your personal values come into play too. What do you believe about the "rightness" of the time you spend writing and in flow? Some writers see it as an expression of the highest morality, and others are troubled by the niggling feeling that taking too much time for their writing is slightly selfish because it's like stealing time from their family. If you identify with that second attitude, naturally you might find it more difficult to let go and focus fully when you do sit down to write.

63

Is there a creative writer's personality?

Scientists, architects, dancers, cooks: all are creative and perhaps all share certain personality tendencies. While I delved into the research on the creative personality, I discovered that each of the studies that had been done came up with a different, sometimes overlapping, set of qualities that seem to make up the creative personality. The terms each researcher used were distinct, too, resulting in a rather unhelpful situation for an individual writer seeking immediate, practical guidance. For instance, one researcher found creative people to be introverted (among other traits), another found them immensely demanding of themselves and others, while a third found them to possess strong egos. Yet another suggests that writers don't have great mood swings during writing, while other studies found writers to be especially intuitive.

More important, though, than any of these specific research results, is the fact that personality traits that tend to lead toward creative accomplishment don't operate like on-off switches. The tests that researchers have done have shown strong trends, but they're not mandates by any means. According to eminent creativity researcher Frank Barron, "There are many exceptions to everything. Like medical diagnoses, they're just probability statements and frequently wrong." In other words, as valuable as it is for the study of creativity as a whole, the scientific research on creative personalities may not have a lot to do with *your* own individual success as a writer.

Barron, in summing up decades of research, much of it with writers, points out something else of value: an intense desire to create is the most common aspect of creative people. In addition, he posits a "cosmological motive," that is, a drive to find order and make sense of everything, including this world.

The natural writer

Let's begin by examining what I like to call "the natural writer." These are the writers for whom, more than for most, flow is a natural state. They claim to live, when daily life allows, in an extended day-long flow. Poet Charles Harper Webb, for instance, says, "It's never a struggle. It's a struggle to be the other way." Prolific romance novelist Phoebe Conn agrees, "I sit down and turn on my computer and work. I wouldn't even notice [moving into a flow state]. There's not a shift." A few spend most of their lives in a parallel world of their own imagining, always in a mild flow around their characters' lives. For some of those who are in flow much of the time, it's as though there's a valve (the prosaic concerns of reality) holding them back from flow. They just have to open it and let themselves go through.

Much of what such an individual thinks of as natural may have been learned over years of experiences, yet it feels utterly inborn. I suspect that getting into flow easily, so easily that you come to believe it's a natural ability, may be closely related to whatever it is that makes one person more intrinsically motivated than another. If you're one of those who believes it's a good thing to be "most fully yourself," flow would tend to be highly self-rewarding for you.

About a quarter of those I studied indicated that flow—losing track of time while writing—is a natural part of who they are. Novelist Madison Smartt Bell, for instance, told me that he thinks he has a natural facility for living in a dreamworld, and that's probably why he became a fiction writer. Diana Gabaldon, whose thick historical/romantic time-travel novels have sold millions of copies, says she feels as though she was "meant to write novels. I've known that since I was about eight. I have always had stories going on in my mind." And so with Faye Kellerman, who says she was always a spacey child who lived inside her head. Frank X. Gaspar, too, finds flow completely unremarkable. "It's about as natural as having breakfast," he says. "My mother would say, 'Frank, you're in the stars. Come back to earth. Where do you go? Your mouth opens, and you're catching flies.' And that's the part of my intelligence, or the kind of intelligence, that writes."

Some natural writers who spend a lot of time in flow may do so in an almost purposeful disengagement from reality. "I remember getting so involved with reading science fiction that my family would disappear," Stephen told me. "I wonder if some of the precursors of my current ease of flow would be simply my zoning out in those jobs where I would be a typist. I would love just simply not thinking, not being."

If losing track of time is an element of flow, then what about those individuals who are out of touch with time almost *all the time*? ("I lose track of time whether I am in the flow or not," asserts Mark Strand.) It struck me that, although I'm used to saying that I have a much stronger reality orientation than my husband, what we actually have is a paradox. When I think of where I am in time, I imagine my calendar book superimposed on my mental space. I am picturing what I have to do today, what's written there that is pressing on me, what day, time, season it is, and so on. When I think of where I am in space, I picture a large map and see myself in this house on this street, in this area of this city, and so on, until I picture, if it seems relevant, where I am in the world and even universe. But those grids are actually symbols for the real things. And Stephen, who has no idea of or concern with his time/space context much of the time, may actually be experiencing himself in reality more directly, without the interference of all those symbols. Here and now, the *real* here and now, unmediated by maps, calendars, watches and to-do lists, may be the most real you can get. Passing much of the day in that kind of *direct* confrontation with time, with *now*, is, at least for many writers, more suitable for creating imaginative works.

Natural writers, then, seem to experience a totally guilt-free escape into flow as often as they possibly can. And, truth be told, they may even be more drawn to stories than to reality itself.

But I'm assuming you're not a "natural" writer who gets into flow whenever you want to. Maybe you don't really have a compelling interest in learning to be spacier. It isn't necessary. Even if you sometimes struggle with ambivalence about leaving the world behind, I can offer you hope for learning to access your creativity. What it takes is putting into practice certain attitudes until they become second nature to you.

In the rest of the sections in this chapter, I'll share what I've found to be the most often occurring and salient of the characteristics and attitudes found in creative writers, and I'll suggest ways you might move toward thinking more like a writer. If you can develop an attitude of sufficient openness to experience, you'll be more able to withstand the anxiety-producing challenge of plunging into your own creative depths and coming up with written work. Being able to get fully absorbed in what you're writing is a personality trait, but it's also an attitude that can be cultivated. In addition, emotional resilience is a necessity in a domain that is, of necessity, so internally driven. You can learn to do the work in spite of fear or anxiety.

Open to experience

What does it mean to be "open to experience?" I think of it as a kind of active passivity. It happens when you allow yourself to consider all possibilities rather than shutting any out automatically. It's a combination of being curious, sensitive to what's going on in the world around you, and having a certain liberal attitude about life. When researchers looked at the relationship between openness to experience, creative

Q. I've always worried just a tiny bit that maybe I'm an oddball. The way I write seems so *strange*. Do my writing habits mean I'm a little off?

A. You are definitely not alone in feeling odd. Many writers have said to me in one form or another: I wonder if this is normal, or I don't know if anyone else does this, or I thought I was the only one who did it this way, or you're going to think this is weird. These expressions reminded me of Gardner's study of eminent creators in which he found a high incidence of a sense of marginality, of not fitting in. Nevertheless, a couple of writers told me they couldn't imagine writers pursuing their craft any other way. One said something akin to "the world, *c'est moi*," though even he felt a bit sad that he isn't able to share the flow experience with his wife. Apparently, writers are so unlike one another that they don't even universally share a common sense of bizarreness.

The fact is that, among creative writers, you are not atypical, but you are not *ordinary*. As Frank Barron puts it so well, "I have spoken, as we psychologists do, of the 'normal' range, but please remember . . . that normality is a characteristic of distribution of scores, not of individuals like you and me. Everyone is odd."

ability and creative accomplishment, they determined that openness moderates the relation between creative ability and creative accomplishments. It's this openness to experience, then, that provides you with the impetus to explore creative avenues and to pursue a career like writing.

Again and again in my reading about and interviewing writers, I found examples of an openness to experience, as well as a blurring of the expected boundaries (certainly the opposite of the typical Western ways of perceiving the world). Often this was accompanied by a fascination with Zen/Buddhist/mystical/occult thought. Such an openness to crossing boundaries may directly relate to ease of flow entry (there's more about this in the next chapter on loosening up).

What do you experience when you get lost? Is it closer to delight or to despair? I always study a map before setting out, and I've been reluctant to take nature hikes if the signposts seem badly marked, unless I'm with someone with a better sense of direction than my own. I detest that uncertain feeling of not knowing where I am in physical space. Novelist Jim Harrison, though, said in an interview, "I told them . . . I'd write them a little piece about getting lost and all the profoundly good aspects of being lost—the immense fresh feeling of really being lost." Award-winning science-fiction author Ursula Le Guin emphasizes the importance of this quality in her own terms:

> Fiction is made out of experience, your whole life from infancy on, everything you've thought and done and seen and read and dreamed. But experience isn't something you go and *get*—it's a gift, and the only prerequisite for receiving it is that you be open to it.

When you're open, you're also more readily inspired by everyday events. You don't need something extraordinary to happen before you feel the urge to write. As poet James Ragan expresses it, "I open myself to inspiration. . . . Everything has the nature of excitement for me, whether it's meeting a new person or being in a new situation, a new city or writing a new poem." I asked him how he thinks that openness developed in him, and he told me:

> I had cancer when I was twenty-six years old and I almost died from that. Because of that experience and going through such a torturous two years of my life, I realized what living was going to be. From that point on, I was openly sensitive to everything because I wanted to be. I had true motivation to realize that my life was almost cut short. And if I was going to write, it wasn't going to be about trivia.

Does this mean you need to defy death at an early age to become sensitive and open to life? I don't believe so. While dramatic stories like Ragan's are relatively rare, you can learn to appreciate and value every moment by paying close attention to the lives and histories of others. I've come to believe that you don't have to hit bottom to learn the lessons of crisis. You do need to be able to imagine yourself experiencing other lives, but then that's what creative writers do so well.

Take a risk

Among the writers I spoke with, I discovered numerous examples of openness to experience, exemplified by a delight in intellectual risk-taking. One that stands out is poet Richard Jones saying, "Risk is *always* fun." Another is Susan Taylor Chehak saying, "I have in mind that it [flow] may be dangerous. But I've always flirted with disaster, it's sort of the way I was brought up."

Q. How does flow fit in with the Buddhist concept of mindfulness?
A. According to Jon Kabat-Zinn, author of *Wherever You Go There You Are*, an aspect of Buddhist-style mindfulness is "non-doing." He describes this non-doing as a particular kind of action, much like flow. For instance, he writes, "Non-doing simply means letting things be and allowing them to unfold in their own way. Enormous effort can be involved, but it is a graceful, knowledgeable, effortless effort, a 'doerless doing,' cultivated over a lifetime." He describes effortless activity as being able to take place in any domain. "Years of practice and experience combine on some occasions, giving rise to a new capacity to let execution unfold beyond technique, beyond exertion, beyond thinking. Action then becomes a pure expression of that, of being, of letting go of all doing—a merging of mind and body in motion." According to Kabat-Zinn, meditation is synonymous with such non-doing, although he equates this with an acceptance that things are perfect as they are, perfectly *what* they are.

Altered states researcher Charles T. Tart says flow and mindfulness practices and states are parallels, if not equals. "My work on mindfulness is about creating a mind set or state of consciousness that is present-centered and applies in all life situations, rather than being induced by a task per se," he explains. When you write in flow, though, there is a goal, an ideal held in the mind to work toward. It's all a matter of perspective.

Buddhist-style mindfulness also includes letting go into the moment and taking a nonjudgmental orientation, which are prerequisites of flow entry, although this letting go is balanced, say writers, with allowing the internal critic back in (later on, usually) to do what it needs to do to ensure the desired outcome. The process of composition can be experienced as a journey. You don't need to know where you're going when you start. You take one step forward, then another, with each step creating the journey. Later, you can look back to see where you've been.

When you're not afraid to risk, you increase your odds of coming up with something novel. Playwright Edward Albee has been quoted as saying about fellow playwright Sam Shepard: "Sam was always taking chances, always being original. Somebody who was willing to fail and fail interestingly. And if you're willing to fail interestingly, you tend to succeed interestingly."

Taking risks, of whatever kind, can be especially challenging to those who can't bear to give up control. If your desire for control is higher than average, you'll naturally have a tendency to try to structure your world so as to avoid *uncontrollable* situations and the stress they cause you. Sometimes, of course, that's not possible, and, for some creative writers, it may not be desirable. You can learn to open yourself to the unexpected, which is such a rich source of creative insight, by giving up control in small ways. Sue Grafton, a self-identified "control freak," describes her own quandary:

> I try not to worry about anything I can't control. I can't control marketing plans. I can't control what a reader reacts to. For instance, I'm looking at my desk. I love tidy, I love order. I love routine, I love regulation. Because all of that contributes to flow. If I look around my desk and I see unanswered letters, pencils out of place, the mail piled up, I go insane. Because to me it's little voices going, Do me, help me. . . . Currently we have construction on the premises. It's madness. So I just look at all of this as a way of practicing. I can't control it, so I have to set it aside. If you can't control your immediate environment, then you have to lift yourself out of it or sink beneath it and go on with the work. It's good practice. I'll never get it right.

Another novelist admitted to me that he gets anxious when he's not in control, that he isn't an adventurous person, that even when he goes on book tours and is in a new city for three days, he stays comfortably ensconced in his hotel room. As such, he is an example of how the need for control and the backing-off from new experiences can, in some ways, work against your ease at entering a flow state. For, although he's a fine writer who has had commercial success, he rarely manages to get into flow, and then only for minutes at a time. He thinks of writing as hard work and doesn't enjoy the process nearly as much as writers who told me they both love risk and spend long periods in intense flow.

Such examples are actually of comfort to me. These days, I'm not much of a risk-taker or an adventurer in my real life. Yet it's possible to learn to be more open to taking the sorts of risk—intellectual and imaginative risks—that lead to creative breakthroughs. I'll share how it began happening for me, and perhaps you can find some catalyst in your own life that will produce similar benefits.

Stephen and I like to play computer adventure games, not the kind where hand-eye coordination is the most vital skill required (blast the alien before it conquers your planet), but the kind where you're trying to figure something out and achieve some goal. When we began to play several years ago, elaborate graphic adventures had not yet taken over from simple text-only games. With the latter games, you can type in anything you can think of, and the machine is programmed to respond, even if only to type back, "I don't understand this command." When we first played these games together, Stephen would come up with outlandish ideas to try in order to get past some obstacle in the game, and I would routinely and predictably squawk, "You can't do that!" I have no idea what I was afraid of, other than the new, the untried, the unexpected. We both still joke about the time when we (us on the screen, in the game) needed to get past a stubborn guard to go up some stairs to get a key to continue to the next scene of the game. We tried everything logical, while a little frog jumped nearby and made inane comments, but no luck. For two or three nights we were stuck and frustrated. Finally, Stephen typed in, "Throw the frog at the wall," and I, of course, was horrified (remembering childhood pals who had done hurtful things to frogs). But it worked. When we "threw" the frog, it grabbed the needed key for us, and so we bypassed the recalcitrant guard and got unstuck.

I thought about my habitual risk-aversion and finally realized there was actually no risk involved in games. Then I was able to loosen up. My real test came when I made a move in a game that resulted in the blowing up of a horse into grisly bits. It would have been thoroughly neurotic to let my guilt at this fantasy play consequence upset me in the least. So I didn't. Since then, I have often considered whether some experimental action I wanted to take was as risky as it usually first feels to me. That's why I know it's possible to become more open. Even if it's your usual tendency to holler, "But you can't. . . !", it's possible to learn to pull a switch in your thinking and allow yourself to do whatever it is anyway.

Many authors, at least in their writing, take extreme risks—emotionally, psychologically, aesthetically. In an interview in which Anne Rice described her writing of *Memnoch*, which is about the vampire Lestat and an argument between God and the devil, she said,

> This book was just as instinctively written as *Interview With the Vampire*. . . . With all the others there was more thought, more doubt, more hesitation. . . . I write now like I did when I wrote *Interview*—all night long. *Interview With the Vampire* was written in five weeks; this was written in about four weeks, and it was the same sort of experience—

just surrendering to the process. And I found myself asking the same kinds of questions. I kept asking, "How *dare* you write these things!"

In spite of questioning herself as to her own audacity, Rice went ahead and stopped fighting the creative process that seemed to be taking her over.

Jane Smiley, a Pulitzer Prize-winning author, is one of those open personalities who is able to get fully into whatever she's doing, whether chores or writing, which is a form of glorious play for her. Even the outgoing message on her phone machine is an astonishing "The answer is yes." When I asked her about how this might relate to an attitude of openness and risk-taking in her personality, she responded, "I'm never afraid to do anything."

> Yet, I have to do it in a fairly deliberate way. I write in a quite deliberate way. I write three, four pages a day, I don't go too quickly. I think my books, though they don't have a lot in common with one another, do have a certain kind of underlying pace in common, a kind of steady forward motion and they do have a kind of belief that any event or phenomenon can be understood and assimilated if you, or if the character, goes about contemplating it in a systematic way. So that's pretty much who I am. In my life, and also in my work. I write every day, several pages, and I don't get too upset—I don't get upset at all about anything having to do with my writing.

Smiley agrees that some of her openness (and her admirable resilience and equanimity) may be attributable to the nonrestrictive way she was raised. She believes that it's hard to be a writer and to have a productive and happy life if what she and a friend of hers call "the committee" is always in session.

> One of the things my cousins and I always joke about is about how we grew up wild. We weren't trained or judged. We had to say ma'am and sir, we were taught certain forms of good manners, not to expressly contradict our parents. But we never had piano lessons, we weren't taught strict hygiene, we weren't given chores, we weren't required to go to church. The list of things we were not required to do is as long as your arm. The result of that is that all of my cousins are happy in their adult lives. They all have a lot of *joie de vivre*. Everybody is relatively creative or interested in creative things. The last thing anybody in my family would ever have said to one of the kids was, "You've got to go out and make a living."

Q. I'm an extrovert. Would I enjoy being in flow for long periods? **A.** For many highly creative introverts, losing the self in flow is an ideal state of mind. They don't have to get anxious about dealing with strangers, nor bored by the ordinariness of much of what passes for social interaction. Rather, for as much time as they can manage it, they get to inhabit richly peopled worlds of their own imagining.

Many outgoing and social people, certainly, are productive and satisfied writers. As long as your strong social needs are met, you'll probably love periods of flow as much as most introverts do. The key is to find your own personal happy balance of interacting with others and playing around in your own brain. Yet it's always possible that writing novels isn't suited to your temperament. Whit Stillman, who wrote and directed the films *Metropolitan*, *Barcelona* and *The Last Days of Disco*, said that although he originally aspired to be a novelist, he found the solitude wasn't right for him: "I didn't like the prospect of an entire life spent writing a novel for four years, having lunch with your editor, getting a telegram that it's published and then going back and writing another. I thought maybe in film I could do something where I wouldn't have to write all the time, where I could be involved in stories in an industrial production line." Only you know which lifestyle sounds better to you.

Nora Okja Keller, in discussing her own kind of openness, said this:

I talk with other writers about how writers think, about what makes our thinking different. Maybe it's an openness in terms of exploring different possibilities, different versions of what people consider as fact, trying to explore what goes on behind the scenes. You see somebody picking flowers in the garden at McDonald's, and you don't just stop there and say that somebody's picking flowers. You say, why is that person there, what motivates that person? When I was taking the bus, it was always interesting to see the people get on and wonder about the various stories. And I like to think of different versions of what could be possible.

Diana Gabaldon, a very open person these days, says that when she was younger, she was shy, constrained and conservative, even picky in her food tastes. "I have a cautious streak that was ingrained in me. It was more of a fear of the expectations of others. I was so brainwashed into always doing things that people expected me to." In her late twenties and early thirties she began to expand a little, and when she realized this wasn't a threat, she became much more adventurous. As a matter of fact, she adds, "I'm a gambler at heart, and it was only much later in life that I realized I've been one all along." When she began writing novels, Gabaldon had no intention of showing them to anyone, and thus, "there was essentially no risk to it at all. I could not fail."

Ellery Washington C. thinks of himself as a person who takes a lot of chances, and he attributes part of this to being what he calls "overly idealistic, one of those people who believes you can sort of make your life in many ways what you want it to be."

> I think that it's important for me to understand what it feels like to be alive. And because of that I'll take different risks. I haven't made usual choices and I've felt comfortable. What I've realized was said better by a famous anthropologist I saw on KCET: they asked him why is it that every culture studies religion, every culture seeks God. He said, "It's not God—they're seeking the rapture of life, to understand what it means to be alive." And that involves things that are physical and sensual, and it involves things that are spiritual and emotional. And I think there's some part of me that's caught up in that, to feel like I'm really living. Because of that, I think it has created in me a really adventuresome spirit. I'm willing to try many things until I'm certain they cause me harm.

A number of creative writers believe their childhood experiences are partly responsible for their current openness and ease of boundary-crossing in their lives and work. For example, Ed Ochester tells why he values having grown up in Queens, New York, in a lower middle-class and working-class family where no one had gone to college before he did, and where it was a challenge to be the only bookish one around:

> Most of the people in my family (sort of a German-Polish family) were friendly and supportive enough, but nobody ever opened up much. I think just the fact that there were a lot of them, a lot of different personalities I could observe, was very useful. When I'm talking about my life to a student, I'll usually say, "I was a teamster for two years." Probably, at the time, I never thought very much about it, but on the other hand, I really have grown to be extremely grateful that I had those kinds of experiences. I comment on parts of my life from other parts. Friends of mine from college who went to private schools, who never

held jobs, who had a fairly easy time of it through the time they went to college, I really envied, but on the other hand I don't envy them anymore. I think there was an impoverishment of experience that they had. That's the one way in which I see myself as occupying different spaces or crossing boundaries.

I hope you're not feeling perversely impoverished because you *did* have some of the so-called benefits writers like Ochester *didn't* have. Even in the most average middle-class background you can find quirk-iness, multiplicity, richness of experience—even if you never noticed it before.

Though I've been extraordinarily lucky to have been able to get as educated as I wanted to be, I've also had the usual horrendous part-time clerical jobs that I thought would drive me mad (including maga-zine sales by telephone for an excruciating half-day, during which I sold exactly one subscription, and felt guilty about it); I've had small needy children cling to me in nursery school jobs; I've met my share of oddities as a social worker for the mentally ill (including one now elderly woman who used to hear threatening voices in her head but who has remained my friend for twenty-eight years); I've wandered the streets of Paris all of one frigid December and clung idiotically to an Algerian boy under a succession of French bridges as only barely ac-quainted seventeen-year-olds can do; I've done stupid things like driv-ing drunk (once) and flooring the pedal on the urging of my co-sixteen-year-old passengers (luckily not on the same occasion as the previous stupid thing); I've met a pregnant woman in a class who, when asked if this was her first, told me that her other children had some years before perished in a house fire; I have a friend who once fought fires, another who flirted ever-so-briefly with the idea of being a stripper, and, not to forget, I used to be married to a Lebanese Arab, which is certainly a major border crossing that is so much a part of who I am that it tends to slip my daylight mind these days, though I occasionally, even now, dream of again visiting the "old country," which isn't *my* old country at all, and of being embraced by my large family of former in-laws whom I'll never see again.

Compile your own list of how your life so far has put you in contact with people unlike you. Think of how you've been affected by these many experiences (and it's always *many*—after all, I'm a relatively shy homebody-type, yet even I have had quite a range of encounters). If you're open enough to register them, any of these experiences and awarenesses might develop into insights, then be made into entertaining stories, poems and perhaps great art.

Fully absorbed

You are fully absorbed when you are deeply enough immersed in some activity as to be impervious to distractions and to have an altered sense of your self and of reality. As a personality trait, absorption reflects the degree of your tendency to become deeply engaged in movies, nature, past events, fantasy or anything else. It's also been argued that high-absorption people are motivated intrinsically, by their own experiences, while low-absorption people tend to be more motivated by outside events. If this theory is true, it confirms that if you're a self-motivating, self-rewarding person, you'll have an easier time becoming absorbed and entering flow. Still, where your consciousness tends to spend most of its time may be more of a habit than a mandatory default.

Interesting connections have been shown to exist between absorption, openness to experience and hypnotizability. It seems that absorption involves a tendency to process information in unusual ways, which is what you do as a creative writer. Absorption and fantasy-proneness may also be related; again, this calls to mind what creative writers do regularly.

If you're a high-absorption type, you're better able to screen out distractions, which is how you enter flow. Robert Olen Butler told me he "can't do anything part way," that he applies absolute absorption and concentration to everything. James Ragan said he believes in "passion about everything, in every aspect of my life. Passion and total absorption." Not surprisingly, then, Ragan discovered early on that he could write poetry in public places. "There's something about people around you in a café experience that is like a library, a library of life. The sounds, the voices, everything about that somehow contributes to the creative process for me." Of course, this could relate to Ragan's having grown up in a Slovak family of thirteen children, with a "constant barrage of cultures coming into my home," with no boundaries, but always a sense of connectedness. Clearly, he learned to work through the noise and bustle and find ways to integrate it into his work and make something positive and passionate out of what someone else might have found overwhelming.

Yet even if you're not (or don't believe you are) a high-absorption person, you can learn to deal with distraction. Jane Smiley told me she's not good at getting deeply absorbed:

> I always answer the phone if I'm writing. I can write while talking on the phone. If the conversation isn't all that interesting, I'll start writing secretly. One chapter of the book I'm writing now, I wrote while feeling very distracted. My bookkeeper was here, my kids were walking through, the cleaning ladies were walking through, the dogs were barking, I had to get up every several minutes to do something, and when I came back to that chapter later, it was great. I was feeling frustrated, but it didn't have any effect on the outcome of my writing.

Ellery Washington C. doesn't think of himself as a person who gets totally absorbed except when he's writing. "But," he says, "if you ask my sister, she'd say, 'you spent hours in your room drawing a plant,' when it didn't seem to me that I was sitting in my room for hours." Then he adds, warming to the subject, "I do have a tendency to push though. I mean I lose time. That's a problem. I have to set an alarm or miss appointments, but the problem is that I turn it off! So I'm still late wherever I'm going. And it's the same with the oboe. You know how people say, 'practice for fifteen minutes a day,' but who can practice for just fifteen minutes a day?"

Judging from the writers I've talked to, it seems there is no commonality among them as to how much absorption they have as a fixed trait. In some ways, flow and absorption are synonymous, so that if you mostly only get into flow in writing, then that's what you're able to get totally absorbed in. Michael Connelly, author of best-selling police procedural novels, told me that when he seeks a short break from writing, he looks for something else that will fully absorb him, such as racquetball or playing with his toddler. If he attempts something less absorbing, like golf, then thoughts of his book are free to bedevil him.

You can be the sort of person who skitters from task to task, but if you feel passionately about what you're writing, you can get absorbed and enter flow as well as individuals who can do so readily in *anything* they do. Diane Johnson told me that she gets into the highly absorbed state more with writing than with any other activity, and that she has a "rather short attention span in other respects. I flit around and change activities frequently." I find such admissions encouraging, both for myself—since I have always been less able to sit still undistractedly for long periods than I thought I *should*—and for every other writer who doesn't fit the pattern of total, forget-everything-else, hours-long immersion in writing.

To recap, then, being a person who gets fully absorbed in many things is a kind of ideal. It means you can experience and benefit from flow no matter what you're doing. Yet if you can only do so in your writing, that's also a felicitous and not uncommon situation for a creative writer. If, though, you are having trouble getting absorbed even in your writing, you'll have to sort out what's getting in the way. I'll offer some ideas in the following chapters, especially in chapter six, "Focus In."

From resilient to confident

Whenever I teach seminars for writers, regardless of whether the advertised focus of the session was marketing or how-to, psychological questions dominate the early part of the group discussion. Beginning writers all want to know, "How do I deal with isolation, rejection, self-doubt?" The writers I interviewed didn't start out naturally resilient and optimistic. Rather, they have all to some degree mastered their weaknesses and anxieties while traversing the career trajectory.

It's not a matter of simply telling yourself, "I love to write." It may be, rather, more a question of reminding yourself, first, that you have succeeded at other activities in the past and so you can at this one too, and second, that, regardless of your past successes, it takes persistence to succeed at anything. If you can keep that thought operating during the most discouraging days, you'll become a more resilient person, a more confident writer and, inevitably, someone who writes more—and that's what it takes to improve your craft. As for entering flow, the more you write, the more likely it is.

Confidence relates to a sense that your skills are suited to the task. As banal as it may sound, you have to believe in yourself, at least often enough and strongly enough to return again and again to the hard work of creating, regardless of results. The writers I spoke to all generally express a sense that they can do what it is they have set out to do.

If you have a healthy and high sense of efficacy, you are likely to be more resilient, which leads to confidence in the long run. Such confidence builds itself on the activities and successes of a tenacious striver rather than the hopes of a wishful dreamer. How much hardship are you willing to endure to reach your goals? Just how much unpredictability can you tolerate? The most productive writers are those who combine a sense of realism about the tough odds they face with a belief that such odds can be overcome with enough effort. While success builds a sense of efficacy, the most resilient learn a great deal from their failures. You take what doesn't work, didn't come out right or didn't sell, and you use that for information on how to do it differently next time. Above all, don't set your goals unreasonably high (i.e., "I'll win the Pulitzer next year" or "My next book will be *the* great American novel; it will be perfect"). This holds true unless—and here you have to know yourself extremely well—you are most highly motivated by unreachable goals, *and* you're not crushed when you don't meet them but are suitably pleased when you get as far as the next milestone on the way.

Here's an example of how attitudes can be shaped purposely: Carolyn See claims to have formed her approach to life, and her way of facing the task of writing novels, partly in reaction to her former husband, who, she says, made a huge fuss about how hard writing was. "He was into like writing half a page and then tearing it up," she says. "And I think as some kind of defiance of him, I just constructed another way of doing it, which would be, oh just sit down and get it done."

A writer's confidence comes in multiple forms. Marnell Jameson, for instance, never doubts that flow will come eventually, "but the unknown is how long it will take. Sometimes an entire writing period goes by and I've written nothing, but I comfort myself by realizing that even when we write nothing, when we just sit and think about the nothing that we're not writing, that, too, is part of the process." Another type of confidence is exemplified by Ellery Washington C., who says a part of him believes that regardless of whether a piece of writing turns out to be great or not, he feels "like I'm experimenting in ways that I don't see everywhere. Underneath all of it is still disbelief. I think that the doubts and the insecurities that I have by far are not strong enough to stop me from doing it, because I realize it's the thing I can do."

On the other end of the psychological spectrum, if your ego is genuinely fragile, you may be so terrified of rejection that, even if you do get around to writing occasionally, you may never have the courage to send your work out. Liz, a friend of mine, writes incredibly imaginative and psychologically profound and lacerating short stories. Yet, to my knowledge, she has never gotten one published. Why? Last time we spoke, she was apparently too petrified to market them in any systematic way. She told me that it once took her a full year to gather up the psychic energy to purchase stamps for some submission packets. And writing cover letters? That felt too much like putting herself on the line.

Let's distinguish between confidence that you can produce work, and an assurance that the work will, at any particular session, be up to your standards. The latter is not a particularly common feeling among a lot of writers. Take novelist and short story writer Ethan Canin, who struggles regularly with a lack of confidence in the quality of the work he is producing on a daily basis:

> Flow happens once a day, no matter how much I hate it, pretty much once a day.
> Q: You hate the struggle to get into it?
> A: Yes, it's the dread of starting. And I don't know if it's fear of failure. Probably mostly fear of failure.
> Q: Do you feel like every time you sit down that it matters?
> A: Oh, yes. Maybe it's perfectionism. And I still have a great fear after three, four books, my wife doesn't even really believe this, I have no idea if it's utterly horrendous or great.
> Q: Among the highly experienced writers I've interviewed, most of them develop a confidence that eventually it's going to come.
> A: Then their work starts to slide.
> Q: That's the perfectionist's fear.
> A: I'm definitely a perfectionist, and that's definitely inhibiting, but I'm glad to be one.

Along similar lines, Michael Connelly said that knowing he is his toughest critic has built his confidence to the point that, once he gets past his own demands on himself, he has confidence in the work.

Some, after a long career, have learned to be confident of the results too, even if they cannot always depend on an even output. You find that if you write regularly, most of what you write won't be up to your own standards—it's been said that the writer's best friend is the wastebasket—but that's reality. Write consistently enough, though, and you *will* get work good enough to keep. The intermittent reinforcement of those stunning, surprising successes—Did I write that?! I wrote that!—is very powerful. In time, you build an almost irresistible urge to persist, so you can experience the thrill again.

Confidence also means having faith that the poem or story you are writing towards is indeed waiting for you at the end, as poet Wyatt Prunty suggests:

> Think of an archaeologist who brushes the dirt away. Rewrite, rewrite, until you reach what's under the surface. Or, put differently, the sense you have at the beginning is similar to standing in a dark corridor. You cannot see it but you know there is an end to the corridor. The essential element of the poem exists ahead of time, and you have to keep working to reach it.

Exceptions, as usual, can be enlightening. Here's Carol Muske, whose great confidence in her ability to enter flow paradoxically causes her some anxiety (reminding us of the addictive quality of flow mentioned earlier):

> When you ask about what leads up to this state, it's really hard for me to answer. I feel like there's something pressing on my brain. I feel like there's something going on, percolating. It's like a miniflow state that I can partially enter at almost any time.
> Q: What is the fear?
> A: This state, that you will go into it and never come back, I suppose.
> Q: But it doesn't keep you from entering it.
> A: Oh, no. Because I trust enough. The fear would be that it's so wonderful, so all-consuming, why bother coming back?

You might be surprised at how many writers mention feeling anxiety and fear, which may be a result of having to satisfy so many constraints at once. They manage to write anyway. It's often a form of confidence that has ups and downs, causing you to feel like you're on an emotional roller coaster. Ron Wallace, for example, who has authored six collections of poetry, has had hundreds of poems in magazines, plus two dozen short stories and three critical books, as well as articles and reviews, writes:

> I don't feel like a writer unless I am *at that moment* writing, and writing well. Whenever someone asks me if "I'm writing," unless I have written something *that day* I equivocate, or I look ashamed and admit that no, I'm sort of blocked. Whenever I finish something, and have no idea of what I might turn to next, I fear that I'll never write again.

Yet in spite of what certainly sounds like a lack of confidence in his own seemingly unending source of creativity, this poet continues to write, and to write daily.

Nora Okja Keller found that anxiety first became her writing companion when she was in high school and had to deal with writing assigned for classes. When we spoke, as she was commencing work on a new book, she described feeling awkward and unsure of both the characters and the plot development. Happily, she's found a productive way to deal with the potential problem: "I've tried to think of my anxiety and fear, reframing it. This anxiousness doesn't signal reluctance, it signals excitement about the work. That's kind of a breakthrough for me."

Few writers, of course, are completely predictable in their psychological tenor, and time spent creating isn't always euphoric. As novelist Hilma Wolitzer, says, writing is a "sickening joy." Aimee Liu told me, "I mean there's a certain amount of anxiety that I'm just not going to be able to pull it off." Likewise, novelist Susan Taylor Chehak describes her seesawing mood:

> I love what I do. I don't think there's anybody happier with what they do. I get to lie around and read novels, I get to teach classes and talk about books. You caught me on a good day though. . . . I'm ready to jump out a window a lot of times. It comes and goes. There's a time when it gets to be extremely lonely. If I'm in a difficult place and I can't figure out how to get out of it, or it doesn't feel like it's going right, or I don't feel good about what I'm doing, then it's so lonely, because there's no one to talk to about it. You can't take your problem to anybody and say, what do you think I should do? Should I change this scene and put it later? That loneliness can really get to me. It's really depressing.

Carol Muske explained that when she was writing a novel with scientific aspects, she felt "in over my head." In order to write the book, she convinced herself she knew enough, constantly fighting her fear that it was "stupid." Even though she sent pieces of the manuscript to a biochemist at Harvard who let her know when she wasn't being accurate, she says she was still "pretty terrified." Then I commented to her, "There may be a point with anxiety where the anxiety is motivating, but when it goes over, it's fear. You may have been straddling that line." She responded, "That's what helps it work."

I'll quote at some length from the conversation I had with Bernard Cooper, as he was unusually generous and articulate in sharing the reality of his doubts and anxieties. Keep in mind that his work, when he does release it to be published, is inspiring, genuinely human, and beautifully crafted.

I'm infinitely scared that the work is somehow bad in a way that I can't see, or that I won't be able to do it anymore, or I'm going to make an idiot out of myself. Believe me, there's a whole slew of things I'm terrified of. But the images, that's where the joy is for me. . . . Part of my process, for better or worse, actually for worse, is that I have to go through this real struggle of doubt and torture before I actually do it, and then it gets to the point where it's actually so bad, and I feel so hopeless, that then I feel a kind of abandonment and I don't care anymore. Because I'm so sick of feeling bad and it's so hopeless, then all right, I might as well just do what I want to do. . . . Someone once asked me when I knew I'd become a professional writer, and I knew instantly that it was when I realized that I wasn't worrying all day and all night after I turned off the computer, that I could reserve a little time to chew my fingernails and reflect on what I did and worry about it, but that the worry would be a part of it. It just had become so familiar and so much a part of the occupation that it no longer consumed me in the same way.

When I get back a self-addressed stamped envelope, I feel as though I'm going to faint as I open it, and it's not so much because, chances are great there *will* be a rejection, but because I just don't want somebody to have written something that will depress me, like, "Well, I really like the last piece but you just didn't . . . " or something like that. It's that sense of bracing myself. I know myself well enough now to know that it will be a hump to have to get over. And when it's just a form rejection, it's "thank you, oh thank you!" I'm so glad.

As you can see, anxiety almost never intrudes once you've made it into flow. It's rather an uncomfortable state that often surrounds flow, a transition you must negotiate.

To increase your confidence when your own criticisms of yourself begin to sap your belief in a project, consider the source of those negative judgments. Best-selling author Michael Crichton once said, "I realized my subjective opinion of whether something is good while I'm doing it is worthless. So when I start, I finish." Crichton keeps a journal during the writing of his books, so that when he starts getting that "I never should have started this, it's garbage" feeling, he looks back and sees that he felt the same way at a certain point while working on previous novels. On your current or next writing project, begin a simple journal of your feelings about the work. Write in it either each time you begin writing, right after you stop for the day or whenever the mood strikes. Or consider keeping such a journal at all times to record your subjective impressions of "how you're doing" as a writer. When you've gone a long time without getting a poem published, for instance, look back to how you felt just before your *last* publication. You'll discover that how you feel about your work at any one time doesn't have a whole lot to do with your commercial or publishing success. Becoming aware of this can increase your general level of confidence and belief in yourself. As long as you're doing the work you feel you were meant to do, it doesn't matter too much how you feel about the worth of what you produced any one day.

I like the following advice from a sports psychologist: Remember your successes, not your failures, and if you aren't comfortable with so-called "positive thinking," all you have to do is "eliminate all the negative thoughts from your mind, and whatever's left will be fine."

Not too mad or manic

You may have wondered how much truth there is to the popular belief that a link exists between genius or creativity on the one hand, and madness or other psychopathology on the other. In other words, do you have to be slightly mad to be a great writer? First of all, researchers who have scoured the biographies of great novelists, poets, painters and other creative folks have indeed found higher rates of all kinds of dysfunction. One study found the rate of psychosis to be 30-35 percent for creative artists as compared to about 2 percent for ordinary people. Another found that 80 percent of a group of 30 eminent writers had experienced an episode of affective disorder, while only 30 percent of the controls had. A third determined that 38 percent of 47 eminent British writers had been treated for manic-depression, and 50 percent of the poets had. Yet a fourth found that members of the theatrical profession, all categories of writers, artists but not architects/designers, and musical performers and composers experience significantly more psychiatric difficulties over the course of their lives in comparison to a number of other professional groups. In the final study I'll mention, it was found that female writers displayed significantly higher rates of all psychopathology, especially depression, than the controls. Furthermore, when you take highly creative individuals and give them personality questionnaires, their answers are weirdly close, though on a lower level, to those of neurotic or psychotic individuals.

What does this mean to any one writer who longs to be (and to be thought by others to be) among those creative greats? Not much. Without going into the possible flaws in such studies, let's agree that highly creative people are a little more likely than average to suffer from mental difficulties. In my own smallish circle of good friends, most of whom happen to be quite creative, it's not at all unusual for conversations to veer into comparisons of antidepressant medications.

Rather than be concerned about whether you're crazy enough to be a renowned writer, or whether you're creative enough to cause yourself mental turmoil, it's much more productive to seek out supportive friends who will keep you from feeling like a total oddity. The fact is, no researcher has yet figured out precisely what the above figures are caused by. We don't know whether it's got a lot to do with the way artists fit into (or don't fit into) society, or whether it's mostly genetic: genes for dysfunction and genes for creativity often marching side-by-side on the same strand of DNA, doing their little two-step with your psyche. As for worrying about whether you're strange *enough*, keep in mind that the majority of writers are quite regular in most ways (if you don't count the fact that they often are living two or more lives at once: their normal lives and the ones they dream up and write about).

None of the writers I talked to admitted suffering from manic-depression, though some mentioned depression, adding that the right medication made a big difference in their productivity. Others described high-energy working habits. Some of these indicated they thought of themselves as at least slightly manic at certain times. For instance, Marvin Bell said, "You will rightly wonder if I am describing a manic-depressive pattern. Only to a very small degree. I am not bipolar officially but do have highs and lows." Jonathan Kellerman told me that he thinks of himself as "definitely somebody who's hypomanic. Both my wife and I have the capacity, if I didn't have kids, I'd write 6, 7 days a week—well, I wouldn't write 7 days a week because I'm an Orthodox Jew—but I'd certainly write 6 days a week, and I'd probably write 2, 3 books a year instead of one." In discussing with Stephen his tendency to become more energized at certain times, I told him that I never hear him sound manic except when he's talking about flow. He responded that this is not always the case, that "a lot of times when you're very engaged and in a state of flow that has more full cooperation/collaboration between your conscious and unconscious mind, there often is a sense of quietude, of peace, of just simply involvement."

Some of the particularly unusual writing experiences that have been described to me (see the section on atypical flow experiences in chapter eight) were those in which writers worked unusually long hours at a stretch. Along with an intense flow experience, you may find yourself with an extremely high level of energy, analogous to a near-manic state. This happens more often if your project is at a certain point, whether in the early stages for some writers, or during final revisions for others.

When you look at the evidence of a connection between creativity and adjustment (or lack thereof), the most rational conclusion is that there are many routes to creativity. Even if you have a predisposition to mental illness, creative production happens most often when you're functioning well.

We have by now seen that the idea of a single distinctive writer's personality is questionable. What do I mean, then, when I say you ought to think like a writer? Being a natural writer—one for whom being in flow is the personality's default setting—is one option. Failing that, you can evolve certain attitudes that will surely help you. If you've got strong self-motivation, an ability to loosen and blur the boundaries in your thinking, can learn to tolerate anxiety and work at keeping yourself open to experience, such attitudes predict you'll enter flow and more easily be creative and productive as a writer.

In the next Key, you'll learn how critical the loosening process is for the actual writing, regardless of how open you are most of the time, and how to accelerate it.

⚷ | *Turning Key Two*

Attitudes tend to involve long-term preparation for writing, rather than being the immediate precursors of flow. That is, you cannot sit down and *decide* to think like a writer right now, so you can slip into flow. The work of making this Master Key turn for your writing needs to be accomplished over a period of months and years. It takes internal and psychological effort, rather than being a matter of trying out a few techniques and routines. Still, there are some tasks you can undertake right now, including:

1. Read interviews with writers. Whether you begin with writers with whose work you are familiar, or dive in anywhere, read as many of these interviews as you can. The more you read, the more you will

grasp the wide variety of ways there are for a writer to think. You will without doubt find ways in which you are similar to some of these writers in your attitudes, and in other instances, you may be inspired to adopt new ways of approaching your work.

2. Notice when you're tempted to say "No," or the occasions that cause you to say or think "You can't do that" or "I shouldn't do that." Are the risks real or imagined? Might you have an enriching experience without harming yourself or anyone else if you choose to do whatever it is, instead of unreflectively heeding your negative impulse?

3. Spend time with people who are accepting of difference. Their openness and nonjudgmental attitudes will encourage your own.

4. Visit an art museum or attend a gallery opening. Reserve judgment. See what you can discern in each painting or artwork that made someone find it worthy of acceptance.

5. Notice how long you tend to stay absorbed in your writing. Try setting a timer so that you can push yourself to stick with it for ten minutes or a half hour longer than your norm. Or, if it suits your temperament better and it's feasible, try extending your work day so you can continue to hop around and yet return to your main task repeatedly and get a lot done over a longer period of time.

5 Key Three:
Loosen Up

Now it's time to put aside thoughts about your long- and short-term goals and your attitudes, and find a way to get fully involved in the writing itself. To allow your creativity, your insights, your inner stories, to spill over onto the page, you'll need to work out—consciously or not—some way to loosen yourself up so it can happen ("it" being, at best, flow, but at least getting some words from your mind onto a page).

Most writers evolve certain individualized routines and rituals that seem to ease their entry into flow. It's hard to know whether all of these specific rituals and routines are truly crucial in order for you to be able to write easily and well. I get the feeling that more depends on these rituals than you might yourself be fully conscious of. By their habitual nature, they help you make the shift into an alternate consciousness and contribute to your creative process. Such habits may also cause biological changes, just as certain sights, sounds and odors signal the start of other altered states, including sexual arousal.

Loose as a cat's shimmer
It shouldn't play into any of your anxieties about the loss of control that comes with flow if I share with you that looseness and the ability to cross mental boundaries are aspects of both schizophrenic thinking and creative thinking. "Schizophrenic thinking is characterized by a

cognitive style that has been variously called overinclusive, allusive, loose or characterized by the term 'mental slippage,' " writes Eysenck, a noted researcher in the field. There is "some loosening of associative thinking, . . . a failure of inhibition that allows less relevant thoughts to intrude into the problem-solving process" that makes people creative and that matches definitions for psychoticism. For the psychotic or creative individual, the concept of relevance is itself broadened. For a writer, such looseness is an amazing asset.

Carl Jung, contrasting James Joyce to his schizophrenic daughter Lucia, said that they "were like two people going to the bottom of a river, one falling and the other diving." Lucia made random uncontrolled and uncontrollable associations, while Joyce, though he pushed language to its limits, knew on some level exactly what he was doing.

Author Joan Didion, who is certainly not psychotic, explains what this feels like:

When I talk about pictures in my mind I am talking, quite specifically, about images that shimmer around the edges. There used to be an illustration in every elementary psychology book showing a cat drawn by a patient in varying stages of schizophrenia. This cat had a shimmer around it. You could see the molecular structure breaking down at the very edges of the cat: the cat became the background and the background the cat, everything interacting, exchanging ions . . . Images do shimmer for me. Look hard enough, and you can't miss the shimmer. It's there. You can't think too much about these pictures that shimmer. You just lie low and let them develop. You stay quiet. You don't talk to many people and you try to keep your nervous system from shorting out and you try to locate the cat in the shimmer.

Notice also how Didion narrowed her field of focus in order to allow this looseness to happen.

Looseness of thinking does seem, then, to be related to creativity, and to the ability of creative writers to access a wide variety of original ideas. If you're lucky enough to have a personality at the looser end of the continuum, you're probably able to leap boundaries in separate parts of your mind, leading to better communication among segments of your brain. Thus you can potentially evoke a more chaotic and fresher series of associations. This looser-than-usual connection between brain sections may very well contribute to both creativity and to flow. Have you often made references in conversations that others seem to find odd? It's a common experience among creative writers, and it comes from this easy ability to communicate across areas of the brain, to make loose and unexpected and wildly imaginative associations.

Crossing boundaries

To facilitate and perhaps even accelerate this loosening process when you sit down to write, regardless of how naturally it comes to you, you'll need to develop your own ways to relax and let go, both physiologically and psychologically. Bringing a sense of play into your work is one gambit. Others stop *trying* and wait, knowing that is what it takes for their minds to become loose enough to get into flow. Phyllis Gebauer makes it sound deceptively simple: "I just relaxed and let go." Eventually, your action and awareness (what you're doing and what you're thinking about it) merge and your writing becomes, if not necessarily automatic, at least not such a struggle.

Every writer finds his or her own way to accomplish this. Maurya Simon, for instance, tends to go outside and have a cigarette during the composition of more difficult poems. "It's probably stress," she says. "It's also an upper. I think it's the breath, the deep breathing in and out, almost a very strange yogic effect. I lived in India and studied yoga. There's this whole sense for me, it's too bad one's breathing in toxins at the same time, but it is, I think, for people who are smokers, part of the relaxations is that long, deep inhalation and that long exhalation. Which does work physiologically to slow the heart down and calm the nerves." Does she actually let go consciously? "It is automatic for me, and I think it's from years of writing," she responded. Nonsmokers, of course, can find healthier ways to relax. Any physical exercise, a long walk, yoga or a hot bath are all possibilities for changing your breathing and slowing you down.

David St. John explains that he "fools around with older stuff" for two or three weeks in order to loosen himself up before beginning on new work. Not that he isn't also initiating some new poems during this noodling about period. "I mean," he says, "I'll be writing poems, I'll be even finishing poems, but they won't be the ones that I end up keeping. But there will come a point at which I really feel that this sense of that conscious determinate mind begins to finally let go. And at that point, this sense of transmission seems much more open and fluid." Or:

There certainly is a mindset that will not produce a poem, and that's a kind of heavy-browed determination to write one. By that, I mean you have to hold the world lightly by the throat. You've got to be deadly serious and playful at the same time.

Q: Do you *will* yourself to be serious yet playful? Do you feel it as a letting-go process?

A: There is a kind of letting go. You don't will your writing as you would for an essay. (Wyatt Prunty)

Poet, short-story writer and novelist Chitra Banerjee Divakaruni told me that when she began working on *The Mistress of Spices*, she was "very open to seeing what kind of book this would become." Such openness is a way of playing with boundaries. And in fact, the voice of her main character came to her a page and a half into the novel, and "I could see it was going to be a much more lyrical book, there were going to be magical elements in it," elements that weren't in her previous book. It's possible that Divakaruni's attitude of openness toward her art is related to the boundary-crossing she does in life: the fact of having emigrated from India has been a central influence in both her life and her art. "The boundaries by which your previous life was defined are changed, so you begin to question boundaries," she explains. While she came from a traditional Indian family where roles and rules were strictly laid out for her, and she didn't rebel against them, she has since done a lot of choosing and picking from among those traditions. Now she says she sees a lot of value in crossing lines, both in life and in her writing.

To loosen yourself without necessarily emigrating from your home country, you might try what Divakaruni recommends to her students: read widely among writers of many cultures who write in various ways and whose visions of the world differ. When it comes to your writing, experiment by writing material that is almost diametrically opposed to what you've been comfortable writing up to now. "The idea," says Divakaruni, "is not necessarily, don't write what you know, but try to look at it from a whole other angle. Write about someone who is absolutely not yourself." In some cases, these exercises may turn into usable pieces, but even if you toss them, you will learn something.

Crossing boundaries in their work comes quite naturally to some writers. Ed Ochester, for example, explains how his poetry is affected by his expectation that border-hopping is what the surprise of art is all about:

Q. People sometimes say "write from your soul." But what does that mean?

A. It's one of those metaphors that either works for you or it doesn't. I take it to mean that you should write after accessing whatever place your creativity resides in, rather than from your more prosaic conscious mind. Yet not everyone imagines his or her soul (assuming belief in the concept in the first place) to reside in the same place, which means everyone's "soul" can't be accessed the same way. As for me, I rather like picturing my soul as being a happy parasite crazily interwoven with the dendrites in my brain, much like the more favorable bacteria that inhabit the human mouth. While some writers insist they don't use their minds, seeking to write only from their hearts, their emotions, their souls or their whole bodies, I feel fairly confident that diverse parts of the brain—that complex and not fully understood organ—are involved in all aspects of the creative process, and that it should be respected, not trivialized, for its role. (See Notes for further discussion of the brain.)

Those who are good at crossing boundaries don't only bring this ability to bear when they are writing. At the end of my interview with Sue Grafton, we were joking around about someday flow being available in pill form. Grafton made a conceptual leap and suggested that maybe the ingredients in the same pill would cure cancer too. (Actually, that kind of thinking is precisely how a number of scientific and medical inventions have come about.) The trick is to allow yourself to joke about serious things, to practice linguistic and cognitive boundary-crossing at every opportunity. Then when it's time to write, you'll more easily throw off the restraints of less imaginative routine thinking (if you indeed ever cross back—some highly creative types never truly do).

I like the notion of trying to range across things. I rarely write a poem that's only in one frame of reference, because it always seems a little bit to me too much like a picture at an exhibition, I think—I want to do what seems to be unexpected because I think that's what poems do and the imagination which is gathering poems does or ought to do. The other thing I'm aware of and probably hasn't done me very much good in terms of reputation is the fact that I have an irresistible urge, and I have for a long time, to mix what is quote tragic and comic, sad and funny . . . It's very hard to confront reality in the United States without often or usually having that sense of what is sad and comic and inextricably linked.

Although most experienced writers don't use exercises in their own work, some do have a favorite exercise or two they recommend for those who need help in loosening up. Pulitzer Prize-winning poet Henry Taylor offered the following, which I found to be effective when I tried it in one of my own classes:

> Remember how it feels to suddenly think of one of the most embarrassing moments in your life: how it surfaces without being invited and makes your skin crawl, and you may have to pull over on the shoulder for a second and compose yourself, but you mash the thing back down into the subconscious where it damn well belongs, and get on with the day. Okay. This time, write it down. Make sure you linger lovingly over the painful details. Be aware at all times that you are not being asked to turn this in.

Taylor adds, "The result is that 99.9 percent of the students turn the things in, because once they've done them, they like them."

Another technique—this one requires a little preparation—is used by poet Lola Haskins with her students. Photocopy some poems or pieces of fiction in other languages (you can get some from the library; Haskins has picked hers up during foreign travels). Then choose a page in a language you don't know well, and "mock-translate" it into your own words. "Type as fast as you can whatever the words bring to mind, which will give you an incoherent page or two. Now highlight the interesting juxtapositions and start over. Rearrange, add, etc. It's a little like a Rorschach. It breaks people out of habitual language-sets," explains Haskins. This exercise, like the previous one, invites you to both cross boundaries *and* play with words.

Play with words

The creative process is sometimes extraordinarily playful. As we'll now see, flow entry is encouraged when there's a playful attitude on the writer's part. And play involves a bit of risk-taking at times.

Those who do creative work in fields other than writing can often provide wonderful examples. For instance, I was reading an interview with actor Jim Carrey and director Peter Weir about the process of making the film *The Truman Show*. Carrey said something about "flying without a net, that's a scary thing for me. . . . I wouldn't know what I'm doing, I'm just going on inspiration or electricity," that those takes often wouldn't work, and he described the crew's embarrassment for him and his own sheepishness about those "failures." But then Weir says: "There was no way I wanted to be cautious about it any more than Jim did. He would say, 'Maybe this is too much,' and I'd say, 'No, it's only film, let's shoot it.' " The lesson here is that there's no need to be careful and censor yourself early on when there's no real risk, which there almost never is when you're creating artistic works.

Sometimes the use of the word *play* is a tip-off to the loosening process in action, as poet Stephen Yenser describes here:

> I think I allow myself more latitude when I'm writing poems compared to writing critical articles. You never know what you're going to say. Of course you don't really in prose either, but somehow I have a sort of framework in my head when I'm writing prose. I don't write down weird thoughts, because I'm thinking this has got to be a compact whole, I'm going to have an argument or something that resembles an argument. Whereas if I'm writing a poem, that's not so true. I know I don't have to rely on argument. The sequentiality is not so important to me. There's more play involved for me in poetry than do this, do that.

It seems to me that learning to let go into flow may be akin to learning to fall asleep. Some infants are "natural sleepers," but many more have to learn to let go into sleep (there are popular books and articles on teaching infants to calm themselves, as well as a plethora of children's books with the aim of easing them into sleep). Generally, you don't remember how you learned to fall asleep. Most writers also don't recall exactly how or when they learned how to surrender to flow.

Preparation can be both the ally and the enemy of flow, depending on the particular situation. The more experienced you are, the easier it is to determine when to stop preparing and let go. David Groves, who is a nonfiction writer, a novelist and a magician, told me that much of the credit for the success of a magic show of his that I had seen was due to preparation. For two weeks prior to the show, he focused on details: where to keep props, where to dump them after he was finished with them, how to transition from trick to trick smoothly, the inflection on certain jokes for maximum laughs, what would be in his hands when he took the stage and so on. "That's very much like the outlining and research that you do in writing an article," he says. "Then, only when you're nine months' pregnant with preparation, can you flow." And later, after seeing a videotape of his performance, he says he had to impose a kind of looseness on himself. "Preparation is antilooseness, and after I had prepared completely, I had to let go of that preparation," he explains. "It's kind of like in writing, when you start out with a first draft that's more formal in language, and then realize that you have to make the language more conversational or the structure more real-life."

Why is it that some people can spend so much time composing E-mail messages to their friends, but when it comes to their "serious" writing, they always find something else they need to do? The answer has everything to do with this facet of loosening up and allowing yourself full rein to play with words. When you're writing to a friend, especially something so seemingly ephemeral as an E-mail message, your internal critic doesn't usually even bother rousing itself to pester you about how well you're doing. The "perfection" of E-mails doesn't matter to most of us; our friends send us messages rife with typos, silly mistakes, unreflective meanderings. So we, too, loosen up and type whatever is on our minds at the moment and push the send key. (If we hear later that our friends are printing and keeping everything we write to them, we probably have a moment or two of dismay. This stuff was never meant for posterity's eyes.)

If you procrastinate over your "real" writing, it may be because you believe on some level that your first drafts have to be excellent, perhaps even perfect. But that's not the way to get yourself to do your best work. When I had a hard time once getting a major paper for graduate school off the ground, one whose complexities hadn't yet worked themselves out in my own mind, I decided to think about who would be reading this. Since, luckily, my professor—the only one who would be reading it—was a supportive and understanding woman, I imagined her quite clearly as my audience. Then I began the paper as though I were writing her a letter: "Dear Libby." I started with my own confusion about the subject, then continued until I had a bunch of pages. Later, when all the information I had was down on paper, I re-read it and began the revision process. I soon eliminated the epistolary first paragraph, rearranged the rest until I was satisfied, and the result was a decent paper. (As I write these words, I focus more on my friends reading it, than on the faceless, and possibly critical, masses. For more on how to handle thoughts of your audience, see chapter seven on awareness of audience.)

If you tend to spend more time E-mailing than writing your more lasting work, consider this: I bet some of those friends who appreciate your work so much would be delighted to have you send them rough drafts of your stories, even though your natural tendency is to hold back until you feel your work is as good as you can get it. And later on, once you've got some confidence in yourself, you can go straight to the work without the intermediary of the letter system.

Also, consider integrating E-mail time into your creative process, thus legitimizing it. When I apologized for distracting Nora Okja Keller by E-mailing her a follow-up question for our interview, she responded: "Don't worry about being a distraction from writing; E-mail actually gets me to the computer and that's the biggest step." Personally, I *always* start my writing sessions by checking E-mail. A diversion? Yes, but unless I get carried away composing extremely lengthy messages, it's a minor diversion that also serves to get the words flowing for my *real* work. I have found that time spent E-mailing is *added* to the amount of writing time/energy I have, rather than subtracted from it.

Another aspect of the loosening process in action is that sometimes you need to be willing to wait for something to happen. Ralph Angel explains: "There's absolutely nothing but the void. And I have two choices: I can get up and walk away, or I can stare into the void in my heart. I think that oftentime's what leads to my trance." Former U.S. Poet Laureate Richard Wilbur doesn't prepare for flow except by sitting down in an undistracting, phoneless indoor place. He finds there are no guarantees: "If I feel clever or emotionally stirred or otherwise poetic, it is not an indication that good work will ensue."

Many of the popular self-help books for writers concentrate on this one key to flow. Numerous exercises invite you to try something new, to play around with possibilities and, in general, to allow your natural creativity to come out by learning to set aside the internal critic. Yet we all come to the task with our own personalities. An exercise that is freeing for someone else may seem constraining to you.

How do you like to play? This is where you can look for clues to what most readily opens you up to being creative. For instance, consider Lillian Hoban, the well-known children's book author and illustrator (she illustrated her husband Russell Hoban's *Frances* series, then later

> **Q.** Why do I get my best story ideas (and sometimes write whole articles in my head) while driving, taking a shower or doing aerobics?
>
> **A.** Lots of writers habitually come up with good, usable ideas while doing something else. The activities you mention—driving, showering, exercising—are all pretty automatic. Your body is absorbed but your mind is still largely free to roam. There's something about rhythmic, habitual, routine physical activity that relaxes and loosens both the body and the mind, thus preparing it to be creative.

wrote eleven books about Arthur the chimpanzee and his little sister Violet). Her obituary quoted her as having once said, "When I am writing, I like writing best, and when I am drawing, I like drawing best. But probably what I like better than anything is just messing around with color." What do you like "messing around" with? Ideas, words, images, impossibilities, characters? Give yourself free rein to play with any or all of those. (You may surprise yourself and others by changing your mind midway; Bill Watterson, the creator of "Calvin and Hobbes," quit creating the popular comic strip after it was appearing daily in 2,400 newspapers. Apparently he decided instead to devote himself to a greater passion, oil painting.)

T.C. Boyle insisted to me that he hates all puzzles and all games: "The only game that I play is writing fiction. . . . The reason why my work is so various and imaginative is because that is what appeals to me in fiction—inventing things, making things up, the game of fun. And everything in life is invented in some way."

Novelist Merrill Joan Gerber suggested the following as among the few worthwhile exercises she uses with her students:

1. For a story subject, remember a "hot spot," something that happened in the past that still compels your attention, something that attracts your thoughts over and over, an incident, a fright, an argument, an insult, some conflict or mystery in a relationship that hasn't been solved or is still exciting over time.
2. Write a letter to someone in your past, to set the record straight, to see the long view of a relationship, and try to get to the heart of it.
3. Write down your dreams. In a dream you will find a scene ready-made

to be described, but there's nothing to plot. By learning to wrap words around scenes in your mind, and doing it regularly, you'll be primed to do it when you're inventing a story.

Once you've been writing for many years, you rarely think about what you do to loosen yourself up. Loosening yourself to write is often largely a subconscious process, one that you usually learn close to the outset of your writing career. According to Robert Olen Butler, if you write every day, *that* is part of the loosening process. But when he *is* having trouble, he makes himself write first thing, "to go from the literal dream state to the artistic dream state with as little time and thought as possible in between."

To sum up, let's eavesdrop onto an E-mail message sent by Stephen to a friend of ours who has experimented with short stories but who often finds himself blocked when he sits down intending to write:

> My own program/tricks for loosening up are: NOT letting myself prepare at all before I begin. If you don't have any preconceived idea, you can't fail. Also, this lets you surprise yourself. Write as if you were telling jokes at a party. Artificially get yourself worked up. Listen to some piece of music, say that Eric Clapton Unplugged album, anything that gets your blood moving. Write something deliberately bad so you can see that you can do it and not implode. Take two ideas at random and free-associate. Write regularly (for a short time!) but don't let yourself read what you've written. You need to build new habits; the ones you have are not working. All these suggestions have to do with dismantling the critic. The devil that sits on your shoulder and says this is shit, this is shit, while poking you with his puny, vicious trident. Remember: preparing is the enemy. Thinking in the usual way is the enemy. Procrastinating is the enemy. You need to get down and dirty. Also, many writers say that the real way, the only way, they improve at their writing is through writing. You can't improve at what you don't do. A vacuum can't be revised.

Turning Key Three

1. What do you think about as you sit down to work? Do you typically worry about how well the finished piece will turn out? Omit all consideration of spelling, grammar, mechanics, word choice and

Q. I write newspaper and trade journal articles for a living, and can't afford to risk investing my time in something more creative right now. Does that mean flow is out of the question for me? I hardly ever get into it.

A. Journalists and nonfiction article writers can certainly experience flow, though it may be more difficult to let go fully when you have highly specific external qualifications for your finished writing output. If you'd like to enter flow more often, try out some of the same tricks we'll be discussing throughout this book. For instance, find a creative way to start or end a piece. Explore character a bit more than you're used to doing. Put something sensory into the work (what did the scene smell like?). By putting your whole self into what you're writing, whether real or imagined, the greater your chance of moving toward flow.

similar constraining and anxious thoughts from your mind. Remind yourself, "First drafts don't matter."

2. I once clipped the following phrase from a time-management article and hung it on my bulletin board: "Trivialize the task." It helped me to keep things in perspective. Relatively few writing sessions are that critical in themselves. Each is only one part of a single day's work. If you can get yourself to conceptualize your writing assignment (one scene, the opening part of a dialogue, a short poem or half a poem) as small and fairly unimportant in the larger scheme of things, it may help you to loosen up. This may seem to be contradictory in light of how many top writers believe that what they are doing is the most important thing in the world, and considering how motivating it is to believe that writing does matter (as we saw in chapter three). The point to keep in mind is that, while writing matters, *no one piece* of writing is that critical. I don't know any successful writers who keep repeating at the start of their day, "This bit of work matters a lot, it's a huge big deal, it will make all the difference." The work goes much more smoothly when you take it for granted. "Oh, here I go again, just doing a little linguistic doodling for a while to see where it takes me." *If you have trouble loosening up,* keep telling yourself, until it becomes your mantra, "It doesn't matter."

3. Imagine yourself sharing your work with the friendliest, least critical person you know. It might be your mother, regardless of whether you'd ever show your work to her or whether she'd get it at all. Or it might be someone who loves you, so long as he or she is extremely supportive and not any more critical than you can bear to think about at this point, assuming you actually will show this person the work.

4. Do some writing in another genre than your usual one, enjoying a freshened sense of wordplay.

5. Every time you hear yourself say about some possibility in your writing, "I can't do that," do it anyway. You can always edit it out later.

6. Jot some ideas on a scrap of paper, instead of your usual pad or computer. One person said that commencing his creations on napkins in coffee shops was freeing for him, since he didn't feel as though he was committing himself to anything.

7. A loosening exercise used by Nora Okja Keller when she teaches creative writing is to start with a family story or some gossip you have heard. Write another version of it, from behind the scenes. Or write out a dream you had, then pare it down and shape it.

8. The poet Thomas Elias Weatherly suggests mechanical exercises to get yourself going. By writing a sonnet or a villanelle, for example, you are distracted from thinking about whether you can get going or not.

9. Choose several apparently unrelated items and find a way to relate them in a poem or piece of a story. For instance, look around your room, pick any item. Then look outside and choose another element. Now grab something from the newspaper or TV. How can you make them all come together in a single piece of writing? Don't even consider judging what you've produced. Use it only to oil your creativity.

10. If the pump needs priming, dig out a childhood snapshot and write a poem or start a story about what you see in it. Be literal, or be wild, whatever works. In other words, if you're holding an ice cream cone in the photo, you can write about flavors, the sense of feeling refreshed, that tingly feeling in your teeth when you bite into something cold, a time you dropped a cone and felt devastated, twenty things you can do with an ice cream cone, and so on.

11. Try this exercise, suggested by Bernard Cooper (who said he heard

it from fellow novelist Michelle Huneven): Write down the story you've been telling people over and over, a story that irritates or amuses or has gotten into your craw in some way, a story that is so strange or so outrageous that you have to keep telling it to kind of corroborate what's happening with yourself. Such an exercise tends to get you writing very loosely and quickly, as it's based on material you've perfected in the repeated retelling.

12. Rage and fury and anger and revenge are huge emotions you can use to loosen up your writing, according to Margot Livesey. Write a character description (or a poem) from the point of view of one character detesting another.

13. Talk into a tape recorder. Even if it feels like babbling at the time, once you've transcribed it, you may find bits useable as take-off points.

14. If you have a friend who always leaves you refreshed after a conversation, bring up the current project, obsession or brainstorm that you haven't yet found a way to get down on paper. Your friend may say something, or inspire you to say something, that will send you back to your desk with newly loosened energy.

15. If you find you're not having fun with what you're writing, don't say, "This is not fun," but rather ask yourself, "How can I make it fun?"

6 Key Four: Focus In

THE PROCESS OF FOCUSING IN, of placing your attention to the work, is another precursor—and the fourth Master Key—for getting into flow. Your whole mind has to get involved in the job of writing, with not a bit of mental energy left over to wander here and there. Only when your attention is fully focused on the task you're trying to accomplish is flow a likely scenario. In this chapter, you'll learn about the quality of that all-important focus, how it differs from a hypnotic trance state, and how long-time writers find their way into such deep concentration. In later chapters, I'll offer some specific procedures you can try if you're not fully absorbed when you sit down to write.

Pay attention to attention

Think about this for a moment: you must put your attention *somewhere*. Typically, if your attention is on your self, you'll start worrying over some aspect of yourself. That, in turn, fosters anxiety, which, as we've seen, is often a sharp detour on the road to flow. Or, if you find your attention skittering around, switching from self-consciousness to thoughts of what's going on in the next room or in the world at large, to ponderings on the past or future, you are also not anywhere near being in a flow state.

While focusing in isn't nearly as simple as merely telling yourself to *pay attention*, you can help yourself enter flow by *deciding* to direct your awareness to a limited stimulus field. Athletes manage it all the time; a journalist who interviewed sports psychologists and coaches discovered that their recommendations for reaching "the zone," or a flow state, include strategies borrowed from meditation practices and the martial arts, aiming to "liberate athletes . . . from their mental and emotional obstacles . . . and point them toward the state of grace that resides at the center of their games."

Since writing is your game, you too can learn to get out of your own way and focus intently and totally on manipulating words. Some people seem to have the knack for directing their attention from inside. They want to work on a story, so they sit down, begin work and some combination of this knack and the work itself makes flow begin. Or they seek out some particularly engaging part of the writing project that makes it easier for them to get going. Character development causing you frustration? Don't begin with that. Instead, write that short scene that's been keeping you up at night. Or, if you keep a writer's journal of thoughts and images that have momentarily captivated you—and you should—peruse it for ideas. When some phrase or idea strikes a note for you, use *that* to get your writing started. If you do, lack of focus won't be a consideration.

It is possible to learn to concentrate better even if it doesn't come naturally. One way is to build your attention "muscles" by meditating. In the typical form of meditation, you bring your attention back again and again to that one word or phrase, or to your breathing, no matter how many times it wanders off. Once you learn how to concentrate while meditating, you should be better at it in your writing too. If you're not interested in meditating, practice directly with your writing project. I can't tell you how many days I force myself back again and again to the work, even if it's just to type one more paragraph, though I'd so much rather return to the terrific novel I'm reading. (Not that I don't take plentiful reading breaks if I want to; that's one of the advantages of having a whole day to work—I just stretch out my workday a bit longer if I've taken so many breaks that I feel as though I haven't earned the right to quit for the day.)

Or you may have to rely on external cues. This means that you find a way to structure your activity (the writing task), so as to produce flow. External cues, for a writer, may mean entering the study, turning on the computer and having a cup of coffee at your elbow. For some writers, having a clear desk and a clear mind are so essential that they spend countless hours trying to "clear the decks." That can mean anything from paying urgent bills to ensuring that all the pencils in the house are sharp and that there isn't a stray piece of paper within sight. When even that isn't enough to allow flow to happen, other measures are called for. Something else is evidently getting in the way.

The writers who write most regularly have learned to block out everything but the work, figuring out ways to restructure their environment so that flow can occur. That is, they take a chunk of reality and get control of it by separating it mentally from the overwhelming mass of daily experience, then respond with intense focus to the feedback the activity offers. Such writers literally pay attention only to what's going on in the work they're creating, disregarding whatever is irrelevant. A researcher found that those who performed well on tests of attentional-regulation were also able to become absorbed in activities and enjoy them intrinsically, "a state wherein our experience seems to 'flow.' "

Consider the current popularity of those tiny magnetic poetry kits. What you buy is a large set of words attached to tiny magnets. I doubt that a lot of serious poets are buying these kits, but I believe the reason they may be so appealing to so many members of the general public is that they limit the field of focus and make it fun to play around with words. Anyone who writes more or less full time knows that you can play around with words in your head any time you want to. What can make it such a daunting challenge is that you have the entire language to play with. When you find yourself limited to a couple of hundred preselected words, it's similar to being forced to write a haiku, a sonnet or some other traditional form. For many people, the constraint lends focus to the task. It's less overwhelming than dealing with the wild multiplicity of possibilities of the whole language. Just these words. What comes to mind if you just move this one here and . . . look, an interesting combination appears. In a way, you've structured your environment in such a way as to eliminate distractions: all those *other* words and their messy and complicating potentialities!

Not long ago I was given a set of these magnetic words by a parenting magazine for which I write, and I decided to stick them on the front of the refrigerator. Although there aren't any words that are even remotely erotic included in this particular set, Stephen and I have gotten in the habit of putting together phrases and sentences that express our mood of the moment. With suitably quirky minds and plenty of innuendo (and a forgiving attitude toward grammar), it's been possible for the two of us to go back and forth for weeks, suggesting and countering. I've been tempted to buy the erotic set or the Edgar Allan Poe set, but that would make it too easy.

For mystery novelist Sue Grafton, the constraints of writing alphabet-themed mysteries (*"N" Is for Noose* and so on) concentrate her creativity in a (mostly) positive way. She compares writing mysteries to a hand of bridge, where you're always dealt thirteen cards, and within those cards you have no idea what you're going to do or where you're going to go. "And so the skill," she says, "is to take the rules and regulations and push them as far as you can." Furthermore:

> There is a curious relationship between me and the alphabet. On one hand, I love the structure. I love the form and the content it gives to my days. If I reach *"Z" Is for Zero*, I'll have to find some new way to invent that. I swear I'll never do connected titles again, though, as long as we both shall live. And I do wake up sometimes and say, What was I thinking! Was I insane? Did I have a breakdown? Was I nuts? But what a wonderful way to stay connected to the work.

Analogously, you have those poets who either typically or occasionally write in forms. When poet Alfred Corn used to teach undergraduates, he would sometimes ask them to write in meter, using rhyme, or to produce a verse form, such as a sonnet. "Oddly enough," he notes, "fulfilling verse requirements leads the psyche to uncharted areas, and the student writer soon discovers that s/he knows more than s/he was aware of having known."

Another way to both loosen and focus your thinking, whether you're planning to write a poem or prose, is to give yourself an assignment such as: Write a series of lines beginning with "I wish . . ." or "No!" or "Alas!" or "Amazingly . . . ," or, as Stephen suggests, "The elephant has big balls. . . ." Give yourself five or ten minutes. Any of these line-starters, or any other you devise, will force your brain to get itself in gear and turn out words. At the same time, you may find yourself tapping into emotions you had no idea were so close to the surface.

Your attention, of course, doesn't stay put on one thing for long, no matter how easy it is for you to get fully absorbed in your writing. Once you get used to a stimulus or situation, say, the novel chapter you've been struggling with for weeks, your attention may begin to wander again. Boredom is often both the cause and the result of such mental distractibility. If you're one of those individuals who is expert at con-centrating, you've learned to complexify your tasks (as well as your relationships and other aspects of your life) so that your attention stays tuned to the activities in which you've chosen to invest your interest.

If you've never thought about complexifying your work on purpose, it's a surprisingly uncomplicated process. Say you've never written from the point of view of an unsympathetic character or from the point of view of someone of another gender. Try it. What if your particular project has clear parameters (it's a travel memoir and you want to stick close to the truth), how might you complexify that? Currently, I need to revise a piece about a trip to Great Britain that Stephen and I took, where we visited a variety of cemeteries of famous writers. I first wrote it as a straightforward round-up (annotated list of stops on the journey), but that was too boring (both to the editors I sent it to and, truth be told, to me). The thought of reentering a boring piece of writing isn't very seductive to my attention. Brainstorming, I came up with the following ways to entice my interest: write a lead that enters the story from an unexpected vantage point, say the evening Stephen spent a half hour picking huge slugs off Sylvia Plath's grave, thinking who knows what thoughts as I watched the sun set over the cemetery walls; or write about my own plans for eventual cremation and burial based on what I learned from visiting all these other famous graves; or write about the compelling urge felt by contemporary literary pilgrims who cross all of Ireland in a single day in the rain in order to stand transfixed for a few minutes in front of Yeats' grave; or turn it all into a poem or short story, putting aside absolute truth in the quest for a higher truth.

Here's where a strong enough motivation comes into play: when you genuinely want to finish the narrative or polish the poem, you'll do what it takes to stay focused on it. The "what it takes" is what sophisticated writers have learned to do, and what less experienced writers must learn to do. It can take anything from moving yourself and your notebook to a garden, to reading a page from another writer that inspires you to climb back into your writing with fresh energy, to any of the many rituals and tricks writers use to get started in the first place, as I've described throughout this book. For, after all, staying with a task is sometimes a matter of finding the will to start again and again.

If it's a matter of gathering momentum to start something new— say you've recently finished a poem or story or novel and you can barely muster interest to sit down and begin all over again—think of complexifying. What would feel fresh and motivating to you? Stephen has told me that he often says to himself, "Now, what haven't I done before?"

If you're distractible, wondering at times if you might be hyperactive or suffering from attention-deficit disorder, your work-style is the antithesis of flow. A form of writer's block that I have experienced personally occurs when I'm having difficulty focusing on a single topic or task. Instead, my mind tries to pay attention to *everything*. At those times, I need to find a way to blot out the distractions in my environment and in my own mind. If you're a writer who believes you fall somewhere on the continuum of attention-deficit disorder, it's not impossible to learn to focus in, but it's certainly an ongoing challenge.

Staying focused is a form of mindfulness. Those with the ability to be "mindful," as described by psychologist Ellen J. Langer, are open to novelty, alert to distinction, sensitive to contexts, aware of multiple perspectives and oriented in the present. Many of these traits coincide with the requirements of flow. Flow requires enough novelty to maintain interest, not so much that a great deal of anxiety results. "People naturally seek novelty in play and have no difficulty paying attention in those situations," writes Langer. As we have seen, flow feels a lot more like play than like work. People who can find the novelty in anything have no trouble focusing on whatever they set their minds, and are rarely bored or distracted.

For example, when my son Kevin was eight years old, he had to wait more than a half hour in the principal's office for a car pool pickup. When asked if he had been bored, he responded, "No, I kept busy looking for pictures in the wallpaper." In other words, he cognitively restructured the task to generate more information, to keep himself attentive and interested.

When asked for any focusing exercises that have worked for him or his students, poet Ed Ochester suggested zeroing in on one particular time in your life, say a single particularly vivid memory from your high school years. "Then try to elaborate it a bit, try to write something visual out of it, try to have one character responding to that thing which you just described." And then he added:

> The best exercise, though, is just to focus on things that you have around you. Instead of doing the rhetorical exercise, saying, I have to write three sentences about this with two visual images, say to yourself, I'm

Q. I just got back from a meandering trip to Texas and Florida, and found that the trip made me more creative, more able to come up with clever phrases and plot twists, than when I'm home and my life is carefully planned out. What can you say about this dichotomy?

A. Two separate writers wrote essays for *The New York Times* in which they extolled the benefits of travel to bring the mind to sharp attentiveness. Mystery writer Lawrence Block describes how he travels all over the world, then returns home and writes another book set in New York City. "I'm sure the time I spend far from New York brings the city into sharper relief when I turn to it again in fiction, that I see more clearly for having temporarily turned my eyes elsewhere." And Letty Cottin Pogrebin finds that "travel is the ultimate time extender. In a strange, new country, the world slows down because we are paying attention, trying to figure things out. Exotic locales elicit the same sharp focus and intense concentration as did all of life when we first encountered it."

When you're away from home and your usual routines, many of the constraints you normally contend with disappear. Some people, when they're on vacation, have terrific sex in strange hotel rooms with their own spouses. Others go so far as to have affairs (not all surrenders have equally positive results). In the same way, if you're a writer, some part of your brain is giving you signals that "this doesn't really count," or "this experience is out of time and place," so that you feel looser than you usually do. Also, by changing your location and the times you eat and sleep, for instance, all of your senses are being freshly stimulated, so that new insights seem to arrive unbidden. As a writer who wishes to write regularly, you need to seek out ways to complexify your day-to-day life so that it remains fresh and inspiring to you. Even those writers who never leave home can find ways to do this. You might consider purposely changing something about your routine to see how it affects your creativity. This won't work for everyone, of course. But even if you believe your daily routine is sacrosanct, you must be finding ways to stimulate your mind and your senses that don't involve physically leaving your desk. Consider, for example, renting a foreign video if you're not in the habit of doing so; taking a walk in a new part of town; calling up an old friend you haven't contacted in years; or even something as pedestrian as hanging up a picture that's been lying around. Even a simple change like this may refresh a jaded psyche.

going to pay attention to the lumps of plastic bags in the recycling container of the supermarket and who drops the things in. Maybe that will lead to something and maybe it won't, but on the other hand, it's looking closely at common objects. Usually just making the choice is some kind of indication that you have an interest in it, or you're making that choice out of the infinite number of possibilities, because there is something there that seems to lead someplace. Instead of working with set subjects, try to be open to what's around you, the flow of the life around you, and where your mind particularly goes, or why you have a certain kind of memory when you're looking at a certain kind of object. Often, I think we just ignore that. It's a mistake to ignore it.

Trance or flow?

I am often asked how flow relates to trances and other altered states of consciousness that seem to focus inward. While some writers use the word "trance" when discussing their periods of flow writing, trance, hypnosis and flow are not quite the same. In "A Special Inquiry with Aldous Huxley into the Nature and Character of Various States of Consciousness," Milton Erickson detailed his careful study of author Aldous Huxley in an apparent flow state. Erickson, who was interested in hypnosis, and Huxley kept and compared daily notebooks throughout the project. Here is how Erickson described Huxley's process:

Huxley then proceeded with a detailed description of his very special practice of what he . . . called "Deep Reflection." He described this state . . . as one marked by physical relaxation with bowed head and closed eyes, a profound progressive psychological withdrawal from externalities but without any actual loss of physical realities nor any amnesias or loss of orientation, a "setting aside" of everything not pertinent and then a state of complete mental absorption in matters of interest to him. Yet, in that state of complete withdrawal and mental absorption, Huxley stated that he was free to pick up a fresh pencil to replace a dulled one to make "automatically" notations on his thoughts and to do all this without a recognizable realization on his part of what physical act he was performing. . . . It was quite common for him to initiate a day's work by entering a state of Deep Reflection as a preliminary process of marshaling his thoughts and putting into order the thinking that would enter into his writing later that day.

By putting Huxley into a variety of hypnotic trances, from light through deep, Erickson concluded that Huxley's Deep Reflection was not hypnotic in character. "Instead, it seemed to be a state of utterly intense concentration with much dissociation from external realities but with a full capacity to respond with varying degrees of readiness to externalities."

To enter a trance state, your field of focus must be drastically narrowed, similar to what occurs in a flow state. A good hypnotic subject is someone who has the ability to give up voluntarily his usual reality-orientation. Similarly, if you can enter flow easily, you can let go of your usual way of orienting to reality. Thus, flow, absorption, intense focus and a mood of persistent fascination with an activity are all varied forms of altered consciousness.

A few writers learn to use self-hypnosis to put themselves into what may be an actual hypnotic state to gain greater control over their creative output. Journalist and novelist Thomas B. Morgan learned from a psychiatrist to hypnotize himself and then used the trance to write daily. He explained that self-hypnosis gave him confidence, "as though I have been authorized by myself to create," and helped him control his perfectionism and fear of failure, but that it didn't necessarily make for better writing.

Sue Grafton, having decided she'd like to be able to work on her laptop even during hectic book tours, asked a hypnotist to make her a tape that would talk her into a light trance. On typical workdays, though, Grafton says, she uses a form of self-hypnosis she learned from a library book. "I think it is a way of suggesting to yourself that the job is going to get done, so you suggest to yourself that there will be a period of concentrated and focused work." She adds, "It's odd when I do a form of self-hypnosis. At first I think, well, this just feels like any other workday, but inevitably I get tons more done, and I feel connected to the work."

Although a true hypnotic trance and a flow state may be arrived at differently, these descriptions make them sound as though they *feel* remarkably alike and produce the same results. Therefore, if you're interested in pursuing self-hypnosis, I'd suggest reading up on the sub-ject or perhaps seeing an expert in hypnosis (first read the section on Meditation in chapter nine). By now you've seen that there are many possible routes to the same goal of more pleasurable and better writing.

Find the silent center

Most writers throughout history have found they need to carve out a sense of solitude for their writing time, whether that entails strict alone-ness or merely psychically cutting themselves off from the activity around them. "It seems as if I have been stripping everything carefully away for several weeks to clear my self for the *ceremonial* undertaking of the commitment," wrote author Janet Burroway. Some have found that working in a small writing room away from the bustle of their usual lives is the only way to focus inward the way they need to. As William Maxwell said, "I wrote the last two sections of *They Came Like Swallows* beside a window looking out on a tin roof. It was perfect. The roof was so boring it instantly drove me back to my typewriter." Playwright Henry Miller, quoted in *The New Yorker*, said he wrote his recent plays in a twelve-by-twenty-foot cabin next to his Roxbury, Connecticut, house, and added, "It's my little synagogue. I sit down there and I pray. If it doesn't go well, I'll be there an hour or two and just leave in disgust. If it does go well, I can go six hours. When it comes toward the end of something, I can go indefinitely."

That doesn't mean that, once you're ensconced in a particular envi-ronment, that you'll remain aware of those surroundings. If the cutting-off process has worked and intense focus begins, all else disappears. Such focus can begin even before the special writing place is reached, for experienced writers. As playwright Neil Simon said in an interview, once he's lost in thought, he is no longer aware of his office. "I never know it's here," he said. "I came in this morning and I'd say within three minutes I was sitting and writing, because you start the process when you're in the car."

Physical cutting-off isn't the only kind, though. To isolate yourself in a deeper sense, you'll have to remove your awareness of your audi-ence from your mind, as noted by Stephen Spender, "The only impor-tant ritual for me is to write in such a way that I shut out all conscious-ness of my public." (I'll discuss audience awareness further in the next chapter.)

Various writers find their own routes to focus. Conrad Richter wrote

Q. Why is it that I'm able to tune out all kinds of noises (TV, kids, barking dog) when I feel passionate about my writing, but that the slightest noise breaks my concentration at other times? A: When you're in flow, you care about what you're doing, and your attention is fully engaged. There's no attention left to perceive all those irrelevant environmental sounds. It might be only writing the grocery list, or it might be a poem you promised to write for your mother for her anniversary, but you must feel something about the task in order to remain in your most highly focused state in spite of interruptions. Some people are easily distractible no matter what they're working on, but you indicate that you *are* able to tune out distractions at certain times. When you're less than passionate about your work, however, you're not in flow and so every little creak and squeak injects itself into your consciousness. When someone asks you a question, part of your mind notices that something is demanding attention, and it eventually returns to reality in time to give a somewhat delayed response.

Apparently, for you, intense flow only happens when you are emotionally involved. If you crave more frequent flow experiences, seek out passionate projects whenever you can. Beyond that, if possible, learn ways to make whatever you're doing more emotionally engaging.

that he had to "prepare consciously for work by tensing the mind to the task of writing—so many minutes or hours of mental tension on the subject in question." Or, as Amy Tan has said, "I focus on a specific image, and that image takes me into a scene. Then I begin to see the scene and I ask myself, 'What's to your right? What's to your left?' and I open up into this fictional world. I often play music as a way of blocking out the rest of my consciousness." Donald Hall calls it "absorbedness": "I enter the page in front of me. Time stops. I am utterly absorbed in the task, in the language, in the attempt to make an art."

Many of the patterns to which writers become attached serve the purpose of centering your attention on the work (as well as of loosening you up, which has to happen at the same time). The very fact of automating your working habits helps eliminate the distraction of the outside world and its expected judgments.

Writers talk about the act of focusing their attention in various ways. For some, it isn't a particularly conscious activity:

> But if I'm just in that attentive—attentive isn't the word exactly, attentive is kind of a Zen word—it's not even that. It's engaged, maybe. I'm not sure that I'm necessarily focused. I just feel like I'm . . . there's energy going through and I'm just not blocking it, not getting in the way of it. (Richard Jones)

What I'm after here is that state of concentration in which everything flows to and from the work. . . . Then, when I walk into my study, I bring this kind of energy with me, readying me to focus inward. . . . There is a drifting in and out of awareness (i.e., I know more openly that I'm involved in a poetry experience), but I try to ignore that knowing. I don't want the spell broken. (Andrea Hollander Budy)

And sometimes it *is* more of a conscious activity, as Diana Gabaldon says, "While I am actually working on a piece, I do have that feeling of needing to concentrate very hard to listen. It's not that they talk to you and you write it down. It's that you're actually working with them." Sue Grafton explains:

> When I think too much about reviewers, reader reception, all those issues, I get scared, and once I get scared, I don't work. So what I say to myself is, "Lower your sights. Quit looking at the end product. Quit looking at leaping four months until your editor is reading the book. Quit thinking about reviews, and will you get another insulting letter about your plotting." My only responsibility is to write the next sentence well. And so I pull my focus down to as small and tiny as I can get it.

Key Four is about bringing your attention down to this tiny, quiet center where you will be able to imagine freely, so you can form the wild associations that will make your poems and stories original and enjoyable to read.

Turning Key Four

You may be unable to write when other people are near, or when interruptions threaten, or when the end of your current writing session looms too soon. Even when such distractions and potential interruptions are a possibility, you can always try the following suggestions, as well as the many specific techniques in chapter nine:

1. Are you someone who is easily distracted or do you get highly absorbed in virtually any task you undertake? If the former, are you less distractible when you're emotionally engaged in what you're doing? Is that emotional passion an integral part of your writing? Think about the times you get most deeply focused and absorbed. What qualities does that activity have? Is there a way to get more of that in your writing?

2. Do you catch yourself worrying about some aspect of yourself (i.e., am I a good writer? am I a successful person?) when you were intending to get involved in your writing? Try to watch for those kinds of thoughts, and rather than berate yourself for having them (it's almost a universal habit), simply notice them and let them go. Then refocus your mental energy onto your work. Do this as often as you need to for it to become a habit.

3. Do you have difficulty zooming into the center of one aspect of your project because too many confusing thoughts about it are buzzing around your mind? Rather than beginning to write complete sentences, make a list of as many of these distracting thoughts as you can. Feel free to jot down words and phrases in any order anywhere on a large sheet of paper. Sometimes it helps to be able to visualize the whole amazing mass of ideas, thoughts and half-formed images at once, before choosing one with which to begin the writing session. Often a few phrases or images will start presenting themselves to you, but you have as yet no way to grab hold of them. After you've jotted down a mass of them, come back a few hours or a couple of days later, and focus on this haphazard "list." A beginning place will usually present itself to you. This is similar to using a writer's notebook for keeping track of all those bits of ideas that aren't yet ready for your full attention. Part of learning to focus in is to know when you're not yet ready to do it.

4. Slice the salami. That's my friend Greg Kamei's favorite term for choosing one small piece of a larger project to focus on, thus eliminating the sensation of being overwhelmed by the whole thing. (Other writers have called this "eating the elephant one bite at a time.") Or try making a loose outline. For some writers this reduces anxiety due to the overwhelming nature of a project.

5. If you're finding it a challenge at the moment to focus in on a particular character, so that your plot can move along, novelist David Gerrold suggests sitting down and having a conversation with the character. Ask: What does he want? What does he like? What's he afraid of? Where's he coming from? Where's he going? What does he need you to know?

6. Get a large sheet of paper and splatter words on it randomly. Write down anything that comes to mind that is in any way related to what you're working on. When you've run out of words, look for patterns or a point of engagement.

7. One way to practice focusing in is to choose something—any-thing—and write everything you can about it. Look closely at that rose and see how much you can write about it. Or choose something that is totally uninspiring at first, say, the pros and cons of gummed stamps, or the personality of a dust mite, and write about that.

7 Key Five: Balance Among Opposites

WRITING IN FLOW IS ESSENTIALLY MYSTERIOUS, a paradoxical and shifty process. Contradictions exist not only *among* writers, but coexist within the *same* writer. For example, while you're writing, you may feel you're in control and not in control at the same time. Some writers feel as though they are mostly in control and prefer that; many more don't, and either prefer that or don't care. Your personal working methods will place you somewhere along the continuum, as you find your own ways of balancing the opposites, making sense of the potential contradictions. Do you think you *think*, or do you believe thinking—at least in the usual way or perhaps entirely—is antithetical to creativity?

Some writers credit inspiration for their work, while others seem to believe that with enough hard work, something—inspiration, flow—will break through (Mario Vargas Llosa said, "Inspiration for me comes from a regular effort. . . . The 'illumination' only occurs during the work."). As for thoughts of your eventual readers, do you attempt to focus on them or to put all thoughts of audience aside? Do you find it difficult to answer such questions definitively? If so, it's because it's not a matter of balancing once and for all. Rather think of this image: you stand legs-wide on a surfboard, ready and able to adapt and shift position flexibly as the waves—your writing projects— require.

When it comes to emotional states, there too, you'll find yourself balancing among pairs of opposites, to find what you need in the tension between two poles of feeling. One researcher found that "writers seem to draw strength from emotional antitheses. . . . Writing often seems propelled by a collision, a tug-of-war between positive and negative feelings, agony and ecstasy." Somehow reconciling all these opposites means you learn to live with some residual mystery. While you needn't be a mystic to enter flow, neither can you demand that flow be reduced to an either-or formula. Lynne Sharon Schwartz says that when she's in it, life is the way it should always be, "freed from time and petty daily concerns and all forms of self-consciousness except the very deepest, which is paradoxically a kind of forgetfulness yet profound awareness of self—but alas, that is not possible very often." Or, as Marvin Bell suggests, "In that other state, or universe, perhaps things make sense and associations seem logical in a way that they might not in the other world, just as dreams have total authority."

In or out of control?

"Write from a white-heat state of mind," one writer in our group advised a friend who asked how to compose a poem for her sister as a birthday present. He had previously suggested she do a clustering exercise to get the ideas flowing, in which she would write down anything that came to mind in relation to her feelings about her sister and their shared experiences, allowing each written phrase or thought to spin off into related ideas. She had loved the exercise and now had two pages of scrawled thoughts and images to play with. What next, she wondered? How to turn this brainstormed mass of ideas and feelings into a poem?

While this advice is excellent—what he was telling her was to write while in a flow state—and her poem turned out quite lovely, there are times when you need advice that is more concrete. *How* do you get from here—a cluster of images tendriling the brain—to here: *sans* thought, *sans* mind, *sans* everything but the piece creating itself out of your deepest self?

That out-of-control state is, after all, what many notable writers find produces their most intense and original work. Yet, writers vary in how much they give up or lose control, and they vary in when the process changes for them into one that is less mindful and more intuitive.

For the most part, writers express more of a sense of control during revision and editing than in first-draft writing. For instance, Howard Norman, whose earlier novels *The Northern Lights* and *The Bird Artist* were both National Book Award finalists, explained recently to a group of readers how *The Museum Guard* reached its pared-down and uncluttered form. In early drafts, Norman typed literally hundreds of pages describing every detail of a cemetery of which, in the finished book, we only see brief glimpses. Nearly all of that description was revised out of existence when he took active control of the novel. Not only that, but once the typed version of one of his novels feels complete, he then rewrites the entire manuscript by hand to get a fuller sense of control over style and voice.

Jane Hirshfield is comfortable with the paradox of being in and out of control at the same time:

> The first draft may at times come almost as dictation, as if the words were speaking themselves in my consciousness, but even here, even when I am at times frightened by what is being given, I don't feel taken over in any uncomfortable way. To offer myself to the condition of concentration is what I want to do, it is a pleasure. It is abandonment and collaboration at the same time.

A few writers are adamant about the necessity of maintaining some control at all times, while others cannot write without feeling they have totally let go. Such surrendering is one way to move into a more relaxed, open and creative place: "Out of control in a lovely way" (Marnell Jameson); or, "I am neither in nor out of control. I am nothing in 'the flow'" (Mark Strand). Suzanne Lummis compares the feeling to her experiences as an actress: "I'm both in control and not. It's like that with acting too, in one's finest moments. You're more in control than you've ever been, yet you're not controlling anything."

Poet Henry Taylor says he feels in control as much as he needs to: "I have some curiosity about what's coming next, and so I just wait and let it come, and then see." Marvin Bell described his own views by elaborating on a favorite quote of his from another writer:

> Four lines from Antonio Machado: "People possess four things / that are no good at sea: / Anchor, rudder, oars / and the fear of going down." The Machado quatrain says it: surrender! That "flow" in

which you are interested is, for some, a highly sophisticated form of surrender; for others, as natural as gooseflesh. I grew up on the water: having anchor, rudder, oars and even a healthy fear of going down sounds like a good idea. If I'd have had enough fear, I wouldn't have "borrowed" leaky boats for the day, and my friend and I wouldn't have caught hell. But Machado says no: his sea is a metaphor for language. Without a rudder to set direction, oars for propulsion, an anchor to keep one immobile, and even a fear of the prospects, one can abandon oneself to the medium (language) and end up places, to use a William Carlos Williams phrase, "heretofore unrealized." (Why go to the same islands all the time?)

More or less control when in flow? I don't think about it. I am out of this world. Am I more in control of the other world? I wouldn't call it control because it's a confidence that comes from surrendering to the materials rather than controlling them. Of course I "control" by making choices, but the rationale for the choices is poetic rather than sensible.

Two writers described their processes in similar ways, resorting to visual/spatial analogies. Chitra Banerjee Divakaruni compared writing to driving through fog. "You only see a little bit ahead." And Bernard Cooper explained it this way:

> Someone once asked me on stage what my writing process was like. I sort of got out of my chair and I closed my eyes and I started to grope around the stage, and I sat down and said, "That's what it's like." I was actually quite serious. It's not that I start off, generally speaking, with no idea, no inklings or impulses, but I usually start off with something like an image or a sort of stray statement or the idea of an incident. Often from memory, though now that I'm writing short fiction, it's not necessarily based on memory. But I think what motivates me is just being haunted by something. Again, a kind of fragment that I don't quite understand and then try to sort of pursue it until it yields some sort of narrative meaning.

Self-control is another form of control, according to Jonathan Kellerman, who makes himself *not* write until a predetermined time. He begins each writing day by rewriting what he did the previous day. He says that takes the same kind of control as when he's outlining for six months and he's really itching to start writing, but he knows that if he waits, it will come out better. He does take notes, and if he really can't control himself, he will let himself write an opening page. "A lot of times the book is determined to a good extent by the way it starts," he says, "but I really try to exercise a degree of self-control because the kind of novel I write has a lot of structure, a lot of story."

In talking about her creative process, Nobel Prize-winning novelist Toni Morrison described that tenuous balance: "Listening to characters—they're like ghosts that are being released—but I'm in control and I'm writing the book. Sometimes I have to shut them up. Everything is knowing when to stop. That's the difference between novice and experienced writers."

Or you may belong in that proportion of writers who believe they are—and must be—in control throughout the writing process. This is how Pulitzer Prize-winning poet Anthony Hecht expresses it: "The state you call 'flow' is always one of authority and control. If it were simply hallucinogenic it would be easily attained by artificial means, and would be an escape from artistic responsibility and conscious art. It might be pleasant, but whatever it produced would be chiefly of medical interest."

Control, in such cases, refers to controlling the content of the work, rather than to control over one's ability to enter flow at will. If you feel you must maintain such control at all times, whether or not flow occurs may be irrelevant to you. I would hazard a guess that those who believe all aspects of the creative process are out of their control probably have a harder time working regularly. It might even be seen as self-defeating, a psychological condition of learned helplessness. In such a situation, you believe you *can't* do something because you haven't been able to before, so you give up making any effort at all in that direction.

The less you fear losing control (in the sense of letting go of your workaday self to move into an alternate reality), and the more you're willing to explore anything without prior rejection, which is a form of looseness and boundary-hopping, the greater your possibility of enjoying the unself-consciousness of flow. At some point, of course, you have to take charge of the work, looking at it a bit less passionately perhaps. Even then, you may not actually be "in control" in the usual sense of the phrase. For some, though, that revision is done in a similar state as the original work, but the internal critic is allowed to tiptoe back in and finally have its say, however intuitively based.

To think or not to think?

In flow, ordinary thinking gives way to an alternate kind. When I discuss with writers what their thought processes are just before they begin to write, they usually either tell me they purposely make an effort to "not think," or they acknowledge that they do think, but not the way they usually do. It's a common misconception that the right brain is the only part active during creative activity, including writing. While it appears to be the case that the left hemisphere of the brain has advantages in dealing with language and that the right hemisphere shows dominance in spatial tasks, brain studies show that those whose brains communicate most richly between the hemispheres are more creative. They are more in touch with their feelings and express them through their creative productions.

Nevertheless, numerous self-help books contain exercises that purport to help you make the left-brain to right-brain shift, and other writers' manuals have suggested exercises to help the would-be writer "not think" in order to cross over to the place where something else does the creating. While it is possible that such exercises may help alter consciousness away from the familiar mode, realize also that the intuitive and the rational work best in a mix. Judgment is intimately involved throughout the process of creating. You do not suspend thought, per se. You merely use another kind of thought, a type that allows you to break away from (or loosen) the usual series of connections to make new ones. You're always making choices, whether you're writing poetry or inventing a new machine, and reasoning is always of value in solving creative problems. The highly regarded humanist thinker Rollo May said it well:

> Ecstasy is the accurate term for the intensity of consciousness that occurs in the creative act. But it is not to be thought of merely as a Bacchic "letting go"; it involves the total person, with the subconscious and unconscious acting in unity with the conscious. It is not, thus, irrational; it is, rather, suprarational. It brings intellectual, volitional, and emotional functions into play all together.

A good poem exemplifies the results of a shift out of standard thinking. Ralph Angel attempts to put words to this ambiguous process that is at the crux of his writing experience:

> Most of the thought process is getting rid of thought processes. Culturally, we use language as a source of information. And poetry is not information . . . Unlearning and getting rid of thought is important to me because I can't really make a poem unless I discover it, discover what it is I'm writing about or actually conveying, whether it saddens

or disgusts or shames me, or whether it presents me with joy or wonder or love. To get to something fundamental in my nature I have to offer up, in the Catholic sense, what I know or think I know. And if in doing that I can touch upon something fundamental about my existence, then I might just make an art object that might just make contact with another human being who I'll never meet.

Can you choose not to think (in the usual sense of the word) or is it a shift that you learn to allow to happen? Are those two acts essentially opposed? You don't have to know the answer to these questions before you enter flow, and most writers I've spoken to have difficulty talking about this clearly. Indulging in one or more prewriting habits is often how you'll get yourself in the proper frame of mind to write. Writing often feels like less of an intellectual exercise than one that taps into your subconscious, with the sensation of doing "intellectual" work more fully belonging to a nonflow state. Some writers find that the definition of flow for them coincides with a sense of not thinking. "I have no 'thought processes.' I almost never think," writes Mark Strand. Says Wanda Coleman: "I feel 'plugged in' and whatever is in my head flows out effortlessly without my having to think about it." Robert Olen Butler says, "The state I'm talking about here has to do with the complete relinquishing of the conscious analytical mind. . . . Art does not come from the head. It comes from the place where you dream."

Here are poets describing their preflow and flow thought processes or lack thereof:

> I try to empty my mind; no, I wait for the mind to empty. TV, crossword puzzles, errands, keeping up on records and bills—such activities allow my mind to empty and to let go of the entirely civic, public, rational, conventional. (Marvin Bell)

> I think I did shift into flow in writing a poem about flow, and I vaguely remember describing the cognitive thought patterns as being kind of sparks that were trying to catch up. The flow process is coordinating an incredible number of things at once that I could not possibly consciously coordinate. It's not that you are no longer thinking, but you become thinking itself. You're no longer watching yourself, you are the activity. And you have to rely on that. I keep forgetting that that is the most important part of the creative process for me. Sometimes I try to go back into the research mode but it's almost always deadly. In some of the more complicated poems, I've gone to notebooks that I've previously

used, and there will be all the data, the puns, the images, there, but you let that other facility take over and take charge of those facts, and it will use them as it will use them. (Stephen Perry)

When I'm in flow, all of a sudden I'm going somewhere and I have no idea where. No idea, none. . . . Flow is not thinking. Thinking is tiring. When you think hard, you have to concentrate, like when you're doing a math problem, or your taxes, or trying to balance your checkbook. You become tense when you think like that, even if you've only been working for five minutes. But if I'm just in that attentive mood—attentive isn't the word exactly, attentive is a kind of Zen word—it's not even that. I just feel like there's energy going through and I'm just not blocking it, not getting in the way of it. A very intelligent energy flows through the entire body when you write, and it's the energy that is concentrated and translated, not the mind. Flow occurs when I don't let the writer in me get in the way of the writing. How do I get in the way of it? I start thinking. (Richard Jones)

If you're a novelist, you too may often experience your work as best accomplished without thinking in the usual sense. According to Carolyn See, once she sits down to write, she's thinking for maybe the first ten lines, and then she's not thinking any more. Peter Clothier explains that the purpose of meditation, for him, is to get out of the regular thinking process and back in touch with his unconscious mind. "At this point," he says, "thought is a distraction. Flow works best for me when I come to it without any intellectual predisposition." According to Ursula K. Le Guin, the only decisions a skilled artisan or artist makes during the work are aesthetic ones, and

since aesthetic decisions are not rational ones, they are made on a level that doesn't fully coincide with rational consciousness. Many artists feel that they are in something resembling a trance state while working, and that the decisions the work involves are not made by them, but by the work.

Yet maybe you *do* think in a way that closely resembles what you've always thought of as thinking. "There's a lot of stopping and just thinking," says Judith Freeman. Carol Muske says that while she works, she walks in circles when she's thinking. Maurya Simon explains that there are exceptions to the way she usually works. "I usually sit down and let whatever happens happen. But [one recent time] I was doing a lot of sorting and criticizing and analyzing which usually happens more in the revision process."

Thinking can be useful (!) in the immediate preflow period, as Charles Harper Webb describes: "There's a pile of books beside the bed, and I pull something out. It's not totally at random because I've left things out that I think might be interesting. Anyway, the books just get me thinking verbally. They get me interested in language—in messing around with it." Hilma Wolitzer also talks about thinking and related mental activities as essential to getting started: "My favorite prewriting ritual is procrastination (no joke intended). This means thinking about writing, allowing ideas, characters and blocks of prose to take shape in my head."

Will or inspiration?

"The terror of writing comes from the fact that there is always something involved beyond mere willpower and conscious labor," wrote poet Edward Hirsch. What is the relationship between willing the work to flow and waiting for inspiration to descend and provide you with both the raw material and the ease to carve it into art? Does any particular piece of writing depend on a certain proportion of the one to the other, something like the *pi* of flow?

When writers use the word "will" to describe their creative process, those thoughts often intersect with comments that indicate the writer feels a sense of control (or its absence). When you talk about inspiration, you may mean that your work seems to come from some alien place within you or, less typically, from some other source. Inspiration has been associated with what has been called the illumination phase of the creative process. You may feel you are entering flow at the point of illumination, if not far sooner.

While you can certainly will yourself to work, it's not necessarily possible to will yourself to enter flow. "I am always grateful for these visitations of clarity," writes Anthony Hecht. "I find I can do nothing to induce them." Nancy Kress, author of fantasy and science-fiction novels, thrillers and short stories, agrees: "If flow doesn't come by itself, I don't know how to make it come. Sometimes I give up, sometimes I work. Sometimes I work and then erase it all in frustration." Few artists, in fact, would insist that everything about their work comes to them from a source over which they have total control.

It's like opening a door that's floating in the middle of nowhere and all you have to do is go and turn the handle and open it and let yourself sink into it. You can't particularly force yourself through it. You just have to float. If there's any gravitational pull, it's from the outside world trying to keep you back from the door. It's not willing. . . . The will gets you to the chair. The not-will gets you to the flow. (Stephen Perry)

I don't understand flow at all. If I knew where it came from, I'd go back to get some more. It has no discernible pattern for me. I can be "hot" or "cold" for weeks or months at a time. I've always referred to the hot or productive state as "inspiration," and generally feel guilty about waiting for it to happen, rather than applying myself in a more disciplined way. (Hilma Wolitzer)

"I don't think there's some scientific approach to 'flow'—the steps one can follow to get there, or, in hindsight, the formula for finding it again," contends novelist and short-story writer Merrill Joan Gerber. She believes that flow

seems to come out of a state of partially "idle" concentration (at least a willingness to work), whereupon, at some point, the imagined idea, thought, scene, invention takes on a sensual reality that overpowers the everyday demand on the senses, those thoughts that always accompany work—wouldn't I rather be eating, sleeping, playing with the cat, etc.? It's not exactly a mystical state, but neither do I think it can be scheduled, prepared for with rituals, returned to by will (as your questions suggest). It's a kind of grace that comes after long preparation, after turning to the subject with a willingness to go there (this is often the hardest part) and also after a kind of maturity settles onto the material you've been mulling about, or even writing about. It's a state much to be desired, like love, but can't be willed into being.

I'll return to this topic—and, in a fashion, partially rebut such assertions—in chapter ten on learning to flow. For I have found that flow *can* be learned, at least by certain motivated individuals. Learning to alter a state of consciousness, though, takes time, practice, knowledge and, sometimes, a spark of native ability. Pure will isn't nearly enough.

Cees Nooteboom, who works in both poetry and prose, experiences the will aspect quite dissimilarly in each form. With poetry, once he has the idea or a few lines or even a few words, or sometimes when he's reading poetry, suddenly something sets off a spark. In his opinion, though, you cannot really provoke that feeling at a particular preset

Q. The only writing time I have is three hours every morning from 5 to 8 A.M. During much of that time, I feel rushed and pressured. How can I get myself into flow more quickly?

A. My answer to you has three parts. First, many writers have even less time than you do. You sound like you may have unrealistic expectations of what you can accomplish in that amount of time. If you've been struggling to write four pages a day, or a whole poem, perhaps you could cut your goal in half. On your worst, slowest days, how much do you manage to write? If it's only one unrevised page, then tell yourself that you will write one first-draft page per day, every day. Then multiply that by the number of days in a year and face the fact that at the end of a year, you will have not only completed the first draft of an entire novel, but you will have had time to polish much of it too.

Second, think about those three hours. By rushing yourself and determining to enter flow before you're quite ready, you may actually be inhibiting flow entry. For the next month, allow yourself one to two hours of loosening time at each writing session. Although you can't absolutely count on it, it's fairly sure that you will get into flow somewhere in that period. Read over what you've written before, play around with some ideas, approach the work through a side door (concentrate on figuring out one character's motivation or, for ten minutes, freewrite words and phrases that come to mind that might be in any way related to your project).

Third, let your subconscious processes do more of the creating for you. Try stopping work when you're in the middle of a thought. This way part of your mind will continue mulling it over when you're away from your desk, and then when you begin work in the morning, you may get into flow more quickly.

time, whereas when he's writing a novel, he will determine to sit down in the morning and work on it.

You may call upon your will to get motivated to begin work. For example, I know that music puts me into an altered place, and so does sex. Yet sometimes I have to actively will myself to begin those activities, in spite of an odd reluctance, rather than continuing to perform chores or work or whatever activities are currently keeping me anchored to my habitual reality. I have to will myself, even when I am not already "in the mood," to allow myself to get "in the mood"— if I am to achieve the altered state that on some level I desire. Similarly, you may need to make a conscious decision to begin doing whatever you have found gets you into flow, though you're certainly not in that altered place when you first make the decision. That's one good reason why habit is so expedient: you don't have to go through the challenge of deciding every time. It can also take a real effort of will to arrange your environment so you can focus inward and onto the challenge at hand. It can be done if writing means a lot to you. When Chitra Banerjee Divakaruni began writing, she did so erratically, when "the passion struck me. As I became better at it and writing became more important in my life, I realized I would have to set some time apart for writing. I just started setting time apart every day." (What she gave up, she told me, was entertainment time, but absolutely not reading time, which both calms her down and is a necessity to her as a writer.)

Moving from will to what I see as its opposite, inspiration, I found that writers operate with a variety of belief systems. While some writers experience their ideas, or whatever it is that goes into making their art, as being the result of inspiration, as coming from outside in some way, other writers are equally certain that if there is such a phenomenon as inspiration, it comes from their own subconscious minds. I also discovered something else, and this is where the experience of others has direct relevance to your own writing life: numerous writers believe they can facilitate their own inspiration by sitting down to write, by willing the process to happen. "Sometimes you begin with the insight, and sometimes you have to find it. You chase the poem until it catches you," says James Ragan.

Jane Smiley, who loves to write and who writes regularly, nevertheless feels her novels mostly come to her somehow, so that she's never been anxious around her writing.

> Fairly early, within a few years of my first published novels, I decided that my writing was not something possessed by me, that I didn't possess my own works. They simply *were*, they passed through me and I passed through them.

Smiley elaborated: her fifth novel, and still her favorite, *The Greenlanders*, was about a true place, the Norse colony on the southern tip of Greenland in the end of the fourteenth and the outset of the fifteenth centuries, with historically attested characters in it. "For me, that book was absolutely a vision or a communication from somewhere else, from them. It took me a while, about a hundred pages, to realize it, and it was pretty scary. I strongly had the feeling that I was *receiving* the novel and transmitting it." I asked Smiley if she tends to be mystical, and she responded negatively. Yet,

> I believe that it's only partially created by the conscious mind. Where the other part comes from, I sometimes think one thing, I sometimes think another. There's a lot of things that you could say. To me all writers have said it's coming to them from somewhere. From the muse, from god, from literature itself, the subconscious mind, the Ur-mind, some kind of Jungian other, from the reptilian brain. Who knows?
>
> I ride horses a lot, and there's a lot that you feel coming from the horse when you're riding it. That's the sense I had that it was coming from the characters. There was a kind of energy. Many of them were actually historical people. It seemed to me that the story I was telling about them was true. Well, so how would I know that? I don't know. It was an uncanny experience, it was a frightening experience, and I no longer felt after that that I possessed my own work in any way.

In each of Smiley's books, she went on, something similar has happened. With her comic novel, *Moo*, she was unsure of her style until she arrived at the end of a particular section. "I looked at that," she said, "and knew this is the style. It has come to me and it is rock solid. I do not to have to think about this anymore. What came to me in *The Greenlanders* was the story. I found *A Thousand Acres* extremely laborious to write, but what came to me was who Ginny was. Every book does feel strongly like it was given to me."

It can be tempting to confound inspiration with flow and to speak of them both in the same way. You may then use the word *inspiration* to indicate whatever it is that propels you more deeply into your work. Poet Sam Hamill agrees that he gets so absorbed in his writing that he often looks up to see that more time has passed than he had expected, and yet

> I'm not convinced that you're talking about anything different from inspiration, which the old Greeks believed in—in a literal way—drawing in the "breath of the goddess" in order to "become pregnant with meaning." . . . And I don't think that inspiration is just this sort of momentary flash where you say, "Oh, I've got to write down this line."

Though that's a kind. But I relate it to Zen practice and the idea of *Ken-sho*, or enlightenment. Some schools of Zen say, "Well, forget about the huge breakthrough and the huge realization. You should have little realizations every day." And I tend to conform more to that description.

Similarly, Ethan Canin insists that "the freeing moment is sitting down and sometimes just writing two sentences and somehow that unlocks this other thing and it comes out. You cannot write a novel out of inspiration, out of a moment of genius. There's no substitute for sitting down every day for four hundred days and writing a page."

Regardless of what you believe, it's a good idea not to wait for inspiration to strike before embarking on work. Rather, you can learn to take matters into your own hands (and mind) and put yourself in a situation where flow can happen. Ralph Angel, for instance, says he doesn't so much write out of sudden inspiration anymore, but that he simply needs to go to his writing room to make writing possible. Nevertheless, you may experience fleeting moments that you can't conceive of as anything besides inspiration. Says Stephen Yenser:

> I think I would say more like 85 percent [of poetry] is revision. I feel that most of writing poetry is a matter of craft. It's not an easy craft, you can't learn it in a year or two. But it's like writing prose, writing fiction, writing music, like painting paintings. I think all these things involve a hell of a lot of work, and a touch of inspiration. And a lot of the craft that I'm talking about is kind of second nature by now. So I don't have to think about writing an iambic pentameter line. So the craft is there inseparable for me from the flow. In fact I wouldn't have the flow without the craft, I think. The inspiration is different. I think anybody can be lucky enough to get hit by lightning.

When told of the preceding statement, my own poet-about-the-house Stephen responded, "I *invite* lightning by playing around in my metal suit."

Hariett Doerr insisted during our conversation that she does not believe in flow as I have described it, but that the following passage (which she translated from the Mexican writer Agustin Yanez after he visited a class of hers at Scripps College in 1976) is a more accurate description of how she writes: "The work of a writer is hard, slow work, like the work of a cobbler or a stonemason. You, the writer, hammer and build as they do, page by page, paragraph by paragraph, phrase by phrase, word by word, until you find the word that flowers on the page."

Inspiration is notoriously unreliable. This is not meant to imply that such bursts of inspiration are not welcomed when they arrive; it's just that they do not predict a polished, or even a workable, piece of art. When Donald Hall, who claims not to enter the timelessness of flow with any regularity, was younger, he "received drafts of poems from the mothership, often a little group of them in one period of inspiration, hours or days or weeks, and then needed to work on the poems daily for a couple of years to get them right." In this way, a burst of inspiration, always a delight when it happens, might need to be followed by years of careful recrafting.

At least equally common is the experience of Cees Nooteboom, who describes that wonderful/awful feeling of having to get out of bed to write down something that may or may not have been worth the trouble in the bright light of the following day:

> In the middle of the night I may suddenly think of a line of a poem and then I have to make a great decision whether I will write it down. Because sometimes you're half asleep, and then I know what will happen, is that once I start writing something down, then there will be more, and I will have to leave my bed and go downstairs, and suddenly I might find myself a few hours doing this. . . . But I still don't think one should mystify it. It's just that you have gotten onto something that you feel may be worthwhile giving up lovely Morpheus for. And quite often, you also have the experience that it wasn't true, that what you find there is not so much utter nonsense as something that is not really very workable.

Whether your scribbled midnight revelations are often worthy of the cold post-caffeine reappraisal you give them, it can't hurt to keep a pad and pen on your nightstand (pencils make scratchy noises that are annoying to light-sleeping partners—take my word for it). Some of my own most frustrating mornings have been spent wracking my brains in a vain attempt to reconstruct an insight—the one that would unlock the mystery of whatever I was writing that day—that, at 4 A.M., I was certain I'd committed to memory. My beneath-the-blanket mantra, "repeat, repeat, repeat, repeat, then let go and sleep," doesn't always work.

Who's watching?

If you're too sharply aware of who is going to read your finished work early in the process of drafting it in the first place, not only will your free flow of ideas be inhibited, but you'll find it much more difficult, perhaps impossible, to enter into a flow state. It's rare indeed for much-published novelists and poets to focus on the eventual audience for their work while they're writing it. "The poem is the audience alone," writes Donald Revell, speaking for many. Still, something more along the lines of "I'm always aware of them in some way—that's part of how I make the decisions," is perhaps even more typical. In order to provide yourself with the internal feedback you need (is this line or scene working?), you may run it by some part of your mind for an intuitive decision, or you may quite consciously ask yourself what your real future audience is going to make of it. The latter scenario is not recommended unless you find such a line of thinking doesn't get in your way.

During the revision process, of course, it's more typical to consider your audience, but even then, it's usually only in the interests of clarity, rather than being concerned about a potentially critical judgment. Octavia E. Butler claims to think of her audience "when I worry about being misunderstood. And that's in rewriting, for the most part." Poet Andrea Hollander Budy, too, only considers audience during late revision. "I may try to rethink the poem from a different perspective," she says, "aware of what a listener may hear differently in one, say, first-person version that he would not hear in a third-person version."

You'll recognize paradox in the way many writers speak of how they conceive of an audience. On the one hand, they prefer not to think of one at all, yet on the other, they know someone will finally be reading what they're writing. For some, that knowledge is integral to the work. When I asked T.C. Boyle if he would still be motivated to write if everyone stopped reading his work, he responded: "It's a moot point. Because I would be dead. I'd just kill myself." Does this mean, then, that he *needs* to reach a significant audience? "Not only that," he told me, "but to have them in your thrall, conquer the world, stun them. Amaze them."

You might work out the duality by incorporating your audience into yourself in a noninhibiting way. Rather it becomes part of the ongoing process of making choices as to what will work or, as Mark Strand puts it, "I never think of my audience. My appeals are to myself-made-other."

Popular novelist Michael Connelly says that his main goal is to write a book that he would like to read himself and that "if I like a book, there's a good chance a lot of people will like it." He sees himself as "pretty much the everyperson, down-the-middle type of reader, particularly in the genre that I write in." Thus Connelly only has to create something he himself would enjoy spending time with. Yet, he says, "I'd say when I'm sitting down and deciding what do I write this time, it's harder at that point to keep out the intrusion of audience expectations, commercial viability of ideas and so forth. I don't let it steer the boat, but I think about it."

Writers consciously manipulate the way they think about their readers. For example, the term "audience" is a frightening one to Susan Taylor Chehak, since it implies the scariness of strangers. What she tries to do, she says, is divide herself in half, on the one hand writing for herself the audience, and on the other hand, "just writing, rather than thinking of some objective person with glasses in a chair sitting in front of the fire reading my book." Alfred Corn says he has internalized an audience, with definite likes and dislikes, "so that the process of writing goes in regular alternation with the process of reading: I write for a bit, then read what I write and respond to it positively or negatively." Or:

> It seems to be all mixed up together, because you're telling this story to yourself but there's part of your mind that realizes that there are strangers out there who will bump up against what you're doing at some point. But I think that as you're first starting and as you're finishing a project, you're more apt to think in terms of an audience. (Gerald DiPego)

Then again, if clarity is a particularly meaningful concept to you, you may never lose awareness, on some level, of those for whom you're writing:

> The audience is always implicit. I write for the possible other. When I revise (which is every day) I need to think of what can possibly get through to another human being and what cannot possibly get through. I need to think of another human being when I remove repetition. I don't want to be boring—and the concept of being boring involves a potential reader. Everything does. (Donald Hall)

In the course of writing it is impossible not to think of an audience, if only because it is desirable to be understood, and questions arise about whether allusions will be identifiable, whether notes will be useful. Some allusions can be left to especially gifted readers, without the need for further comment, while others may have either to be eliminated or annotated. These alternatives become serious when they affect the body of the text, and sometimes require revisions anywhere from minor to major. They can determine a great deal about the final poem, in consequence. (Anthony Hecht)

What effect does audience awareness have on flow? It can be inhibiting, pulling you right out of flow, especially if the audience is envisioned as critical: "You can't write for the market" (Phyllis Gebauer); "Consciousness of audience while writing is fatal to the work" (Ursula K. Le Guin). Chitra Banerjee Divakaruni once said in an interview that she tries not to think about audience, because once she begins to wonder what might offend particular readers, she "often comes back to thinking about what my mother would have to say, and that really freezes me."

An aside: It seems that ape painters may also be vulnerable to audience awareness. In the late 1950s, Desmond Morris worked with a chimp who apparently was a self-motivated artist. Once the chimp began to be rewarded for his efforts, he would simply scribble and extend his hand for the reward. "The careful attention the animal had paid previously to design, rhythm, balance and composition was gone and the worst kind of commercialism was born!" said Morris.

To counteract the negative possibilities you can make a point of imagining (and finding!) positive, nurturing audiences to help you clarify your thinking (something chimps can't easily do). If you don't feel you get *enough* feedback, and the right kind of feedback, for your work, and if your own internal feedback is not sufficient—and it often is not, sooner or later, for many writers—consider joining a writing group or workshop, or find a compatible writing friend with whom to share feedback. Find one or more persons whose style of criticism suits you: do you prefer comments that are soft and tentative, or do you like them more head-on? You'll also find it most advantageous to seek out someone who reads and appreciates the same kinds of writing that you admire, as well as someone who can offer you specifics rather than global judgments. That way, you can better trust each other's responses.

Some writers are fortunate enough to have spouses or good friends with whom they regularly share their work. When my husband used to get upset with my comments on his work ("Why is that comma there?" or "I'm not sure what this means . . ."), a friend, Frank X. Gaspar, advised him, "Never show your work to anyone you sleep with." The emotional dynamics of a relationship can get in the way of aesthetics. That advice notwithstanding, some wives and husbands do make good readers of their partners' work, and if they don't always know how to do it automatically, it's possible for them to learn to give what is needed by their partner. (In our case, Stephen stopped handing me his poems to read myself, since that seemed to put me naturally into proofreader mode, and instead began reading them aloud to me, so that they seemed to roll over me and through me, and I was then able to have a more sensual, intuitive response, which is what he needed from me, and which has worked for several years now, for the most part.)

As a nightly routine, Robert Olen Butler reads what he has written aloud to his wife, the novelist and playwright Elizabeth Dewberry. "It's an intimate part of the process. I hear it myself at the same time. She is such a wonderful listener and we are so in tune aesthetically, she is like another set of my own ears." Yet when Butler is writing, he never thinks directly of an audience, not even his wife. "I think of audience in the sense that I'm putting these things on paper in order for someone other than myself to enter into it and to understand the vision, but it is also for me to understand the vision."

Ed Ochester says he shows everything he writes to his wife of thirty years. "If there is something she is enthusiastic about, I can pretty well trust that, and if she is polite but not particularly enthusiastic, then I know I ought to go back into it and take a look at it again. It usually is confirmed by experience with other people, including a couple of friends in Pittsburgh whom I really trust."

Another, if now poignant, example of felicitous husband-wife sharing is that of Donald Hall and his recently deceased wife, the poet Jane Kenyon. In an interview some years back, Hall described his process in a way that many impatient and less experienced writers might learn from:

> I work on a poem for a long, long time without showing it to Jane. I may be desperate to show it to her, desperate for that praise, but I know that once I show it to her, it is no longer something that is absolutely private to me. When a poem, any work, is private to me, its spirit and possibilities are limitless. Once I show it to anyone—Jane is always number one—somebody else's spirit, psyche, tone of voice has entered that poem.

Margot Livesey wrote most of *Criminals* during a particularly productive three weeks at an artists' colony. The most worthwhile aspect of those three weeks was that a good friend of hers was there and they exchanged work in the evenings. "That was an extremely exhilarating factor. Knowing I was going to lose her critical response after the three weeks helped me be more productive." I asked whether, when writing the book, her friend was in her mind, and she answered, "It liberated me to try certain things because I knew someone would shoot them down if they didn't work." That's a perfect example of the positive effect of having a "friendly" audience. Barring the reality, some people simply invent one. Says poet Wanda Coleman, "I block out any thoughts about my audience because they inhibit me. If I feel I need an audience, I imagine it as an understanding intelligence responsive to what I have to say." Or, as Judith Freeman says, it's quite rare for her to think of an audience at all when she's working on a story, and yet

occasionally I think I might single out a person whom I admire or whose opinion matters to me, and they will come into my consciousness. A friend usually. But sometimes that's only as a prompter, someone who might say, "go ahead and be more brave, go ahead and try this," or so-and-so would appreciate the idea that I could try this because I remember him or her saying this was true for them. I do not think of masses of people and how to please them and get them to buy more books, and if I shape this story this way, would it be less offensive or more appealing?

You'll become aware of the audience-awareness balancing act working itself out if you ever argue with yourself over market forces. Will this be acceptable to its intended audience? And if not, should you write it anyway? Here's how David Gerrold describes the internal dialogue many of us sometimes contend with:

There's a couple of times when I've said, "Gee, I'd like to write this scene," and what comes up for me is I'll think, "My God, the audience will freak if I do that." Most of the time, I say the hell with them, a couple of times I've put stuff in that I know they'll freak, and sometimes the freakingness is nowhere near what I'd expected it to be, and sometimes they go way overboard. But I have never really held back. If I do think of the audience, I say, "Well, if I'm going to try this, let me see if I can sell it in a way that's tasteful or in a way that they'll get what I'm working for." The "they" I'm thinking of is the

Q. Are these processes the same for other kinds of writers, say those who work in TV or film?

A. I asked Melanie Lee Johnston, who interviewed a number of television writers for her book, *Getting in the Hollywood Writing Game: How Television's Leading Writers Wrote Their Way to the Top.* She told me how the writers she spoke with experienced and balanced the opposing requirements of entering flow:

> Most television staff writers are also producers, with responsibilities beyond writing their own scripts. Their week may be filled with rewriting script assignments submitted by freelance writers, plotting future storylines or, in the case of sitcoms, sitting around the writers' room improving or "punching up" jokes. Yet when they carve out time to write their own scripts, often by waking up early, their goal is the same as every writer, which is to write a story that pleases them, shutting out the pressures of an audience, at least while they are creating their first draft.

Korby Siamis, an Emmy-Award-winning writer for *Murphy Brown*, told Johnston:

> To me writing was best done in bed in my pajamas with my legal pad and pencil. And it still is. But I've learned to be able to do it in a room of people. That was the biggest shock about working in television—seeing how much had to be done as a group. I always need to work really hard to shut out the thought that millions of people will watch a show, and instead think that what I'm writing on this legal pad is just for me. Otherwise it makes me nuts. Then I allow myself to say, "Okay, it's for the other seven writers in the room." Then I say, "It's for the 120 people in the live audience." To think about the influence you have out there becomes kind of surreal. Mostly you don't think about it while you're doing it, because you're just too busy trying to get a script ready.

Johnston also discovered another kind of flow, that which goes on in the writers' room, where every sitcom script eventually lands to be rewritten by the entire writing staff. Robin Schiff, screenwriter of *Romy & Michele's High School Reunion* and co-creator of the CBS sitcom *Almost Perfect*, told Johnston she enjoys the verbal jousting that characterizes a writers' room that's found its flow. "I love to work in collaboration," Schiff says. "When you're doing something funny, you want to at least try it out on that person across the table. You just throw out lines. A lot of writers are very good writers, but they shrivel when they have to talk. This way you've really got to be loosey-goosey, which is a big part of the writing room—people making fun of each other. But I may say something stupid that may stimulate you to come up with the solution."

These "anything goes" collaborative sessions seem to play a similar role to the kind of word play solitary writers use to loosen themselves for their writing. Whereas sitting among an audience that *will* make fun of you could easily be inhibiting to a novelist or poet, these television writers have apparently learned not to take such jibes personally so they can benefit from the creative stimulation provided.

faceless masses. I sort of imagine them as a crowd with torches and pitchforks. I've met them—I do speaking at conventions and I kind of imagine that room.

Awareness of one's audience, then, is a complicated process. If you can manage to eschew such an awareness, with its implied critical judgment, you will write much more freely. Or you can let the awareness trickle back in during the revision process, where a more critical stance serves the best interest of the story or poem. I especially find it appealing to take charge of the audience by constructing one that feels approving, either made up of intelligent (i.e., intuiting what you're trying to accomplish), though faceless, masses or an understanding friend or two. Instead of or in addition to the rest, you might incorporate the sense of audience into yourself, becoming writer and reader at once, shifting imperceptively back and forth throughout the creative process.

Considerations of audience are closely related to the whole notion of intrinsic and/or extrinsic motivation. It is impossible, or certainly inaccurate, to separate the two kinds of motivation. They interact in a complex way for most creative individuals.

Finding your place on this particular balance, as with the other aspects of the process, may involve fine-tuning and adjustments on a project-by-project or daily basis. You've no doubt made such decisions regarding audience awareness, up to now, on an unconscious level. Since the creative process is a fluctuating and complicated one, audience awareness is often a fluctuating process too.

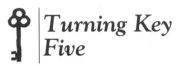

Turning Key Five

1. Is your personal balance among the opposing forces in this chapter a stable one? Do you always feel in control or out, or do you sometimes purposely take control more actively with a particular project, genre or kind of writing?

2. If you suspect your need for control is inhibiting your writing (i.e., you can't get started until you've outlined every detail), see if you can develop a looser form of outlining that will enhance your sense of freedom and let you begin. If you've become dependent on the kind of outline we all learned in school, complete with numerous subheads, opt for a simple list of major points. If the linearity of a list constrains you, use a larger sheet of paper and jot down initial ideas anywhere on the page. Draw lines to connect related themes if that helps you.

3. What happens when you try not to think, when you just try to let a piece of writing happen? Can you do this more readily in one kind of writing than another, say, in poetry rather than stories? Become aware of that sensation of letting go and try to recapture it in all your writing.

4. What is your personal pattern of feeling inspired? Does it happen more often the more regularly you sit down to write? Does it sometimes happen, when you're totally involved in something else, that you get a sudden inspiration and feel the urge to write immediately? What happens if you don't? Notice your pattern and become comfortable with it. Even if you find you don't have to write every day without fail in order to continue being productive, it's still rewarding to keep reading and stimulating your mind with the sorts of materials from which your writing is ultimately composed. Now, if you find you are able to get at least initially inspired by the writing

itself, stick to a regular schedule. Forget about waiting around to get inspired.

5. It matters greatly who you conceive of as your audience. Even if you believe you don't consciously consider your audience as you write, few writers write in a vacuum with no intention of being read. Who, in fact, is your audience? Is it yourself, the art of poetry or fiction itself, a friend, a particular editor, a famous writer either living or not? Purposely and consciously change your audience and see how this affects your writing. Write a short piece imagining it will be read by the most compassionate and forgiving angel in heaven; by your best friend in high school; by your lover. Compare your sense of freedom with how you more typically feel while writing. Does your typical imagined audience serve you well, that is, does it allow you total freedom to write your first drafts fearlessly? Does it also give you an excellent standard to work towards in your revisions? If not, invent some other way of envisioning your audience, one that supports your writing vision fully.

part three

Making Flow Happen

8 Everything You Wanted to Know About Writing in Flow

MOST OF US—READERS AND WRITERS ALIKE—are fascinated by how the best writers "do it." We're curious about how imaginary people and events can be repeatedly brought to life so that we willingly suspend disbelief, sharing fully in the mental construct of another. How difficult *is* this endeavor? "The process is both less understood and more seat-of-the-pants than some wish to let on (fear of being found out) and can be accomplished with simple materials such as you would find around the house," Marvin Bell wrote at the start of our E-mail conversation, only slightly electronic-tongue-in-cheek.

This chapter should amply satisfy your deepest curiosities and lead you, as well, to a greater awareness of your own process. I'm going to tell you how the regularly writing and publishing writers I surveyed do it: when and how often they enter flow, how long they stay there, how the circumstances of a life affect flow, and how flow states can vary from time to time. This information will help you, in turn, begin to take just the right amount of control over your writing habits to enable you to write more regularly and more enjoyably.

The specifics of "when and how often" you write and enter flow are directly related to the "how." This is because you often choose to begin writing when the likelihood of entering flow is greatest for you. Though you don't usually make such choices randomly, you may only occasionally make them consciously. Becoming aware of those choices can help you decide whether they are the most effective ones possible for you.

First, we can get a good overview of the elements of the creative writing process by examining the following passage by novelist Melody Stevenson. My comments in brackets point out how her words illustrate the universal experience:

> How do I write? Generally in great haste and quiet desperation, and with borderline-manic joy [her emotions are highly engaged]. . . . I do my best work when I can begin in the morning. . . . I feel most at ease and productive when I can be quietly, peacefully alone [notice the ritual of starting in the morning, and her preferred environmental context: alone and quiet, to improve her focus] with the hum of my PC or the scratch of my pencil (occasionally supplemented by Barber or Bach or Debussy) [notice the use of music as an aid to flow entry] and the solitary snap snap of my fingers on my teeth. . . . My favorite stuff—short stories, poetry and essays—all begins for me with word-formings and slippages. I start with that and then just try to keep priming the pumps until I find out if I'm heading for the Pacific or just a small vase full of stagnant water [she uses water imagery for flow]. . . . These preliminary notes were deliberately haphazard and illegible—something like freewriting. . . . Often I would just play with the sound or shape of certain words or names, without having any idea how or why I'd ever use them. Or I'd rough out some chronologies just to find out what might happen [pay attention to the "risk-taking" openness to experience, the hunt for novelty]. . . . My husband and children became adept at determining when I was "gone again" (something about my glassy stare and sudden deafness clued them, I guess) into my other world [the obvious external markers of flow]. But by learning to gossip about my fictional creations with my real family, I developed something like a technique for incorporating these people who are most important to me into the pre-writing process itself [a nice strategy for idea-generating]. On a good day, I felt fortunate just to be able to hold those many strands of lives in my hands at the same time, and it gave me indescribable pleasure to braid them into something intricate and multicolored [she is describing the thrill of intrinsic motivation, of the pleasures experienced by a self-rewarding personality in being able to struggle with a challenge]. On a bad day, I dove into other, less creative projects. I found that focused digression gave my mind a chance to tether in those twisting, swirling images that were not quite ready to fly. Which is a positive way, I suppose, of dealing with what is essentially writer's block [she has re-framed writer's block in a positive way]. . . . I brainwashed myself into categorizing the novel, mentally, under the "must do" rather than the

"want to do" list in order to ease my feelings of guilt over actually enjoying myself [she has balanced her need for extrinsic motivation with her self-rewarding personality in a way that works for her]. . . . An awkwardly worded sentence will paralyze me completely [anxiety pulls her out of flow]; I obsess that I cannot ever in my life write another word until I untwist, retwist, rethink, cut and amplify that sentence into the right shape [she is driven to make her writing match the ideal she intuits for it].

When and how often does flow begin?

Flow doesn't necessarily begin at the beginning of an activity, but numerous writers have told me they wish it did. That way, you could skip all the anxiety-provoking hesitation and misery over whether it—the good writing you want to result from your labors—will happen today. An actor told me that actors performing at auditions have no time to dither and consider, so he learned to get into flow *instantly* in order to be fully there at the start of an audition. As a writer, you don't usually have that immediate pressure. Sometimes flow takes its own sweet time to arrive.

Once you begin writing, whether morning, noon or night (see the section Timing Matters in chapter nine), flow may eventually follow, and the range and variety of flow entry times is wide. A sampling: "Maybe a half-hour after sitting down?" (Marvin Bell); "I'd say it's usually between fifteen minutes and half an hour" (Samuel H. Pillsbury); "A lot of times I kind of ease in slowly. It takes an hour or two of struggle" (Aimee Liu); "If I'm going to write at all, flow begins within fifteen minutes of my beginning to fiddle with my notes and typewriter" (Donald Revell); and "I'm in the work right away, if it's going well, but it will be not a completely submersed flow state right away. It'll be more conscious in the beginning. If I'm lucky—it doesn't always happen—somewhere around, oh, I don't know, twenty minutes or a half hour I'll get really with it" (Nancy Kress).

How often can you expect to enter flow? The serious writers I spoke with write on a regular or semi-regular basis, whether daily or several days a week when their other responsibilities allow. A few produce in cycles, binges or spurts. For some, flow happens nearly whenever they write, while for others, it can be more elusive.

Regardless of how often flow occurs for you, it makes sense to keep doing the work, as you can see by this varied sampling of quotes in response to the question, "How often do you experience flow?" "I think it happens every time" (Ralph Angel), "more rare than I would like" (Octavia E. Butler), "I guess I must experience flow nearly every day" (Peter Davison), "I experience flow every day" (Phyllis Gebauer), "Every day I write, 100 percent of the time" (Jonathan Kellerman), "I manage to get into it maybe once a week" (Henry Taylor), "It happens every time I write" (Maurya Simon), "Sometimes I go weeks without feeling that sense of looseness" (Lola Haskins), "I have, alas, no patterns of 'flow.' I wish it were daily, even weekly. I have sometimes passed ten and thirteen years between books" (Anthony Hecht), and "It's much harder to lose track of time if time isn't going to lose track of you. If I have to be somewhere, it's less likely that I'm going to fall into it, because I know I have to fall out of it" (Margot Livesey).

Flow doesn't necessarily depend on how regularly you write, but at what point you are in a particular project. For some, flow happens near the start of a new project, while it occurs further along for others. For instance, for Billy Collins, "This kind of experience seems to happen only at a certain stage in a poem's composition, usually when it is far enough along to assume a definite shape and direction, though the destination is still unknown."

How long do writers write and stay in flow?

Less experienced writers frequently want to know how long they should write. In other words, what's *normal*? By examining how long serious and successful writers write in each of their writing sessions, and whether or not they are in flow most of that time, as well as whether they quit for the day when flow ends, you can see how wide the normal range is. This should free you to find your own edge-of-comfort level.

Among those writers who are fully aware of how long they write, answers range from "an hour or two or three" (Donald Hall), to "a few hours at a stretch" (Marnell Jameson), to "I've written thirty to forty hours at a sitting" (Richard Jones), with every kind of variation in-between. Determining how much of that time is actually spent in flow is difficult for many writers, though not for Ethan Canin, who *only* writes in flow. He says that once he's out of that altered mental place, he can't get back in. "I'm a one-idea writer. I write one burst a day. I write for about twenty-five minutes."

Humorous short-story writer Steve Reynolds explains his fine-tuned process this way: he sets his watch timer for forty minutes and writes.

After "doing a forty," as he puts it, he takes a short break, perhaps for ten minutes, washes a window or some other chore unrelated to his present writing project, then returns to the computer. Sometimes, if he has entered flow—no guarantee he will—he reaches over and shuts off the buzzing watch, resets it, and goes for "another forty."

If you have no idea how long you write, that's not unusual either, considering the nature of flow and how it makes awareness of time disappear. For you, perhaps, like Ralph Angel ("Could be hours, could be all night"), and the following writers, work time lasts as long as it lasts, and that's all you can say about it:

> I haven't observed any regular pattern in the arrival of this state. I wouldn't say it happened very often, mainly because I have very few days in which to work uninterruptedly. On the other hand, I think it's true to say that there have been short intervals of "flow" within a larger block of time that didn't fit that description. I mean that during more conscious, labored periods of work, I have sometimes had a brief interval of "flow," lasting five to ten minutes, but probably not more. (Alfred Corn)

> I think the flow begins simultaneously with the writing; it does not come a half hour later and certainly not during editing, for editing is drudgery to me and writing is not. And the flow continues until I am spent when I stop writing. I have oftentimes worked as many as ten hours without stopping. (Myra Cohn Livingston)

> "The flow" is a stop and flow thing. I write slowly. I am engrossed in possibilities. (Mark Strand)

I especially love the following description of science-fiction writer David Gerrold's writing practices, as it made me feel much better about my own up-and-down, scattered-but-eventually-get-a-lot-done system:

> The pattern is . . . Have you ever seen any films of monkeys copulating? Did you ever notice that what the male does is he goes for about four seconds and then pauses and looks around? That's me. I go for about fifteen minutes and then I just stop, refill my cup with tea, answer the mail, et cetera, for about five, maybe ten minutes, sometimes even as much as a half hour, then come back and go for another fifteen minutes, take a break, then fifteen minutes. And over a period of eight hours of work, the spreadsheet will show that I've done three to four hours of actual writing.

Gerrold uses a spreadsheet (were you surprised to learn that a vastly imaginative writer is drawn to such a time-management tool?) to tally how many hours a day he works. About every fifteen minutes he does a word count (note to non-computer-users: the ease of doing this is one of the joys of computerizing). He sets himself a daily target of about two thousand words. It's a toss-up whether you'll find it more compatible with your personality, and thus more motivating, to count words or pages written rather than hours spent tap-tapping. Do you prefer the concept of piece-work, where you get paid (psychically speaking) by the word? Carolyn See does: "I figure one thousand words a day, or four pages, and sometimes I'll write more." Or do you feel less pressure putting in your time each day without feeling obligated to reach a particular word goal? If you haven't yet settled into a fruitful routine, try them both.

The length of time you write may be hard for you to define, since you may consider yourself "writing" even when you're not actually putting words down. Some writers live in a parallel world of their own imagining, always in a mild flow around their characters' lives. It's all part of the process, as Carol Muske explains: "While I'm making coffee or making toast, I'm writing. I write sometimes on envelopes, on telephone message pads. . . . I've never thought of flow as a separate thing. I live in that state a lot. I think it's there almost all the time." In describing her writing process, Judith Freeman makes a point of mentioning that when she's very engaged with an idea, she's thinking about it constantly. After she spends four hours at the computer, she goes into the garden and starts weeding, or she's riding her horse, and suddenly she begins to find herself "drawn away from the physical world again, into that imaginative realm."

Perhaps surprisingly, there weren't any major differences as far as length of time spent writing among the poets and fiction writers I encountered. Poets told me they tend to spend anywhere from a half hour a day to forty hours at a sitting, but those extremes are admittedly rare. More common are those poets who work at their craft for a few hours (one or two) up to many hours (four to eight). The length of time novelists say they work ranges from less than a half hour a day (one respondent) to "all day" or twelve hours. More common responses range between two to three hours and four to six hours.

These more extended writing periods make me think of the potentially addictive quality of flow. I haven't talked to any renowned writers who said they are actually afraid to let go into flow, but several said they are sometimes aware that, once fully in that altered place, it will be difficult to exit. I have been told by a number of "casual" writers that they fear that altered place and make no efforts to get to it. And, of course, not every oft-published writer enters flow when writing; some are quite insistent that they never depart from their usual form of consciousness and that they have no need or desire to. One poet told me that losing himself in flow is a "bad" thing, though he enjoys it, because it causes him to forget appointments and thus be rude to friends and family.

How does the context of the writer's life affect flow?

If your long periods of flow have a tendency to impact on those you live with, the reverse is also true. Whether you are male or female, the context of your life is bound to have a significant effect on your writing process, regularity and output, and thus on your ability to get into flow in the first place. Family pressures and the necessity of earning a living both impinge on a creative life. Like every writer who has been writing for a number of years—and who intends to continue—you have to come to some sort of accommodation to these pressures. You have to decide, either on a daily basis or once and for all, what your priorities are (and if you have two main priorities, you *can* get used to feeling split some of the time, without necessarily suffering the torments of the damned).

Novelist and short-story writer Lynne Sharon Schwartz, for instance, claims that the older she gets and the more practical responsibilities she finds herself coping with, the less she seems to get into a flow state. "Daily concerns are constantly interfering, and the more I try to get them out of the way, the more they impinge," she says. And even if you decide to opt primarily for human connection and give up some of the creative output that might result if you lived alone, you may yet find yourself uneasy on some deep level. I mentioned to Richard Jones, for example, that he seemed like an especially responsible person who might put the needs of someone else first if something were asked of him. He responded:

> Unfortunately, yes, I will. But I think that often this is a big mistake. I think that my sense of "responsibility" has been programmed in me, and this "responsibility" is not necessarily moral or healthy or wise.

Often I have the dreadful sense that meeting someone else's need is *immoral* in a profoundly existential way. . . . There is a famous story about Rilke not attending his daughter's wedding; he was working and refused to abandon his writing. That doesn't sound very loving or very moral or very healthy to most people. And yet I would love to be more that way: I wish I respected my gift more and honored my gift more. I'm not like Rilke, yet when I don't honor my gift I feel that something is wrong. Rilke's grand sense of responsibility to the art probably seems grandiose to most people, but his example is important to me. I think of the thousands of smaller times when "someone needs something" from me, or thinks they do, and how these duties and tasks and responsibilities accrue over a lifetime and take up thousands and thousands of hours. And the thing is, I give away my time gladly, because the needs of others serve a purpose: they serve my cowardice. Making art takes courage, involves risk, is often deeply unpleasant. If I am "responsible" to others, then I don't have to leave the comfortable world of responsibility and go to my desk. I don't have to get into the flow—and all that means. Instead, I can say, "I'm a nice, good person. I'm much more considerate than Rilke. I'm willing to help other people, to give them my time." You see what I'm saying? I'm spinning out logic against my soul.

If you have children, of course, you know they are more demanding of a writing parent's time than any other responsibility. When I spoke with novelist, short-story writer and journalist Marnell Jameson, her two children were three years old and six months old. "I've written almost no fiction lately as a result," she said. Jonathan Kellerman, who has several children with his writer/wife Faye, said, "The only thing that's a problem is if I get a lot of constant little breaks. The only thing is when my kids are home. Because when they come in I have to engage with them."

Although it takes Michael Connelly about ten or eleven months to produce a book, it actually takes him about three or four months of intense work, being in flow most of the time—"I'm in the tube, and all I see is the water, the story"—to write most of it. That three-month period is "the best period of writing, the most fun." Then he adds, "It was never hard to do this until I became a father, then you get feelings of guilt, you have to pull yourself out." When Nancy Kress hears the voice of her children at college on the answering machine, or of her boyfriend or her mother, she'll pick up the phone, even though it tends to wreck her flow pattern. Aimee Liu tries to schedule child-related appointments at the beginning or end of the day, whenever possible, finding that she can work around such distractions much more easily than at other times.

Even without children, we all have to find a way to make a living, which often takes a major toll on the time available for creative work. According to most surveys I've read by writers' organizations, full-time writers who make a living at it are the rare exception. I'm sure many of us can identify with Bill Mohr, who, when asked what keeps him out of flow, responded, "Having to go to crappy jobs."

I and other writers have discovered that it's possible to live a much simpler, less expensive, less stressed life by thinking seriously about our priorities. Rather than describing my own nonmaterialistic philosophy in detail, I'll only share what my son Kevin suggested to me a few years ago: when deciding whether to buy some appealing new item, don't ask if you "need" it. Instead, ask yourself, "Can I live without it?"

The best of all worlds is to learn to come to an unambivalently cheerful acceptance of the reality of your pressured life, working out ways to get the writing done in whatever time you have, like Carolyn See: "I just constructed another way of doing it, which would be, oh just sit down and get it done, and get it done in the time it takes a baby to take a nap." Or like Marvin Bell, who finds that the more he does, the more he can do. This may sound strange, but I'm sure you can relate to the phenomenon of work filling up the time available, and sometimes, the work getting done in a shorter time when it absolutely must be. As Bell expresses it, "So I can write nothing when there is nothing else that absolutely must be done and all there is is late movies and mundane errands and an orderly existence. But when it's time, I can do everything at once and each thing feeds the other."

Are there different kinds of flow?

Think about your flow experiences. Do they sometimes seem deep and heavy and sometimes short, shallow and easily broken out of? Flow does appear to occur on a continuum. It generally takes a low-intensity form during activities offering few challenges and using few skills. The highest intensity and deepest flow seem to occur when both the challenge and the skill required are greater (assuming you have the same amount of time in both instances and there are no telephones ringing in the periphery of your consciousness). Here's how Marvin Bell

Q. What can you suggest regarding how torn I feel between my family and my writing? I'm so glad the children are back in school. The interruptions were unreal, and they make a lot of noise. Of course, I know someday I'll miss them.

A. I know exactly how you feel! When my sons were little, I began writing touching essays on parenting. I would spend weeks polishing one article or story and found the whole process highly gratifying. The problem was that reality too often intruded in the form of a child who wanted to be played with. I blush to think of the number of times I said, "Not now." And now that they're grown and we communicate most often by phone and e-mail, I wish I could go back and try again. This time I'd figure out a way to be fully there for them more often, putting aside my work and living with them in the moment.

Yet I'm sure I did do some things right, things you might like to try. Once they were school-age, I included my children in my work whenever possible. I'd ask for their opinions and input, sharing with them what I was working on when that was appropriate, even going so far as to choose topics to write about that I felt would interest them. That won't work for you if you're writing a novel about some of the more adult aspects of life, of course.

I read good books to them. Rather than bore myself by reading them supermarket junk books, I chose some of the fine children's stories written by famous adult authors, such as e.e. cummings' *Fairy Tales*, Donald Hall's *The Man Who Lived Alone*, Russell Hoban's *How Tom Beat Captain Najork and His Hired Sportsmen* and *The Marzipan Pig*, Aldous Huxley's *The Crows of Pearblossom*, and others by Eugene Ionesco, Randall Jarrell, Ursula Le Guin, Sylvia Plath, Mark Strand, Leo Tolstoy, Richard Wilbur and many others (I devoted a chapter in my book *Playing Smart* to this subject). This way, my own creative mind was stimulated while I read to them, and I could then carry that stimulation over into my writing.

I also introduced my children to brainstorming techniques ("How many unusual endings can we think of for this story?" or "What might this character do next?"), and we had thought-provoking conversations about what was right and what was wrong and why, based on characters in books and on television and in the lives of those around us. I'm convinced that such exercises kept my own mind from coagulating into oat bran.

Those are a few things you can do to accommodate to your children. As for the rest of the family accommodating to you, you need to believe, first of all, that you deserve a little compromising on their part. Believe that your writing matters to you, and that what matters to you matters to your family. Your partner and your older children ought to be brought into a discussion of your particular needs as a writer. Have a room or a corner of a room dedicated to your writing. Agree on sacrosanct writing times that are to be respected, unless there's an emergency or if a child genuinely needs your attention. If you feel this loophole is being unnecessarily exploited, talk about what "genuinely needs" means. For instance, *you* genuinely need to write.

If your child is still quite young, you'll have little choice but to rethink your workday. At a book fair not long ago, a young mother asked me, "How can I get into flow with a two-year-old?" The first question I asked her was, "In flow with your child or in your writing?" She meant in her writing, of course, and the simple answer is, "You can't." Babies and preschoolers need a lot of concentrated attention, so, of necessity, your writing time will be broken into smaller chunks. The good news is that it is possible to learn how to enter and leave flow—even if not the deepest flow—for short periods of time. Once you get the knack of doing this, you can enter flow in your interactions with your child as well as in your writing, regardless of whether you have only a short time available. Practicing getting into a totally focused-on-your-child flow state may even help you to learn to enter flow in your writing, when you finally have time to do so.

And never forget that both women and men have always had to struggle with the work/family compromise, regardless of the form it takes in our lives. Inevitably, just as we lose sleep when our kids are tiny, we lose flow when they're growing and needy. No one will know *your* story, though, unless you make time to get it in writing. Finally, try thinking of your quandary this way: how lucky it is to have *two* things to love passionately, when both—your child and your art— add meaning and purpose to your life.

describes an episode of deep flow: "You're in flow when you don't know you're in pain."

You may have the ability to sustain your focus for long periods of time, or you may more typically enter and leave flow frequently, "writing in spurts" or "coming up for air." It's not inevitably true, though, that a longer, more consistent flow is a deeper flow.

The depth and intensity of flow depend on high skills, high challenges, emotional involvement, clarity of goals and immediacy of feedback. You might enter a deeper state of flow when you are aware that you have sufficient time to let go into that altered state. While some people possess the ability—and desire—to enter an extremely deep flow state quickly, others hold themselves back from entering deep flow either due to their perception of time available, due to personality factors, or because they haven't learned how to.

It seems to me, as a person who experiences flow only in short bursts, that how you experience flow is also who you are. I experience flow the way I sleep, the way I respond sexually, the way I feel hunger, the way I study—lightly, nearly always ready to have my attention distracted by my surroundings. My own physiological responses dictate how I will experience flow, but it *is* flow, nonetheless.

Adding to the subjective flavor of flow is the fact that some writers believe editing is the hardest part of their work, regardless of whether they say they're in flow then or not, while others claim editing is the easiest, most emotionally thrilling part. Writing in different genres can also affect flow entry for a particular individual, and some writers say they have a harder time when writing nonfiction than when writing either poetry or fiction.

Since challenge is an integral part of flow, as is pleasure, it's hard to say where one person's flow begins and another's ends. What's more, some writers apparently experience flow as something they get into after crossing the threshhold of a doorway, or flipping an on/off switch. Others describe it as more like moving or settling along a continuum, somewhat the way light changes during dusk. Flow can also be experienced in varying intensities during separate writing sessions. As Stephen once said, "Sometimes you don't get to kiss the angels, you just get a hand job from the muse." Depth of flow is unpredictable.

It can be expedient to learn to recognize where you are, flow-wise, at a particular time, though less so, perhaps, for a writer than for someone whose life depends on such an awareness. An amateur rock climber, a woman who'd only been climbing for two years, told me she definitely gets into flow when climbing: "There's just you and the mountain. If you're thinking of anything else, you can't do it. But if you're not *on* that day, you stay on the lower levels and work on more basic skills. If you can't get really into it, that's not the time to reach for the top."

When you're writing, the intensity of your flow may depend on the kind of writing or the stage of the writing process. For instance, Nancy Kress told me that if she postpones her morning writing, she probably won't avoid it, "but I can't get into it as deeply." Carol Muske said that she gets "images, parts of phrases, and somehow it begins to co-alesce. And then there's a moment when you really know. It deepens again." Well aware that his flow state changes its depth depending on variables such as time of day or stage of the creative process, novelist and screenwriter Gerald DiPego says it's hard for him to get deeply into flow "if I'm starting at nine, but I know I have an eleven o'clock meeting. It doesn't feel as complete, as deep. But you've taken some steps into it."

Here's Carol Muske again, describing how she is pulled from a deep flow to a lighter flow due to interruptions:

> I hate the sound of that intercom. Somebody will yell up on the inter-com, "Is this chicken thawing for dinner?" It takes me a while to come back and think, Chicken! What does that word mean? Thaw? . . . But the problem is, it's life. There are things that have to be answered. Whatever happens, it does take me a while to resurface, to figure out "what world is this?"
>
> Q: And then it takes some time to get back in again.
>
> A: Oh, yes. And then people don't understand that. I know I've said crazy things, like to the mailman. 'Cause I can't get back real quickly sometimes. People call it scatterbrained, which is a very telling word. I have to do one thing at a time, ultimately, but I'm still conscious of the other things on my mind.

The process can reverse itself, too, with flow becoming less deep after a period of writing, and then getting deeper again. According to Philip Levine, "The firing [his term for flow] seemed at times to lessen, about halfway through the poem—which is maybe eighty lines long—and then I got hot again and the language began to cook again."

You may experience another depth of flow depending on whether you're working on a first draft or are revising. Some writers say they get into a deeper flow during first drafts and only enter a semiflow or light-flow state while revising their work. As Andrea Hollander Budy puts it, "Over the course of subsequent revisioning, which usually takes place for several hours directly after achieving a primary draft, I'm likely to fall near the flow state, but not exactly in it." Here is how Henry Taylor describes this phenomenon:

> As I enter more deeply into the situation of the poem—the fictional setting, so to speak—it starts feeling easier to write, things come more quickly, and I am not concerned about whether they're good. At that stage I am doing essential stuff, whatever may later become of it. . . . But the subsequent processes of revision, especially with poems presenting very interesting or complex technical challenges, also go best when I am in a state of such deep concentration that I am unaware of myself concentrating; I am again out of time, but what happens is happening very slowly, as alternatives suggest themselves, get tried out, rejected and so on. It doesn't feel much like what I think of as "flow." I accept, though, that we are probably talking about the same thing in either case.

Or it's possible that you get into flow more readily and deeper while you revise and edit your work than when you do first drafts, like poet Stephen Yenser, who said, "I love rewriting. Original writing is much harder for me than rewriting. I can rewrite forever. Alas." Frank X. Gaspar says that when revising a poem, his trancelike "gaze is almost more intense. The choices and revisions come from that same state. You have to go back into it." Bill Mohr loses track of time easily when rewriting: "There's something to swim into. Sometimes the blank page is like diving off a high board onto ice. Gee, wait a minute, I'm supposed to hit water."

But don't be surprised if you notice no special difference between one kind of flow and another, especially if your writing process involves going back and forth between so-called first-draft composition and editing:

> I write for a bit, then read what I write and respond to it positively or negatively. I usually revise right then if it sounds wrong to me. Then I press on and write another passage; then read. And so on. The act of reading doesn't really interrupt the "flow" process for me because, for me, an internalized audience also belongs to the creative process. (Alfred Corn)

I usually enter flow four or five minutes into the work. It also happens during editing. I come upon a description or a line of dialogue that cries to be changed, so I start writing above the line. Then in the margin. Then on the back side of the page. Then on the first clean scrap of paper I can find, then on another one—realize I have to put numbers on these sheets or I'll never be able to type them up—stop and number, but don't stop writing. (Phyllis Gebauer)

Besides, adds Marvin Bell, "It's hard to say how, when or why one moves from one stage to another because the awareness necessary for pinpointing it would, I think, prevent it."

Another major distinction is between the level of absorbedness you experience in your primary creative writing and other writing, which might be nonfiction, essays or, for a poet, fiction. When Stephen recently wrote a short story, for example, he experienced flow while "playing around with the characters." But, for him, this flow differed greatly from writing poetry and "kind of scratching off the skin of reality and finding something else." Donald Hall told me that he enters that altered state, but less so, when he writes essays or headnotes for an anthology or children's books. "It is typical that the prose is less absorbing—because there is less to attend to, less to take care of," he explains. Aimee Liu says she never reached flow in her nonfiction collaborations. "It's donkey work," she says, "though one of the books had stories in it, case histories about love. You can get to that point in those. And that was the best writing in the book."

Fascinated by this topic, Stephen decided to write a poem about flow and see how long he could keep himself in an altered state. Here is an excerpt from our debriefing on that atypical experience:

I did free writing for about five pages, for about forty-five minutes, in as intensive a state and as continuous a state of flow that I could get into. Usually what would happen when I reach the end of a poem, there will be an acceleration of flow, an intensification of flow, an intensification of involvement at oneness. That will combine into a very heady feeling that produces the conclusion to the poem. And there were several points in this freewriting where it would have ended naturally but I still let myself go. I very strongly connect the flow process with not thinking. If you totally successfully outrun thinking, you may not lose flow, but you may lose the poem because the sense of the shaper itself can be totally lost. The shaper is there only in a very ghostly kind of form, occasionally whispering "Don't go this way," "Don't go that way, this is a cul-de-sac, this is wrong." Which may be a critical voice, but it's also a kind of shaping voice too that can keep you on the aesthetic track of things. So there were wanings and waftings in this piece where I'd be deeper and less deep.

Having that level of control over a subconscious process reminds me of lucid dreaming. For more on this, see the sections on Will and Control in chapter seven. Finally, I'll let Steve Reynolds have the final word on kinds of flow:

Everything else shades in and shades out, so why not flow states? There's not just one kind of caterpillar. There are fuzzy ones and there are other kinds.

Are there atypical flow experiences?

You can also learn something about flow entry by examining the more unusual writing sessions that you and other poets and novelists have experienced. Writing for an atypically long time often means you are also experiencing greater stretches of flow than you're accustomed to. You might be able to write intensively for a whole weekend because of changed family circumstances, or you might drop into a deeper, more sustained state of flow because of something within the particular project, either its especially compelling nature or its nearness to completion.

For example, read how Martha Soukup wrote a Nebula Award-winning short story, "A Defense of the Social Contracts":

> I wrote [this story] over a long weekend. . . . Each morning I got up, put Rene Dupere's *Saltimbanco* soundtrack on the stereo, on infinite loop, and wrote. During breaks I treated myself to most of Steven Brust's Taltos books, a lot of reading. . . . When I got tired, I turned off the stereo and the computer and went to bed, and when I woke up, I started all over again, all day. Three days later, I had a different story than I'd expected. I wish they all went like that.

When I asked them, many writers had an atypical flow event to describe. For instance, Richard Jones says, "I've written thirty to forty hours at a sitting. When I wrote the initial draft of *A Perfect Time*, I wrote it in very long sittings." Can we extrapolate that he was in flow all that time? I would suspect that he was in (and perhaps occasionally out of) a more prolonged, intense flow state than usual, and it is the energy from that altered state that allowed him—pushed him—to persist for such long periods. Jonathan Kellerman told me he can write for twenty hours straight if no one bothers him, and that he once completed a one-hundred-page screenplay in only two days. He added, "I definitely have those creative bursts of high energy." Are "creative bursts of high energy" the same as flow? In many cases, they do seem to be. You're so engrossed in the writing that you just keep going and going if nothing on the outside stops you. There's no sense of having to force yourself to keep working.

> If you want to see a book where flow really kicked in big time, look at
> *A Season for Slaughter*. The whole book was written in an extraordinary
> state. I had no idea where it was going. I was aiming somewhere else
> and chapters kept adding themselves to the book and finally where I
> was going was pushed so far back that it got all pushed into the next
> book and this book became this thing of its own. (David Gerrold)

> At this particular time—it was Saturday afternoon and my daughter was
> gone somewhere—I was able to work from noon until I looked at the
> clock and, amazingly, it was about 6:30 or 7. I had no idea. . . . I was
> finishing the book, and there's a particular feeling about finishing a
> book, the momentum. Oh god, it's like rolling downhill. I knew that I
> had it. (Carol Muske)

Is it possible to write *too long*? In other words, have you ever wondered if you'll court burnout by writing in a flow state, either on a single day or many days in a row, until you're exhausted? Although one researcher who has studied ways to contend with writer's blocks advises writers to avoid overdoing it, learn self-control and write only moderate amounts each day, many highly creative and illustrious writers counteract this advice by their own example.

One of the writers I interviewed described to me how he wrote a short story all in one day. He felt he kept being called back to it, though he had other plans that day. He found he didn't like the lack of balance engendered by that kind of writing, and said he doesn't think this is a style that will work for him in the long run. Here mystery novelist Faye Kellerman describes her own quandary:

> There's times when you're more driven to write than others, sure. Flow
> can last longer. It can and it does, but at great cost to your health, if
> you're in one of those kind of manic states. You're staying up late and
> you're not getting enough sleep. Sometimes I'll put the kids to bed and
> go back from ten to three o'clock in the morning, and then I'm up again

at six. It's at great cost to my health. I'm a very high-energy person. I cannot exist if I do that any more than a day or two. I'll wear myself out.

Still, unless you're finding that your entire life is out of balance—the people you live with are regularly unhappy about your slipping into your imagination for extremely lengthy periods, your bills aren't getting paid or you're courting ill health—I'd go with the flow. But don't be surprised if, after a particularly intense writing period, your psychic energy has to recharge itself and you produce less than you've come to expect.

Besides those occasions when you become immersed in writing for much longer than usual, there are times when your entire writing process changes for some reason, as Henry Taylor attests:

> The most recent experience was atypical in several ways. I entered it very soon after getting out of bed one morning, and I went straight to the computer, fired it up and put the rough first draft of a poem into the machine via the keyboard. I have never done that before: I usually do my rough drafts with a pen on legal pad, and carry out all subsequent revisions with the same equipment, until I get the poem to where it might be useful to see it printed out. Now, this poem was based on something that happened in my presence many years ago. I have recalled it many times since. One day about a month ago, as I was standing before an undergraduate class, it suddenly came to me how I might deal with one of the problems the material presented. So I told the students that I had just thought of something important to me about how to write a poem I had occasionally wondered how to write, and then we went on with whatever poet was the focus of our attention that day. It was about a week later that I had the wake-up call.

For some writers, as Philip Levine describes here, being in a deep-flow state is itself atypical:

> I don't recall—on that last occasion I truly fired—what was going on in my head before, I do recall that it happened quickly, maybe less than ten minutes after I started scratching on a legal pad. I noticed no physiological changes; in fact I didn't notice a damn thing; in fact a few hours later when I had a first draft of a poem I had no idea so much time had passed. . . . As for the typicality of the experience, I'd have to say it was not; I don't achieve that level of total concentration very often. (Philip Levine)

For most writers who work regularly, though, flow tends to be such a routine event that it becomes difficult to recall the details of any particular writing session. That may be why those writers who described atypical flow sessions were able to do so with more detail and concrete particulars than the way they talked about their typical flow writing sessions. Some of these stand out in memory as akin to peak experiences. The examples of atypical flow experiences described above nevertheless fit the usual definition of flow. The essential difference may lie in the fact that *one* of the aspects of flow predominates in a way it usually does not. For instance, the sense of timelessness may become prolonged, or the losing of self in task may be much more intense than usual. The motivation to begin may be less clear in origin but more compelling, seeming to derive from unexpected and unexplainable inspiration.

Or the bonus of an atypically long flow session might purely be the result of environmental conditions allowing it to happen. If the context of their lives allowed, some writers would spend a great deal more time in flow than they typically do. Would you?

9 Specific Techniques for Luring Flow

READ THIS CHAPTER THE WAY AN ADVENTUROUS COOK might read a book of recipes: feel free to reduce the salt, add a pinch of cilantro to taste, or wholly revamp the directions. When it comes to writing advice, what works for your best friend, or your favorite novelist, may not work for you. You'll need to discover or design or evolve your own individualized procedures. Now that you've considered the logic underlying the Five Master Keys, you're ready to put into practice any of the concrete techniques in this chapter. Mix and match as you wish, keeping track of the outcomes so you can duplicate the ones that produce the most memorable results.

I found that writers tend to fall at either end of a variety of continua: for instance, some feel that deadlines are good, while others believe they are deadly; first drafts flow best for some, or flow occurs during rewriting only; quiet is required, or quiet is irrelevant; inspiration (and flow) come when they will, or the will to work hard and regularly are precisely what give the writer control over the writing; regularity is crucial, or writing only when the urge is most powerful will produce flow and good work.

As I discuss the actual mechanisms and techniques you can use on a regular basis to propel yourself into flow, take note of my use of the word "propel." It brings my own bias to the fore. I did suppose, and what I have learned in the past few years of studying writers' flow has confirmed my theory, that those who write regularly have indeed found ways to *get themselves* into flow. They make a decision, whether experienced as a conscious commitment or not, to enhance the mental state where writing—and flow—can then begin in earnest.

Like most humanists, I rebel against championing behaviorism too strongly. Yet behavioral techniques often work efficiently in the short run. As Maurice Sendak expressed it, "It's like developing any specific set of muscles." They may also provide a running start, the momentum needed to change behavior in the long run. (After all, you can't simply talk yourself out of a dysfunctional love addiction, for instance, and the last time I actually lost weight, I did it with behavior modification, by writing down the caloric value of every single bite and weighing myself every morning—nothing else has ever worked as well.)

Rituals and routines

Ritualizing your behavior enhances focus on the task at hand. Instead of thinking about the end product and whether it will be well received by the outside world, it works much better to set about constructing a predictable environment where all that matters is the poem, story or novel itself. Once you've managed to do that, you no longer have to consider anything else, nor will you have a gram of attention left over to squander on nonessential concerns. As Sue Grafton expresses it, "I show up at my desk at nine o'clock every morning, and I think part of the issue of flow is presenting yourself for the task. I think your internal process needs to be geared to the fact that you will show up for work at a certain time every day. From the point of view of your subconscious, there is a preparedness."

Some writers perform certain activities before jumping into the actual writing of the day, such as getting up at a particular time, having breakfast, exercising, then entering the study. Some write for a preset number of hours per day, while others do not stop writing until they have fulfilled a word or page requirement they have determined for themselves. Sometimes the schedule is much looser, and schedules and rituals change over the years. Often ritualized delays are aspects of the routine. Gore Vidal succinctly wrote, "First coffee, then a bowel movement. Then the muse joins me."

Most of the sets of rituals— the total routine—writers described to me included within themselves the techniques—call them tricks—that

I'll be covering in more detail in the following sections. First notice how unmystical the daily rite of a working writer is: "My prewriting rituals are waking up, reading the paper, drinking coffee and having breakfast," says Donald Hall. Or Donald Revell, who always begins by drinking tea, followed by clearing his table "of all except notebook, notecards, manual typewriter and one pen. I play music very loud, either Ives, Schoenberg, Prokofiev or Shostakovich." Phyllis Gebauer offers more detail than most:

> I pour myself a second cup of coffee, go into my office, close the door, sit down at my desk. This tells my body and mind I'm ready because I try to get to work the same time every day. What I do is sip the coffee, enjoy being alone in my room, look up at my bulletin board with pictures that reinforce, in some weird way, who I am and what I'm about. A picture-page from a calendar showing two women in blue shawls sitting on a red bench. An Oscar Larsson calendar-picture of an 1890s artist in her studio, contemplating a blooming daffodil. Picture postcards: Frieda Kahlo, Edith Sitwell, Katherine Mansfield, a 1920s psychic (grim-faced) by a sign reading Cryst-L-Gazers. Einstein with the quote about being universally known and yet lonely. Anyway I sit, stare, and sip. Start writing, four, five minutes I'm gone.

I suspect that those who deny having routines don't like the thought of being the least bit predictable, even to themselves, and that this "freedom from routine" is liberating to their creative process. Robert Pinsky, for example, says, "I have (or prefer to believe that I have) no routines, habits or customs: whenever, whatever. No 'typical writing experience.' No personal patterns." Of course, unless we put a camera in the room, we couldn't be sure whether there is truly nothing repetitive about the way such writers work.

You also need to know that *almost anything* can become routine and thus precipitate flow. When Robert Olen Butler began writing, he did so under trying circumstances: he was living on Long Island and working at a demanding job as the editor-in-chief of a business newspaper in Manhattan, and he was in the midst of a distressing marriage that he says he tried to hang onto for the sake of his son. Thus, at home, he spent a lot of time with his son, and the only time he had to write was while commuting:

> I wrote every one of my first four published novels longhand on legal pads on a Masonite lap board, using a certain kind of thick lead drafting pencil, on the Long Island Railroad. And I would write four hundred

polished words going in and four hundred polished words coming out. At first it was dreadfully difficult, needless to say, with all of the physical distractions. The commute was about an hour each way of uninterrupted time (the commute itself was longer than that). It took some very difficult transitional time, but ultimately something kicked in. The commute actually became an aid to my flow state because as soon as I sat down on the train, I got out my lapboard and pad and drafting pencil and wrote fiction. And that's all I ever did in that place with those objects. So eventually, as soon as I was in that place and engaged those objects, I was in the state.

How crucial are these general routines to getting into flow? Although I've made the effort to distinguish between strictly behavioral rituals and routines, such as re-reading the work from the day before, and pseudo-superstitious rituals, such as only writing with a certain pen, it's quite difficult to determine how dissimilar the two actually are. It seems to me that the latter are more akin to thinking a rock keeps devils at bay, and being afraid to try to live without the rock (or like wearing a lucky dress or carrying a rabbit's foot). The particulars of such rituals are somewhat fetishlike. There's the deeply held belief that whatever worked once will work every time, and that one mustn't dare deviate. While the sensible routines serve a real purpose of helping shift consciousness, do the odder rituals do the same thing? They probably do.

Your chosen set of rituals are habits that on a biological level cause other activities or processes. In that way, they may be similar to the instant arousal a person might experience when looking at something he or she thinks of as sensual. Eat the lucky bagel, touch the lucky computer and, presto, the words begin flowing. (And when you lose your talisman, there will be an adjustment: when Robert Olen Butler finally got his college teaching job and started writing in a stationary position, he says he thought for a while that he would have to put a little electrical motor on his chair to jiggle it back and forth.)

You may swear by your daily ceremonies but some claim they're a matter of convenience and comfort only. Cees Nooteboom articulated his strong feelings on the matter:

> These things are *not* important. It's just pleasant for me that these books [red leather notebooks with vertical lines purchased in Spain] exist and that I have this pen, and if I wouldn't have the pen I would write with a pencil on cards, or I would type or I would write on that thing [a computer]. I have the right to make it pleasurable for myself in a certain

way, but you cannot overestimate those things. I mean, people make too much of this. "Nabokov wrote standing behind a lectern." Oh, very impressive. "Proust wrote in bed." Somebody else writes on a computer. My honest conviction is that it only matters to me. It shouldn't be of any consequence to any reader. . . . I would say to a beginning writer, "Try the next five things: try to get a little bit of asthma, lay down in bed half-suffocated, line your room with cork and write *Remembrance of Things Past*. As soon as you see that it doesn't work for you, try a lectern and smoke a pipe, or then again, before you commit suicide, go big-game-hunting and then from time to time write a novel about life. Or, well, whatever, do like Nooteboom, go to Spain, buy notebooks and write five hundred words a day, with a fountain pen, Mont Blanc of course." This happens to be *my* way of doing it.

Still, it became clear to me that your own familiar procedures—in particular, their habitual nature rather than any particular order or kind of activities—serve the specific purposes of helping you shrug off mundane reality, move into another mental place, train your subconscious to do the desired work, and even help remove ambivalence from the writing project. Prewriting rituals also relieve anxiety by enveloping you in a familiar routine, helping you take for granted a familiar, i.e., productive, outcome to the day's writing. As poet Anthony Hecht said about his prewriting rituals, "They usually are evasions, i.e., ways of distracting me from what ought to be the main task of writing, but which often have soothing effects of relaxing anxieties and thereby allowing the unconscious to make known its own life."

Now on to the techniques themselves.

Away with clutter (maybe)

When he's ready to immerse himself in writing poetry, Stephen Yenser likes to begin with a clean desk, devoid of unrelated papers. No matter what else he's been working·on earlier, he puts those sheets away someplace so he doesn't have to be confronted by the middle of a half-completed essay. "I'd have just a pen and a stack of paper at first," he explains. "But I have a lot of reference books right next to me, and if I really get something going, then before long I've got stuff all over the place, having to do only, however, with that poem."

A nondistracting environment *can* be critical for getting focused on writing, but what that means varies. It may mean an uncluttered desk or a day in which there are no residual tasks cluttering the mind.

Maurya Simon, for instance, always does "the chores" first in order to free her mind, "and also in some ways to kind of legitimize my having some time to write. I feel like I have to take care of some other things that need to be done. It's almost like I would feel guilty if I sat down to write and didn't do those things. And to clear my mind in a less pragmatic way maybe."

A sense of clutter can also be attached to the sounds and interruptions of daily life that interfere with hearing whatever it is you're listening for, as this poet expresses:

> Quiet is seen as a preamble to the real utterance, a necessary situation for true articulation. Silence is the blank page. When I sit down to write, I try very hard to listen for something that will carry me into the flow. Then I *don't* try very hard, and the words come like a little piece of interior music; then I just have to follow it, keep up with it. But the initial quiet is actually necessary just so you can hear what it is you really need to say, so you can cut through all the surface thinking, the surface clutter. And there's so much clutter. (Richard Jones)

Or you may be one of those few who finds disarray downright welcoming to your creative process:

> I like the familiar jungle of my desk, the clutter. It's very nestlike, very comfortable, disorderly. I find it very, very comfortable. It's sort of like my unconscious, everything is there. It's like a mulch pile. The clutter is very soft and friendly to me. And I think it means I'm not in that orderly sharp world anymore, I'm in the world of dreamscape, and I'm in the world of trance. All my junk says "yeah." (Frank X. Gaspar)

Some people don't care one way or the other about clutter. You may learn to achieve an internal focus without undue regard for minor details in your environment that others find horribly distracting. While he claims to appreciate an orderly environment, Stephen can work in what seems to me to be the center of a whirlwind of books, notes, pencils, and half-empty soft-drink cans (not to mention piles of undealt-with paperwork and unsorted mail). And I've recently discovered that there are times when even I—someone who thinks the perfect in-box is an empty in-box, everything handled, paid, sorted, filed, listed and otherwise tended to—even I can block out all else and write. When an image or line leading to a poem snaps my head around, for example, I don't feel compelled to stop and analyze what else I should be getting out of the way. Along with the inspiration comes the focus and the drive to write it down. But for those more routine times when you want to write and you're not yet fully in your imaginary world, nothing beats a spare, uncluttered environment, writing tools and reference books near at hand. Unless the creative mulch approach suits you better.

Timing matters

No matter how unusual you've thought your own preferences might be, some other writer has succeeded using similar routines, as you'll see now. First of all, you may have a better chance of getting into flow if you can arrange your schedule to allow for expanses of time in which to work or think about working:

> I don't write by the clock. There are periods when I work in the morning and periods when I work at night. Oftentimes, until recently, until the last few months, I required great spans of time. I would screw up my life enough so that I would make sure I had great spans of time. Hours, days, cause I'm so slow. (Ralph Angel)

> Most mornings I'm aware that I only have an hour or two before going out for appointments or errands. I've had these trancelike states only when there was an unbroken stretch of time before me. (Alfred Corn)

Have you found a particular time of day when your writing seems most fluid? Writing in the mornings (sometimes *early* morning) is chosen by writers about three times as often as writing at night. Stephen used purposely not to allow himself to wake up fully, keeping his brain in that sleep-altered place, "trailing the dream world after me as a comet does its tail." He says he would try to not think about things too clearly, like "keeping a kind of gauze barrier against cognitive thought. If there are real-world activities, like the clanking of a gruel pan, that can serve as a kind of reality alarm clock and start to pull me out. But I can keep myself smothered in cotton." Charles Harper Webb finds that by writing in the morning, he is his most imaginative and patient: "An average day tends to wear on my nerves—driving, bills, demands. I get restless and irritable. Writing, especially revising, can be real irritating, so I work best in the morning, when I have more patience." Donald Hall says he went through years of depression and drinking when he wrote only at intervals or only when he felt like it. "Now," he says, "I feel like it every morning at about six A.M."

Bernard Cooper explains his system thus:

I really will do my damnedest not to let anything disturb those morning hours, and I usually won't take a shower or change my pajamas. What I like about it is that I'm waking, so I feel some sense of being alert, but I'm still a little too groggy to be really censorial, to be as critical as I can be by about noon, with myself. . . . My partner and I have pretty much adapted now to where we both go our own ways, we have a few brief exchanges. There have been some mornings where I'm so steeped in what I'm doing that he could ask me, can I set your car on fire? and I'd say sure, go ahead. I'm just not there.

As you can see, mornings are conducive to creative flow because the regular scheduling of daily life often *makes* that the most convenient time; the morning mind is fresh out of the dream state and more easily moves into the alternate reality of a flow state; you may have more energy and patience to contend with the challenge of writing at that time; and when you work in the morning, procrastination never has a chance to take over.

Night writers, too, have reasons, such as the lack of concentrated time earlier in the day, the silence that gathers around at that time, the lack of interruptions expected to intrude and the special atmosphere late at night that is so unlike that of the daylight world. You may even find that your mind at night has a natural tendency to be closer to the altered mind-set of flow, as Marvin Bell explains: "I prefer to write late at night partly because I can't keep from thinking and it's only after a period of letting down from the day that I can reawake to the feeling of limitless prospects."

If you choose to write at night, it is often by default because of family responsibilities, as Stephen Yenser explains: "When I am traveling and when I don't have stuff to do in the morning immediately, then often I do work. But around here I usually don't. I've got a lot of obligations at the university, and of course, now that we've got Helen [a baby], why she's . . . a morning person."

To be sure, no one time is right for everyone every day. You may find yourself shifting your schedule as circumstances demand. Maurya Simon tries, like many writers, to write when no one else is around, whether that's after the kids are at school or late at night when everyone's in bed. Henry Taylor sounds a bit frustrated by the current demands of his job: "I have had very little time to let go of the MFA program this semester. What I really need is the illusion that I have some free time ahead of me—a couple of hours at least. There's little pattern anymore to when I snatch those, except that I do almost no work late at night. In my twenties I did almost all of it late at night."

I used to think of myself as a morning person. But as I get older (and don't sleep as well), I find that it takes me longer to develop momentum, so I more often find myself being highly productive, even creative, late in the afternoon, early in the evening or sometimes later in the evening. But I usually don't have *two* productive writing sessions per day. I go easy on myself after I've had one, afterwards allowing myself time for fun and relaxation. Some writers, of course, treat writing like a nine-to-five job, putting in long hours daily. Find what timing works for you by trying out various schedules. Don't assume the way you've always tried to do it is the only way, particularly if it isn't working that well for you.

Just do it

You're lucky if all it takes is starting to work for your mind to come into sufficient focus to bring on flow. Plenty of writers find that once they've been writing for some years, that *is* all it takes. Listen to the following writers describe how just starting to write makes time stop: "The flow begins soon after I get to work. It takes me a few lines to get warmed up, to establish the rhythm for the day" (Peter Clothier); "I believe that I have to be actually writing, I mean, putting words on the page, before the trance takes over" (Alfred Corn); "I enter the page in front of me. Time stops. I am utterly absorbed in the task" (Donald Hall); "As soon as I turn the computer on and start typing. I think the act of typing [does it]" (Jonathan Kellerman).

What may be happening is that something occurs inside your mind directly related to the work, such as an image or series of images forming and pulling you into flow. The work incubates, you think about the subject, and the next row of steps becomes clear. You may feel that the work is only one step ahead of you, its creator. Also, the sheer regularity of putting words down habituates your brain to make the shift into flow instantly (if you're lucky). Still, you may find you need to perform a few other minor ritual tasks just before you begin to write if this immediate flow is to happen once you begin putting words down. Read on.

Hearing and seeing things

One way to be drawn into your work involves the senses. When I speak with writers or read interviews, I often find references to "hearing" something that causes the author or poet to begin entering flow. For instance, "When I hear it, when I finally hear it in language, then I put it down" (Ralph Angel), or "The most important thing to me is that the language be sensual and material. And that the music drive it" (David St. John). Novelist James Lee Burke, quoted in the *Los Angeles Times*, said, "Characters seem to have origins of their own. I hear their voices. Hear dialogue. . . . The story is already written. I've never understood it." A screenwriter told me that her characters mumble to her, but later, after she's compiled an outline, they scream, making it easier to hear them and thus easier to write in flow. Wyatt Prunty explains how important these aspects are to him in creating poetry: "You're drawing from your imagination in a visual way and in an auditory way. Things have to be both visually coherent and auditorially arresting."

For some, the visual sense is pivotal. Playwright Willard Simms said that when he was working on a historical play about Leonardo Da Vinci, he would get out a book of Da Vinci's paintings, as well as books containing other paintings he loved. Then he would try to get "involved in the paintings" to heighten his visual senses. Once he was well into the piece, he didn't need to do it anymore. Madison Smartt Bell finds that starting a new chapter or section tends to be a bit more difficult, so he tries to picture the opening scene clearly, to have a distinct sense of the action and of what the opening lines are going to be before he heads for his pen.

You may or may not be as "sensory" as the individuals quoted here. If you are, seeing or hearing something may be just the technique you need to turn the keys of loosening and focusing in. You might try to tune in more closely to what your inner ear or inner eye are perceiving. Try practicing this by devoting five minutes to doing nothing but listening intently to what your mind is saying. If all you hear is your grocery list, stop (maybe you should write it down so you can safely forget it) and then try again. Then spend five minutes watching the movies in your mind, even if they're quite rudimentary at this point. Some people only manage to see disjointed images, or cartoon characters, or bits of scenes, while others say they see whole stories playing themselves out in their heads.

Stephen has said,

Sometimes, I've called poetry "a nonverbal art form." Or have told my students to "live your poem or story." What I mean is that you need to project on the Cinerama dome of the inside of your skull the scene you want to write about. You need to try to actually see what you're writing about, listen to it, participate in it. If you do this while writing, oddly, the words will take care of themselves.

I find Diana Gabaldon's system for constructing a novel quite appealing. If you're having trouble getting started on a big project, her process might loosen you enough to get you started into flow. Once she'd decided to write a novel, and having selected a particular time period more or less at random, she realized that, for her, the only crucial task was to get words on paper. The rest, in her own words:

> I don't normally write any of the stuff that I write from the beginning and work straight through. I will pick up some bit of resonance, I call it a kernel, in terms of fiction it's a very vivid image or line of dialogue or an emotional ambiance (in nonfiction it's a striking idea or turn of phrase), but anything like that that I can put on paper easily, I put that down first. And then you've got something to stand on when you're working backwards and forwards. In its own good time, the first sentence will come along and you can put it where it belongs. Consequently I developed a habit of just starting in anywhere where I could hear or see something.

Gabaldon further explained that her "kernels" or "chunks," while not geographically next to each other in the finished book, would eventually start sticking together and forming a kind of framework. Once the connected chunks became a long enough sequence, say one that might run 150 pages (her manuscripts and books are unusually long), she'd be more able to see what was going to happen next. "They would be long sequences connected to each other like continents rising out of the ocean. First you just see the tips of the islands, the volcanoes coming up, but then as the whole land mass rises, the contours become evident. You can see where one valley leads into the next mountain." And all this starts with a scrap of dialogue, a mood or a vivid image.

Poet Ed Ochester explains that when an image or a particular sound occurs to him, he writes those down on a scrap of paper or in a notebook and lets them rest for a while so his subconscious mind can mull over them:

> Very often, when you put it on a page it serves as a kind of irritant around which the pearl grows. I was coming back a couple of weeks ago from some time I spent in Vermont and I was thinking of just one particular image when I was leaving that morning, and I actually got to

the point, which rarely happens to me, I had to pull off the highway driving back, because I had to make more notes towards another draft.

Musical aids

Music often comes up when writers talk about flow, as though somehow this particular sense has become associated with fluid writing. This may be because the senses generally tend to operate from a different part or combination of parts of the brain from the logical, linguistic part. Flip on the music, smell the incense, taste the tea, whatever—perhaps these simple sensory acts can help you make the switch from active thinking to "letting it come." (Also see the previous section on Hearing and Seeing Things.)

Writers, more typically poets but a few novelists also, who talk about having a strong sense of the importance of rhythm and sound in their work are much less likely to listen to music. Actual musical rhythms coming from outside your mind may interfere with the inner voices and cadence you're listening so intently for, especially for poets. Also, as we'll see in the next section, silence may be of utmost importance to your personal creative process.

Some writers are no longer aware on a conscious level that they depend on these sensory rituals. Novelist Susan Taylor Chehak, for example, didn't mention her routine use of music until late in our interview, at which point she elaborated: "I actually even on Fridays go out and buy music for this purpose. Not like old rock and roll. Modern stuff. I listen to the radio in the car purposely for songs that I think will be right."

If you decide to try using music to pull you over the edge into a flow state, choose music without words, as verbal content might interfere with your own linguistic struggles. As David Gerrold told me, "I might have a disc of the world's greatest television commercials, but that's not what I'm going to put on."

Music-for-writing preferences vary. More or less anything you like is usable. For example, mostly jazz or classical (Ralph Angel); classical or rock ("a Beethoven symphony or some Bach two-part inventions, or chant") (David Gerrold); Ives, Schoenberg, Prokofiev or Shostakovich (Donald Revell); "Shostakovich, the preludes and sonatas. It's meditational music. And it might even be more avant-garde, as long as it does not become explosive or with great changes. Then it draws too much attention to itself" (Cees Nooteboom).

Carolyn See wrote her last three novels accompanied by different albums of Van Morrison. "I play the same album over and over until the people in my house are ready to kill me," she says. And interestingly, the music works so well for her that she doesn't dare play the same tunes while she's driving, because "it zonks me right out, into a real profound daydream."

Of course, once you're in flow, forget about hearing the music you've so carefully chosen. Your brain will literally tune it out. Says David Gerrold, "I'll put a CD on and it will run all day and then at the end of the day I'll say, 'What did I put on?' "

If you find music an interruption and would prefer silence, but your immediate environment is anything but quiet, you can always play nondescript and overly familiar pieces. Philip Levine says he uses music to camouflage intruding noises: "Often I put on a tape of music I know so well I don't hear it; I use it to keep out other sounds."

Simple silence

"What's important is the certainty that you won't be interrupted, no one will pound at the door, no one will call. I think having emptiness and silence is terribly important," says novelist Harriet Doerr, echoing the preference of numerous writers. Silence—a total absence of disturbance in any form—may be your prime prerequisite for focusing in and being able to enter a state of flow.

Steve Reynolds, after he first put on a pair of sound-deadening headphones to block out his downstairs neighbor's radio and indeterminate other scrapings and bumpings, reported the following in an E-mail message he titled, "Headphones and Nirvana":

> I've now stayed up forty-five minutes after I decided to go to bed, just so I can type and sit here in silence. I just can't tell you how great it is to hear nothing (but to know that I still *can* hear something if I want to). I've already noticed that my eyesight has become more . . . shall we say concentrated, on the screen. Remember how you could look up and focus on one star in the sky and get the others to blank out? That is similar to how I'm able to focus on the screen now. It's a very novel experience and rather spectacular.

Ralph Angel explains the purpose of writing in a totally separate room: "When I'm there, I don't have a telephone, I don't have interruptions and my friends know not to disturb me there. It's a place to be alone. I think that's first and foremost. A place where I can divorce myself from the material world." Poet Jane Hirschfield explains why a sense that she is not going to be disturbed is such an integral part of her process:

> Concentration comes to us in two ways—one is as an irresistible demand, as in the concentrated condition of falling in love, or in physical or emotional emergencies; the other, which is I think closer to what is meant by "flow," is from an immersion in the act of attention. Poetry can come out of either, but for that second kind of concentration to arise, we need above all to feel safe, both physically and in the psyche—giving our attention to the task at hand, we are taking it away from the outside world. An acute focus in one realm is a vulnerability in another. Writing demands that vulnerability, that transparence to the inner life. It demands that we be able to drop our guard. That is why the physical situation of non-disturbance is so essential for me as a writer.

Telephones come in for an amazing amount of verbal abuse by writers, as their ringing is one of the more common and infuriating interrupters of flow in progress. "I've been known to not answer it" (David Gerrold); "Late at night, the phone isn't going to ring; no one is going to knock on the door. Even during the day when the machine is on, a ringing phone still feels like an interruption" (Richard Jones); "If I have to answer, even if it's the most mundane question, it's just an intrusion of reality upon your imagination" (Faye Kellerman).

Unfortunately, it may not always be enough to screen calls for later. Once the phone has rung, the interruption in concentration has already occurred. Turning off the ringer while you work may be the best solution. If you have several phones throughout the house, though, it becomes too much of a chore to go around turning them all off and on again.

Besides, some of us (admittedly a tiny minority), isolated enough as full-time writers, don't want to miss any stimulation from the outside that might turn out to be energizing. (Perhaps this is my own form of being open to experience.) I found in Carolyn See a kindred spirit, as she was nearly the only one I spoke to who enjoys telephone interruptions. "I pray that the phone will ring so I won't have to write. I love to get out of it. And if the phone rings, I say, 'Thank God, somebody called.'" You have to realize that See says she has the ability to enter, leave and return to flow easily, so that the procrastination time afforded her by a phone call (in effect—forgive the pun—she's "off the hook" for a few minutes) doesn't necessarily interfere with her day's writing progress. Novelist Margaret Atwood has this to say on the same topic: "In order to actually finish a novel I have to isolate myself from all distraction because if it's a question of a choice between the work and the distraction I'll take the distraction every time."

I'd suggest, then, that if telephones and other noisy intrusions keep pulling you out of flow, you have a few options. You can learn to deal with the interruptions quickly and efficiently and then to re-enter flow again and again without becoming agitated at the interruption (while your adrenalin's pumping with fury over the latest unwanted telephone solicitation, you won't be able to relax into flow—unless, of course, you have an angry scene to write and can channel that energy into it). Or write late at night, early in the morning or in the library or some other place where no one can find you. Turn off the phone and put a sign on your closed door, and respect your own boundaries in order to encourage others to respect them. You might like ear plugs or sound-muffling headphones. I've tried the latter but they make me feel buried alive. Some of us *need* a little outside input, perhaps because we're not as good at hearing and seeing all those enthralling scenes in our heads.

Meditation

We've seen that you can ease entry into flow by changing your environment to fit your skills. Another way is to regulate your internal state. Some writers find that meditation is one way to accomplish this, as the essence of all meditative disciplines is to exclude distracting stimuli, focus attention and move yourself away from your regular habits of thinking.

"I sit daily *zazen*. Is that 'preparation' of some kind?" asked Sam Hamill, indicating that mediation is a routine part of his life that he doesn't necessarily think of as directly writing-related. Yet even some of those who don't meditate as an immediate prewriting ritual suggest that it aids their writing fluency, and a few meditate to solve specific writing problems:

> Sometimes I meditate before writing: seated with straight back, no shoes or watch or belt or tight collar, etc., no motion, eyes closed, not moving, concentrating on breath and one secret word. (Robert Pinsky)

I come to the process of writing as a long-term practitioner of *zazen* (specifically, the *shikantaza* meditation of Soto Zen)—this means that what you refer to as "flow" and I myself call "the mind of concentration" underlies every part of poem-making for me, from the silence that precedes the first word to the final stage of revision. I use no specific rituals before writing, and in general when I am sitting down for actual meditation as opposed to sitting at the writing table, that does not lead to the mind of poetry. While both are conditions of concentration, *shikantaza* ("just sitting") is not word-based, while poetry is a concentration that lives in the meeting of the mind of language with the deep river of the entirety of one's life. (Jane Hirshfield)

Self-hypnosis is another possible option, as we saw with Sue Grafton in the section on trance in chapter six. Here are some other examples of the ways writers integrate hypnotic or meditative practices into their writing system:

I was in Jungian therapy with hypnotherapy for about fourteen years, and I learned to do it on my own as part of the therapeutic process, and it had to do with getting at material that was otherwise inaccessible and trying to find emotional patterns that are interesting. I wrote the last two books with that. . . . Mostly, sometime or another in the day, I do an hour of the meditating, the self-hypnosis kind of thing. Not necessarily including writing time. It may replace it. You know, I don't really make those divisions. . . . And at other times, I'll just want to get down to it in the morning, depending on how troubled I am by my day thus far, the day before, how much shit there is to get through.

Sometimes there's just dialoguing. Sometimes it has to do with just following an image and watching the image and what it's going to do, without words necessarily. Almost always there will be a piece of language that will isolate itself and be very good or very pointed into the poem. And so I isolate that. When I am out of the hypnosis I am able to write. The hypnosis is partly a healing kind of mechanism and partly a creative one, partly active and partly passive. (Brenda Hillman)

The state I go into with self-hypnosis is really pretty shallow, it's really just a matter of getting in touch with myself, making suggestions. One of the things I did with my last novel, and I hadn't intended to, was ask myself a question. I realized on some level that I needed to ask myself this question, and I didn't have an answer. At that point I understood completely why the novel had gone haywire. (Octavia E. Butler)

You may not think of some of your prewriting practices as meditation, though they are essentially meditationlike behaviors. For instance, you may find yourself opting for music that is meditative or hypnotic, as Cees Nooteboom does: "I play the same thing over and over. Shostakovich, the preludes and sonatas. . . . It's meditational music." Madison Smartt Bell notes in a recent essay that "what happens as or just before you are putting the words down on the page must inevitably involve a process of autohypnosis—not that the practitioner would be likely to call it that. You could be doing it without knowing that you were. . . . You might call it meditation. You might not call it anything." He adds that the sometimes strange rituals that writers have "belong to a process of autohypnotic induction."

It appears, then, that while meditation may not actually put you into flow, it can contribute to the relaxation process. It can also help you focus attention and thus lower the threshold for entering flow. If you're practiced in meditation, you may also experience a loosening of boundaries and the beginnings of the self-transcendence that are so much a part of flow.

Going back to go forward

Honesty may be the best policy, but it's all right to fool yourself into getting down to work. I recommend saying to yourself, in effect, "Oh, I'm just going to noodle around for a few minutes with this bit I wrote yesterday. That's all—no pressure at all to branch out from there." This way your subconscious—or however you think of the creative activity of your mind—is gently returned to the same state in which you wrote the previous day's work. From there, it's an easy glide into new writing.

At the start of a writing interlude, Marnell Jameson re-reads what she's written up to that point, "and any related fragments to see if that sets me rolling again." You may stop at re-reading, or you might be more inclined to do some revising as well. Mystery writer Jonathan Kellerman likes to begin the day by rewriting and revising the previous day's work, and, as he is doing that, he segues into new material. "It doesn't take a lot of time," he explains, "and there's a real magical feeling to it." Madison Smartt Bell typically prints out whatever he wrote last and begins the next session by going over the typescript with a pencil: "From there it's usually an easy, imperceptible shift back to the notebook and continuation."

Novelists use the technique more often, but poets use it too. The "going backward to go forward" habit is so natural and organic a way to get into the "feel" of the writing that you may be doing it without realizing it. Some writers rewrite the last page, such as Octavia E. Butler, who insists that "this is not just a matter of mechanically doing it over. It's the lead-in."

Be prepared for doubts to creep in when you re-read your own work, especially if you're prey to bouts of low self-confidence. Nevertheless, the technique can get you past the initial resistance to starting, as it does Mark Salzman: "With me, 99 percent of what I write is crap. I have to rewrite it so many times, so when I re-read it, it looks so awful, sometimes that's discouraging. But it's usually what I've got to do. I've got to read at least the last couple of pages to remember what it is I intend to do next."

Going over previous work helps you get back into the same mental state you were in the last time you were in flow. The characters start moving again, you regain a sense of the rhythms of their speech, and environmental and internal distractions begin to fade.

Experiment with ways of going back to go forward, such as re-reading a single paragraph, one page, one section or one chapter. See how far back you need to go before you're drawn fully into the story. Depending on where you are in a project—just getting started or closer to ending— you may only need to re-read a few lines of what you've written. Almost immediately the ideas will begin to jell and, before long, you'll be lost in flow.

Allegiance to the tools of the trade

Whatever writing tool you choose becomes personally significant, but it doesn't seem to matter what you use so long as you like it, have easy access to it, it doesn't let you down when you're depending on it and, finally, it becomes invisible to you as you become immersed in writing. Writers describe their attachment to their preferred tool with terms varying from the prosaic, "It's just what I'm used to," to the impassioned, along the lines of "I couldn't work without it." It was uncommon to have a writer tell me about his or her writing implement without including the words "always" and "never."

Whatever you use to get those words down, it soon becomes integrated into your regular writing routine. "I never write first drafts of poems on a computer. I use this instrument only after numerous handwritten revisions, and then only to try out different lineations, stanza breaks, etc.," says Andrea Hollander Budy. Maurya Simon says she uses a lined yellow legal pad and any pen that doesn't give her trouble by stopping its flow and hers at the same time.

It sometimes happens that the specific requirements of a particular writing tool may take on special properties that contribute to the creative process, as Madison Smartt Bell explains: "I write with a pen, a Kohinoor rapidograph which I use for fiction only, or almost only. It requires a certain amount of futzing around, cleaning, coaxing, etc., . . . writer's block can be displaced onto these procedures." Here is Ellery Washington C. describing his choice of pen:

> Sometimes it's a Uni-Ball Extra Fine Bic pen, though I actually prefer a technical pen, a Staedtler .01 Drafting and Writing Pen. The key thing is it's a .01 pen. That comes from doing technical drawings for architecture. Sometimes I'll start writing a little bit on the [grey legal] pad, and sometimes I write on the computer and on the pad at the same time. And also it allows me to sketch as I write. I often sketch rooms or things that I don't know the name of exactly, like for example, in this scene where there's this lava lamp and it's sort of melting these kinds of things inside of the lamp while the characters are talking, and of course the lava lamp is like a cloud. You see what you want to see, so the things you see in the lamp are important, but then it becomes helpful for me to sketch the lamp so I can see it in my mind.

It's typical for advocates of handwritten work to experience that as somehow more "organic," though for some it depends on the kind of work, whether poetry or prose. Brenda Hillman says that when a poem is close to being completely finished, only then does she put it on the computer. "I'm very superstitious about that," she insists. Poet Wyatt Prunty articulates his own reasons: "When you're working on a poem, writing in longhand allows you to review previous choices, which, taken in the aggregate, may suggest what direction you should follow."

Some writers express a lot of emotion about the way they work. Carol Muske describes one way she feels she maintains unbroken flow:

> If you saw my handwriting on a page, it would look like a lot of bugs squished. I write in the margins. I'm terrified to leave a page. I'll write all around, in the corners, in the margins, before actually turning a page. It seems clear to me that I'm afraid of losing something. It's like a spark,

and there's a fire there. Sometimes I think I notice—maybe I just jinx it—that if I go to a new draft, a new sheet, I lose something.

Computer aficionados explain their choice by stating that the technology simplifies both writing and revising. Something about the computer itself may make flow possible. Says Lola Haskins, "I've always written using a keyboard because it's impossible for me to get out of myself any other way. Pencil and paper are absolutely useless, and always have been." Frank X. Gaspar has been using a computer since 1986, and now, he says, getting into flow is almost synonymous with just calling up the page he's working on, and then "just noodling around with it a little bit. It enhances the trance almost. I guess it's the hum, the soft green characters; of course, they're not green anymore." Stephen offers two additional reasons for his allegiance to high technology, one being the "sculptural" aspect, that sense of the shape of a poem being "right" when he sees it on the screen. He explains the second:

> Like other people have books above their desks—as I do too on my rolltop desk—I also have more instant access to randomized and non-randomized kinds of material inside the computer itself. Within the electronic OED [Oxford English Dictionary on CD-ROM] I can look up certain words in the Definition category that may then lead me to odd and strange words. For instance, if I entered "genital," I would get "ridgel," which means an animal with one testicle. Now that might be stimulating to the poem. That also happens when browsing through electronic encyclopedias for something that just sparks your interest. Or it can be more specific. What if I want to have an African tree in a poem? I can find one instantly using the Encyclopedia Britannica on my computer. I choose a name that has certain sonic qualities, symbolic or imagistic or even humorous possibilities, or is simply evocative, like African "sandarac" tree. For me, since the process of creation is fiercely combinational, this adds odd combinations into the mix.

Jane Hirshfield explains that all she wants "is a transparent tool between the inner speaking and the page. (And typing, like writing, does require the words to flow through the hands in any case.) If I need to write longhand, I will, but the computer, or typewriter, is second nature to me, and the small hum it makes is a friend to the process of flow, a companion."

Then again, what you use to write with may be of no consequence, as Ursula K. Le Guin says: "I compose sometimes with a pen and notebook, sometimes on the computer; it makes no difference. If all I had was a chisel and a rock I would write on the rock." That seems to me to be an enviable condition of being highly motivated to write, to the point where you are totally flexible and will do it no matter how. I sometimes like to remind my friends of how productive some of the classical novelists and poets were, long before the easy days of high tech. Robert Pinsky is another writer who considers tool choice a non-issue: "Sometimes use a computer, sometimes pencil, sometimes smear words in own excrement on walls of dungeon. But all are mere notation for phenomena of sound that come out of mouth, go into ear." I like Jane Hirshfield's rational explanation for why, after all, "a tool is just a tool":

> There are also poems that have been written almost entirely in the mind itself—poems that have been composed while walking, for example, and are only later put down on paper. I doubt that a reader could tell which poems were written in memory, which in longhand, and which on a computer—I don't think that, at least for me, the inner speaking is altered by the way it is recorded. Any form of transcription is already distant from that first, silently heard voice.

How much attention, then, ought you to pay to your writer's tools? Keep in mind that the ultimate purpose of consistency is to help you narrow the field and focus your attention on your work, making writing easier and more habitual. While the choice of, or attachment to an implement or machine shares some aspects of fetishism or superstition, at least for some writers, at bottom it is regularity and routine that are the most meaningful aspects. After all, if your trusty tool is ready and waiting for you, you can at least count on that one predictable part of what is a highly unpredictable process. Yet consider that if you can't write at all because your favorite pen is missing, your computer is in the shop or you've run out of your favorite notebook paper, you may have become too dependent on the tool and might benefit from expanding your flexibility.

Reading to write

When Carol Muske wants to write poetry, she picks a volume off her crowded shelves. She finds it helps prepare her if she reads a poem by certain authors; Sylvia Plath and Louise Gluck, among others, are dependable favorites. Her process starts to make sense in the following conversation:

This thing that's going on all the time is so organized that I will come down here if I can't find it in my library upstairs, and pick a book out at random. I will open that book to a page, and I will find something that I can use. And not only will it be exactly what I'm thinking about, it will point me to a direction. Where that comes from, I don't know, but for some reason, it's like it's already organized.

Q: It inspires the poem or it just puts you in the mood to be able to write?

A: It inspires the poem. I'm already in the mood. It's almost like a bit of information. Information is not the term. It's like food. It really is almost like the process of finding something I can use for fuel. I take it in.

Q: Maybe it's the match?

A: That's exactly what it is. It's the match, the spark. And suddenly, that's why you just go "whoosh," put the book down, and I won't even be conscious of this, because I realize now that I'm describing something I haven't even thought about, but I must get from the book across the room to the keyboard.

Reading is such a mundane habit to many writers that it's barely noticed as happening just before the writing takes off. For a wordsmith, what better way to prepare for manipulating words than by first spending a short time with another author's words? Says Marvin Bell, "I do invariably come awake by attending to something in words: it might be a letter, nowadays E-mail, or a poem."

I have a little ritual where I wake up and read something; it doesn't matter what.

Something interesting, not newspapers, but something—it might be poetry, it might be fiction, it might be an interesting magazine article. It's like priming the pump, waking me up without *really* waking me up. (Charles Harper Webb)

The only inspiration there is, as far as I'm concerned, is reading. . . . The only thing that inspires me, and infallibly, is reading. Which is not to say every book, because most books don't. But when you find a writer that you like. . . . There are certain writers, when I couldn't think of what to write, I'd read a few paragraphs and there would be such an explosion of energy . . . that made me want to write. (Ethan Canin)

Have you had the experience of suddenly losing your writing momentum? You may be able to parasail yourself back into flow by reading, whether novels, poetry or some kind of nonfiction related to writing in general or to this particular project, as Susan Taylor Chehak does:

"I kind of come to a stop and I don't have anything to say anymore. I run out of words. Sometimes I can get over it very quickly just by picking up somebody else's novel and reading for a minute." Reading can provide grist for your whole mental mill. Ralph Angel explains that when he's in his study, although he's not putting down lines most of the time, "the whole thing is making poetry. When I'm down there reading, when I'm down there frustrated and thinking about every distraction and violation of my life, when I'm down there listening to music, I think it's all part of the process of making poems. If I didn't do all those other things, I probably wouldn't have anything to say."

Ed Ochester elaborates on the reading connection:

One really useful thing is reading novels or from certain poems that I really like—Ray Carver poems and James Wright poems—is that what you're getting when you're reading those is a kind of, I don't know if it's practice, but observation of the ways in which people maintain tone, in which people maintain the level of character discourse. And that I think is very useful, even if it's very different from your own. I was just reading a novel of Jane Austen's that I haven't read for years, and obviously I'm not writing Elizabethan English or trying to, and just having that control of the speech and sensibility transferred in some crazy way with the poem that I was working on. What people call serendipity very often is just the fact there's some kind of trigger that leads you in a certain direction. I remember, when I was in my twenties, looking at a poem by Galway Kinnell or by Elizabeth Bishop and asking myself, Well, how do they do this? This effect, this is wonderful. And I don't do that much anymore. But on the other hand, I think it's more a matter of, if you're talking, say, about maintaining a tone of voice, just about getting in the groove. And you get in the groove by reading some other things that are working in the same part of experience as you want to work with in your poem.

Reading can also be a flow-enhancing relaxant, as Samuel H. Pillsbury explains: "Often I'll read just a little bit, and then I'll get up at 7:30 or 8 P.M. and start writing. I feel like I'm ready to get something done. The reading is just sort of getting into the mood, of getting calmed down and not quite as wired."

Reading works for several reasons. For one, if you read for layers of meaning and patterns, you're stimulating the parts of your brain that find interesting connections. Reading is a pleasure, so it relaxes you and helps you begin the loosening-up process. Reading fiction or poetry helps focus the mind on creative, imaginary linguistic activity and away from more mundane, linear thinking. Reading inspires creativity because it makes the creation of something from nothing seem feasible all over again. It also inspires because it reminds you of the power and meaningfulness of good written art. Reading, of course, is easy, portable and absorbing, while not necessarily so engaging as to distract you, the determined habitual writer, from your own preset goals.

Walking toward flow

Can't face writing at the moment? Get up and walk. As you travel further from your desk, you could literally be moving in the direction of flow. Whether undertaken as an occasional adventure or as a habitual ritual, walking before writing is one of those familiar behaviors that many writers incorporate into their schedules without ever considering how relevant it is their creative process. While you're walking—running counts too—you might be composing in your mind, as Joyce Carol Oates has said she does first thing in the morning, all the while seeing the story happen on a stage, or like a little movie. Then she comes back home and writes on scraps of paper whatever scenes come to mind in a nonlinear fashion. "It's very messy," she says. "It looks like a bunch of chickens." Then she types up the scraps and organizes them into an outline.

Or you might do some precomposing while you walk that will eventually turn into written work. Brenda Hillman likes to think of herself, when she walks, "as a hunter-gatherer for a poem, for the work of the poem." With each step she's assembling images and, to her, that "counts" as writing time. Jane Hirshfield has written poems almost entirely in her mind while walking, which she only later puts down on paper.

Sometimes it helps to get out for a walk if you're seeking some stimulus that is missing, some nonverbal input you need to get the writing going again. It should go without saying that walking can also be relaxing, both physically and mentally. But the benefits may go deeper than mere relaxation. Maurya Simon, for instance, tends to take two- or three-hour walks with her dogs before writing. She says, "Sometimes I'll get an idea then, but I don't intentionally try to compose when I'm walking. I walk to free my mind of other things, so I can think through my teaching and all the other things that are going on in my life, so that frees me to come back and write poems."

But don't think you need to take miles-long hikes to get ready to write. Try getting up and walking around the house, or pacing back and forth, while trying to work out something mentally, as the following authors do:

> Part of the process of writing is walking back and forth to the kitchen. Or when you get a block and you walk around the house and sort of look stupid. Usually when I'm in the middle of a scene and I'm trying to figure out what the character is going to say next, I might get up and walk around. (Aimee Liu)

> I do like to get up and pace around the house, talking to myself, trying to stumble upon the breakthrough idea that will get me back into a piece. (David L. Ulin)

How do you balance on that fine line between pacing as part of your procrastination routine and walking to stimulate flow? Ethan Canin hasn't figured it out, exactly: "I write for about twenty-five minutes. I leave [the writing office] in an hour. I mean, sometimes it takes two hours, because I'm so dreading it, I walk around for an hour."

Walking can be an integral part of your writing or revising process. Here's how it sometimes works for Steve Reynolds:

> Let's say I've sat down at the keyboard and am typing a story. When I want a break from that I'll print it out and come into this room here [his living/bedroom, next to his study], then I'll start reading it out loud. And I just walk around. Always walking around. Remember *Butch Cassidy and the Sundance Kid*? "I shoot better when I move"? That's how it works. You walk around and you can actually get into a flow state for sure, rapidly, reading the story.

Walking can also relax you after a bout of flow, or it might lead you back into some more writing, as Gerald DiPego describes: "I'd say I work three and one-half to four hours in the morning. And then I take a long, long walk. And the walking sometimes evokes more thoughts, so in the afternoon I may make some new notes, but I won't usually try to plunge into it."

The repetitive movement of walking puts your mind into somewhat of a meditative state, beginning the loosening process. It also begins the process of focusing inward, away from everyday reality. While you walk, you're free to think about the writing you'll be doing. Depending on how hard you walk, you might be releasing brain chemicals, such as endorphins, that contribute to better mood and greater concentration.

Stephen has recently switched from writing directly upon awakening from a dream state, to writing directly upon returning from a rigorous walk around the lake near our home, which he always does while listening to classical music on his portable headset. He told me he sometimes begins to think about what he's going to write on the last portion of the walk. He finds himself breathing hard as he enters the front door and purposely strives to remain in that state a while longer. He grabs a glass of iced tea, closes the bedroom door and begins. It seems that some combination of music and walking serve to put him into an intensely altered physical and mental state, which then makes writing flow automatic once he's at the keyboard.

As with all of these techniques, what works for one person may or may not work for you. When I come back from a hard hilly walk, I'm sweaty and out of breath, and I want nothing more than to lie down for a few moments or sit and glance at the newspaper or check my E-mail. The last thing I'd feel like doing would be to sit and be creative. I am also aware that another type of walk might feel more compatible to me, say, a long walk in a cool forest (my favorite natural setting). (I also wonder what would happen if Trader Joe's ran out of Darjeeling tea—the kind Stephen decided he liked best when he first encountered it last year on a Christmas cruise to the Carribbean with his parents in celebration of their fiftieth wedding anniversary.)

Eating and drinking

Before settling down to write, you will eat and/or drink, or do neither, based on a personal equation: What will get your mind and your body's biochemistry to the place where flow can happen? If, like me, you wouldn't dream of writing without eating first, you may be the sort of person who hates to do *anything* before breakfast. Or perhaps you've found that your blood sugar lags if you try to work too long without food. Once flow begins, it will sometimes continue for a long time. If you routinely neglect to eat ahead of time, you'll only realize how hungry you are when you exit from the altered state.

You may choose not to eat before writing in the morning because you want to stay as close as possible to a dream state for as long as you can. Some people find that, regardless of when they write, the digestive process slows them down. According to Stephen Yenser, "Often I have a cup of coffee with me, and if it's in the evening, I might have a drink with me. I don't have much of an appetite when I'm writing. And often it seems to me that the appetite is antithetical to thinking. I get kind of heavy, I think, after I eat."

Rituals related to food and drink serve the same purpose as other rituals: they turn a difficult task—creating—into a habit. Do this, then do this, no need to labor over whether or not to do it. The muscles of the body and brain and will become used to the pattern, making flow entry easier. Michael Crichton, for example, has said that eating routines are vital to his process. While writing the screenplay for *Rising Sun*, he ate a plate of buckwheat noodles (*yaki soba*) every day for a month at the same Japanese restaurant. For *The Great Train Robbery* he relied on tuna-fish sandwiches with pepper; for *Congo*, it was an open-faced turkey sandwich with mashed potatoes and gravy. (One man's meat . . . and so on.)

Certain elements of the food or drink (often caffeine) may stimulate mental processes, as mentioned by Annie Dillard: "To crank myself . . . I drank coffee in titrated doses. It was a tricky business, requiring the finely tuned judgment of a skilled anesthesiologist. There was a tiny range within which coffee was effective, short of which it was useless, and beyond which, fatal."

You may or may not be conscious of how the food is affecting your body, but then once you get into the flow of the work, you'll forget all about the food you carefully chose:

> I eat while I work. It's back and forth. If I hit a block and I can't think of anything to say, I get something to eat. I do find, if I think about it, that protein is really helpful. I mean, generally speaking I choose carbohydrates, but if I can get it together, instead of eating a bagel to eat a piece of meat or an egg or yogurt or something like that, it usually settles me faster. If I eat that, then I usually forget about it and it actually gets the flow going. On the other hand, it's not as satisfying in a way. But it carries it, sort of hits the brain center. (Aimee Liu)

> I get up, when I get hungry around 10 or 10:30, I wander out and have a bagel. I don't really leave the work. I bring the bagel with me. I just kind of gnaw on it. Sometimes I don't even toast it. It's just to keep something in my stomach. Or a bowl of cereal. Nothing I really have to cook. Simple. (Nancy Kress)

Liquids can be vital to the flowing writer, from keeping a glass of water nearby ("Water is very important to me. I get dehydrated very easily. It's sustaining somehow to have something liquid there," says

Q. Why, when I'm in midflow, do I have no appetite, but then, when I come to a dead end in the middle of work, do I need to stuff my face to motivate me?

A. I'm glad you asked, because now I'll have to consider why this happens to me as well. Are you someone who typically eats when she's anxious? I know I am. It's an effort at self-medication, raising the seritonin levels and all that. When you're in flow, your attention is fully taken up, with no space left to bother about minor bodily discomforts like hunger (I suppose you'd eventually realize your stomach was growling, and then you would choose to exit flow if you weren't one of those who gets into it so deeply that even intense hunger won't pull you out). But when you reach a stopping point in your work, you quickly get anxious, which pulls you straight out of flow. And then you turn to food for a bit of temporary comfort and relaxation. It's possible that when you calm down again, your subconscious then figures out what to write next, so that it seems the ingesting of food is what motivated you to get back to work. It can also be a simple habit. You've eaten because you were hungry or it calmed you, and then you were able to work, so your mind and body have now connected those two acts.

If you want to disconnect these two things and not feel compelled to eat just so you can write, I can only suggest you substitute some low-calorie munchy to fool yourself into thinking it's time to get back to work. When I find myself delaying the start (or restart) of work, I often grab a piece of bubble gum to ease the transition. Sometimes a Tootsie Pop will do it. As with all overeating, certainly, it would be best to focus on what's making you anxious and deal with it directly. If not knowing what you're going to write next is what's making you fret, realize that this is all part of your creative process and quite normal and nothing to get distressed about. Seek out a new angle of attack, pick up the work at some other point entirely, or put it aside and take a walk or read a story to loosen your recalcitrant neurons.

Carol Muske), to the ubiquitous cup of coffee in this coffee-drinking nation. You may find you can rely on coffee or tea as stimulants for entering, prolonging or reentering flow, as poet and novelist Frank X. Gaspar explains:

> I wait 'til [my son] John goes to bed or 'til he's down, reading by himself or something. I make up a cup of very strong coffee, and I just sit down, and I'm sure that over the years I've acquired these signals to my subconscious and whatever apparatus it is that produces that mind-state. . . . I think the caffeine is really something that I look forward to, it's a lift. It's late, I've had a long day, I've sort of been beaten up by the world all day and so forth, and so after dinner, a nice sweet strong cup of coffee and I sit down. It's a signal to me that it's okay. I've waited all day for this. It's my time now. . . . I usually have a little sugar, a cookie or some dates. But it's definitely coffee and a sweet.

My son Simon tells me about the morning he drank a couple of cups of strong coffee, unusual for him. He then entered a kind of manic state, in which he wrote and wrote. The result was a fine essay about how the stimulant made him feel, which was later published in his university newspaper. And while the experience was memorable, and he is pleased with the written results, he has not chosen to replicate it as he works on his novel. It's possible that such unaccustomed intensity is better suited to one-time short projects that don't require much planning, organization or synthesizing.

Q. I've heard that caffeine helps you concentrate, so it ought to help a person get into flow, right? But all an extra cup of coffee does, usually, is make me more distractible. I can't sit still though my mind may be racing.
A: If you have a tendency to be jumpy and distractible, caffeine beyond a certain point only intensifies that effect for you. Experiment with increasing your dosage, when you want the extra push, but increase by only a quarter of a cup at a time. You may find the optimum amount that will let you focus but also allow you to sit still.

What about alcohol, which popular lore credits as being integral to the creative process of numerous writers? While a number of famous writers claim to have written while under the influence of alcohol (perhaps easing flow entry by silencing the internal critic), many equally well-known writers probably wrote *in spite* of their drinking habit. Novelist James Lee Burke said in an interview, "It took me years to realize that I had written in spite of alcohol, not because of it." Malcolm Cowley, who personally knew many of the most famous writers of the 1920s and 1930s, wrote that although Hart Crane, F. Scott Fitzgerald, William Faulkner and others drank a lot in order to open up creative visions, they each did a lot of revising when cold sober. "But usually the writer is sober when he writes. He had better be," added Cowley.

Few of the writers I talked to mentioned imbibing alcohol in relation to their writing. Perhaps this is related to the fact that so many more writers prefer to work in the morning, and alcohol is typically used in the evening to shrug off the anxieties of the day. Those who found it to work on occasion, such as Wanda Coleman, believe it does so because it's a relaxant: "Red wine, particularly merlot, does seem to be a facilitator because it relaxes me almost immediately." Not all experiments are equally successful. Carol Muske said she has tried to write with a glass of wine: "But I can't write. Of course, you think you can, but then the next day . . . It's like a dream. People mistake the dream for art. But it's not art, it's just the fuel, the raw material to be transformed."

The use and effect of alcohol, of course, have a lot to do with your emotional state. If you're depressed, and you drink, it's possible (but not guaranteed!) that you'll write movingly out of that state:

> When I used to drink, one of the best things I've ever written, when I was absolutely without a doubt in a flow state, was when I wrote "On the Road with the astronomer." I was so drunk that it was hard for me to type. My fingers were as liquid as my brain was. In that state, the poem was also propelled by extraordinary despondency and extraordinary self-criticism and self-evisceration. I became the crippled astronomer. (Stephen Perry)

At other times, alcohol is used to quell great anxiety, such as what Carolyn See describes happening when she goes to a hotel to finish the final draft of a novel:

> You want to be able to remember everything and keep it all in your mind, and the only way to do that is to go through it one last time or two last times where you really want to be sure, for instance, that words don't repeat or scenes don't repeat or stuff like that. It's very concen-

trated work. It's also very taxing and very nerve-wracking. And so what I do during that time is usually go onto a diet of red wine and tomato soup. They're the two most tranquilizing things I can think of to eat and drink. Red wine is very calming, brings you down, and again, it kind of keeps you in your chair; if you drink enough you don't want to go gallivanting. You're so anxious that you're never going to get sleepy because you're a nervous wreck.

None of the top writers I interviewed mentioned writing under the influence of drugs other than caffeine, nicotine or, perhaps, Prozac and similar antidepressants. One writer I know did mention a time a friend of his gave him what he thought was some cocaine, but which he later found out was actually crystal meth. He describes what happened: "I wrote and wrote all night, until my hand hurt and I had to stop. I think it was just rambling though. Nothing special came out of it."

Like other writers' routines, then, eating and drinking may contribute to making the process of setting about work habitual. Other than a possible dependence on caffeinated beverages (and notwithstanding the occasional alcoholic insight that survives the sober editing eye), most of your eating and drinking habits are otherwise fairly incidental to flow entry.

Stopping today to start easily tomorrow

One of the more reliable tricks is to take advantage of a kind of psychological momentum by leaving your work while it feels incomplete. Then—and this makes sense in the context of some of the metaphors writers use—you don't have to "gear up" all over again each time you sit down. Instead, you're already "rolling." Hemingway is well known for using this technique: "I learned not to think about anything that I was writing from the time I stopped writing until I started again the next day. . . . I would read so that I would not think about my work and make myself impotent to do it." Although some prolific writers write until they can no longer write comfortably ("Once the energy flags, I walk away"—Marvin Bell), and others stop when they reach some natural ending point ("I stop when the 'spell' is broken by closure of some kind"—Andrea Hollander Budy); "I find a good place to stop, at the end of a scene"—Phoebe Conn), many others make a point of ending their writing session in such a way as to ease flow entry the next time.

> I've usually left the work in some way that there's something to go to, that's left hanging. I would purposely leave something that I would

probably be mulling over while I'm whipping mashed potatoes. It's taken a long time to evolve this. (Susan Taylor Chehak)

I figure one thousand words a day, or four pages, and sometimes I'll write more, but I'll try not to. Because I think you don't want to exhaust what it is you're writing about, so the next day you have to gear up for a brand-new scene. I don't stop writing at the end of a scene unless it ends at one thousand words. (Carolyn See)

If I can, I don't end a day on a wrap-up, like the end of a chapter. I like ending the day in the middle of something. It is sometimes hard to adhere to, but it works very well the next day. Psychologically, for me, it's very hard to start a new chapter, in the morning. so if I can, and I can pull myself out of the loop, or the tube—I have a lot of different names for the groove of writing on a certain day—and leave it in midthought, it's easier to take it up the next time.

It's part of the writing exercise to keep your head in the story even when you're not at the computer. So I will just purposely, if it's three o'clock and it's my turn to take the baby and I happen to be at the last sentence of a chapter, then that's just like bad coincidence, that can happen. But at ten of three, if I'm at the end of a chapter, I will start writing the next chapter, the first paragraph, the first page or whatever. I'll get into that, so then I'm thinking about that when I'm feeding the baby or that night when I'm going to sleep, I'm thinking about what I'm writing in the morning. (Michael Connelly)

Notice, by the way, Connelly's desire to stay mentally involved with the work, which is the opposite of Hemingway's method. David Gerrold uses the same procedure *within* a day's work:

That's when I'll stop and take a break and let the subconscious perk on that for a while while I just do something else. I come back and the appropriate comeback will have occurred to me. Usually it's in dialogue where I stop. Let the subconscious work—I'm lazy. The idea there is really to stop in dialogue because you can't leave a conversation unfinished, so that forces you to come back and conclude it.

When you stop work without a sense of closure, you're building in a powerful motivation to resume work the next day, even if only to get that gratifying sense of closure at some point in the writing session. You are also setting yourself a mental challenge: how can I make this scene work out to my satisfaction? When you have a goal or tentative plan in mind, even a vague one, with which to begin the writing session, flow entry tends to come more easily, at least for some writers. It's especially beneficial if you hate facing a totally blank, and therefore sometimes terrifying, page.

Miscellaneous methods

As unexpected as some of the already-discussed techniques are at first, rest assured that even more unusual ways can be found for propelling yourself into flow. One of my students, a screenwriter, described an unfailing ritual in which she burns incense, puts out aromatic oils, and lights a candle to get herself into her writing mode. She has also used a sound machine to cover up distracting outside noises and exert a calming effect.

Andrea Hollander Budy's ritual involves choosing a book of someone else's poems at random, opening it at random, copying the first line of the poem by hand into her own notebook, then (after noting the page number and name of the book on her notebook page) replacing the book on her bookshelves. Then she writes as if the "given" line were her own first line. After she's written a draft, she removes the borrowed line and creates her own first line.

Madison Smartt Bell finds that sitting at other people's fiction or poetry readings—the sound of someone reading aloud—can induce the sort of light hypnotic trance, or flow, that helps him invent his own stories. David L. Ulin uses a preliminary process of jotting, in which he puts down "shapeless, even unconnected, ideas and letting them swirl around on the computer screen. I am concocting a soup into which I can disappear. Sometimes, I'll play with one idea for a while until I see it begin to take shape; at others, I'll jump around from point to point, flitting across the surface of the screen like a hummingbird or a bee."

For Malcolm Cowley it's fatigue: "I found my imagination worked best on fatigue. That's another form of intoxication . . . to set yourself writing, and keep on writing until after two or three hours the subconscious takes over." Marvin Bell also finds that tiredness works creative wonders: "I know that I can heat the pot by . . . staying up so late my brain goes partway south."

Ellery Washington C. has a first-thing-in-the-morning habit of writing his general thoughts into a journal he keeps by the bed. Whether it has to do with a dream or whatever occupies him first thing in the morning, this journaling clears his mind so he can enter his fiction. "If there are things that I'm writing in the journal that pertain directly to the novel," he says, "then after I've eaten and done my routine to get ready to write, I just take my journal with me, and I'll continue writing from that." He also finds he can only manage to write in the afternoon if he naps or plays the oboe first. "Playing has a definite physical end for me. I start to feel tired. Then I put it away and sit for a minute, and then I can write."

John Irving says he wrestles daily to get the flow going. Diane Johnson finds that knitting or needlepoint helps, "because it keeps me sitting still, but it's not demanding enough to require real concentration, so that, I find, frees up my peripheral consciousness. . . . Sometimes I reach a stopping point and knit some more." Weatherly uses a word-game ritual: "Basically, it's like practicing the scales on a piano. I say to myself, all the accented syllables in this piece will have long *a*s and short *e*s. I start doing it, and if nothing happens, then I have practiced. But very often when I'm doing it, suddenly, boing!"

Bernard Cooper finds that while he's working out after a writing session, taking a break by getting back "in his body," he's actually still ruminating on some level. "I will get whole exchanges of dialogue, or ideas about what should happen will come to me unbidden. I'll put down the dumbbells and there it is. I'll say ohmigod and I'll run and write it down. I usually stick the notes in my gym shoes."

If you happen to be working on two projects or in two genres, you can use this to good advantage. Diana Gabaldon, for example, who is working on a glossary to go along with her hefty and complex series of novels, finds that working on the nonfiction book helps her get into the more creative work. It may be easier because it's more mechanical and you simply have to push yourself to do it, regardless of your mood. "It's work," explains Gabaldon, "but it's not shoveling rocks uphill, which the fiction writing sometimes is. You know you can do it, there's no fear to it. It's sort of nice to have that as a kind of a fallback."

A vast catalog of idiosyncratic behaviors has come down to us through the historical record. Some of these you might find a way to adapt in one way or another for your own use. All of them can be explained as contributing to a loosening, focusing, shifting-out-of-the-ordinary mental state. For instance, Dame Edith Sitwell is said to have lain in an open coffin before writing. You can't narrow your field of environmental focus much more than that, not to mention how contemplating one's mortality is known to concentrate the mind. Schiller, the famous poet, inhaled the scent of rotten apples to inspire him, probably having discovered by accident that the sharp smell opened some source of creativity for him. Amy Lowell and George Sand smoked cigars (and the latter wrote directly after sex, as well); Victor Hugo and Benjamin Franklin wrote in the nude; D.H. Lawrence climbed naked up mulberry trees to loosen his thoughts; Colette picked fleas from her cat before focusing on writing; and John Ashberry would spend a couple of hours photographing the decaying parts of the city each morning before writing. I can only suppose that focusing his camera lens on something so particular somehow focused the poet's mind, while perhaps the entire lengthy but engaging process relaxed him enough to inspire a later outpouring of words.

Here's a final method I include because of its singularity, but I have to add, "don't try this one at home":

> There is something about the monotony of driving yoked to the visual stimulation of the world passing by that sometimes stimulates the imagination. There have been times when I placed a legal pad in the steering wheel, and jotted lines as I drove along. If I felt I had something really promising, I would station myself behind a truck and let my peripheral vision of the back of the truck keep me on the road while I worked on the poem. (Wyatt Prunty)

10 Learning to Flow Past Blocks

MOST OF US HAVE HAD DAYS LIKE THIS: Flow? What a joke! You can't even get started. Your mind feels like sludge. Your will is rusty. You sit, nibbling on your pencil or the lip of a coffee cup, but no words or images gush forth. You sense that, even if you manage to scribble a few words, they won't be worth the effort. You would like nothing more than to be as far away from your desk as you can get. Do you scan the want ads, reevaluate your life, go back to bed and pretend you were never born? Or do you persist?

Writer's block is the bane of a writer's existence. Based on my conversations with fellow writers, published writers' interviews, popular advice books for writers and personal experience, I find that writer's block is a widely shared and heartily bemoaned experience, particularly if you're relatively new to the craft.

To be sure, all writer's blocks—and all periods of nonwriting—aren't experienced alike by all writers, a fact that should serve to keep your panic at bay. The definition you use can make a big difference in how you perceive the phenomenon. The definition I use here is a period of time when you feel unable to write although you wish that you were in fact writing. When you say you're blocked, you might mean you *can* write, but only by painfully forcing yourself to produce line after line, and what you expect to result from such a reluctant session isn't going to match your standard.

Of course, if you're not putting words down, you haven't a chance of entering any form of writer's flow. Yet few writers write all the time they *could* be writing. The crucial variable in how you deal with a nonwriting period is the emotion such lag times inspire in you. Not being able to write can feel terrifyingly negative, or it can leave you neutral. Like temporary impotence, an occasional inability to write can precipitate a crisis if you're anxious about it. The words won't come, so you get worried. Then you tighten up, and then you *certainly* can't make it happen. Telling someone to relax under these circumstances— telling *yourself* to relax—is useless.

We could stretch this analogy a bit further. Think about writing blocks being divided into categories depending on when they occur in the creative process. As sexual dysfunction can be divided into a range from an inability to become aroused to an inability to climax, writing might similarly be divided into a range from a lack of ideas or of whatever impetus typically causes you to sit down and begin, to the inability to produce acceptable writing, to being unable to get into that beyond-the-ordinary state where the words flow freely. You may be better able to choose an appropriate remedy once you've zeroed in on what your anxiety really consists of.

A writing stalemate (like a sexual snag) turns out to be a touchy, gut-level subject. A poet told me he felt nauseated when I mentioned one of my early hypotheses, that "successful writers don't believe in writer's blocks." He suffers from occasional slow times, so this possibility frightened him and shook his already unstable confidence. My premature theory turned out to be as inaccurate as saying, "All successful salespeople are extroverts." If you were an introvert with a sales job and you heard such a statement, you might as well turn in your sample case and go home. Other writers feared "jinxing" themselves, or "knocked on wood," or laughed nervously as they said they didn't have blocks.

Ironically, learning how *natural* it is to be unable to write well each time you'd like to can be soothing and liberating. Then writing, and with it, flow, is a renewed possibility.

A difference of opinion about writer's block

I've divided into four categories the clashing opinions writers express about blocks. Think about where your own beliefs are reflected in this selection. First, some writers don't believe in the concept of writer's block at all. Others believe it exists, but say they never experience it. A third group is composed of writers who feel that not only do they sometimes experience writer's block, but that when they do, they feel helpless and miserable in its grip. A final group—and an especially noteworthy one for our purposes here—contains those who sometimes experience block but have learned how to cope without much alarm.

Representative of the first group, poet Sam Hamill is adamant on the subject: "There's no such thing as 'writer's block.' " Novelist, screenwriter and nonfiction author Michael Ventura shared what he thinks *others* mean when they speak of blocks: "I don't believe there's such a thing. I think if somebody calls it a writing block then they have no patience, or they haven't learned the importance of patience in doing this." Ventura, though, when asked, "What keeps you out of flow?" responded, "Stuff in my life, too many people, or things not going well, or I just don't feel like it." He seems to be saying that when external forces keep him from writing, and when he doesn't *feel* like writing, he still doesn't think of it as writer's block. Others agree:

> What is a "writing block"? Do cabinetmakers have blocks? Do dancers have blocks? Weavers? Quilters? I think this is another case of reification, endorsed by writers who (being wordy people) are terrified of the wordless silence of germination. (Ursula K. Le Guin)

> I've never had a writing block. I work [as a therapist] with people who have those, but truthfully, I don't consider "writer's block" to be real. I think there are always good reasons why people don't want to write And if you can just figure out what those are, then you'll find out that it's not that the person can't write, it's that he doesn't want to write. Now he's got to figure out whether he wants to write or not. (Charles Harper Webb)

Writers in the second group do not deny the concept of writing blocks, but claim not to have such experiences themselves: "I don't have writing blocks" (Gerald DiPego; Donald Hall); "Never. Knock on wood [laughs]. No, I never have. I always feel like I have so much to write about" (Maurya Simon); "I've never really experienced that" (Judith Freeman); "I don't have writer's block. I usually have several projects going at once. . . . So I am more apt to feel guilt over incomplete projects than to feel blocked" (Wyatt Prunty).

Some writers, as Carol Muske describes here, avoid problems with blocking by only sitting down to write when something's already "coming":

A block would be if I sat down and the flow didn't come, or if I write but I know it's terrible, junk. You know that you're not on, it's not really happening. Of course, I have times like that when I'm not writing very well, but I have not yet experienced an inability to get into flow. It's not whenever I want. I would probably say to you that I don't go up to that study unless I know something's coming. . . . I don't know how I know. But something must be telling me.

Q. Why is it that certain topics are a struggle for me and others aren't, even though I know the same amount about both?
A. The answer has less to do with the mass of information you've collected, or the preparation you've done, than with your emotional connection to the subject. When you care, you're more likely to get engaged in the ways that lead to flow. If you can't find a way to connect, to care, about a particular subject, it's going to remain a struggle. Even if it's not appropriate, for some reason, for you to inject yourself and your interests into the work, that doesn't mean you can't *think* about it in a personal way.

Perhaps you can identify with writers in a third group who admit they suffer from the affliction and manage to overcome it with varying degrees of efficiency. For instance, Peter Davison admits he deals with these inevitable breaks in concentration "the way one deals with life—roughly, ineptly and inconsistently." Ed Ochester says that in his twenties and thirties, his writer's block was agonizing. He would play rock music at the top of the dial in order to blast everything else away,

and I imagined that if I did that I would get rid of concerns of things around me, I would be able to get consciousness going and get the poem on the page. It worked at the time and later on it seemed to me just unnecessary to do that, it seemed too much of a—what would you say?—a totem, I guess. What is agonizing now, of course, is just to get down to the point of getting serious, and if you're going to write more or less regularly, you have that all the time. I mean, sometimes it's a joy, but usually because of one's self-doubts or because it's really work or you really have to use body English in it, what I find is I have to drag myself to it, and the way I do that is to say, "OK, I've got two weeks now when I can work, I want to do two hours every morning, and starting at 9:00 after my second cup of coffee, I will sit down in front of the machine."

How do I deal with writing blocks? Productively: When the phone calls or letters or chores pile up, I take a morning or a day and just do them. Get them out of my hair and my head so I can return to what I love best. Or I go to the "Y" (three times a week) and swim. Let the endorphins build up. Get my energy back. Or I go to a bookstore, the library, even shopping in a mall. A change of scene, a change of purpose. Nonproductively, I say, "no way am I going to let x, y or z, interfere," sit down and write, no matter what. But it doesn't work. I can edit when I'm stymied or feeling frustrated or worried about the market; I can't write funny, "enchanting" new stuff, it just won't come. Also, I verbally "stew" to my husband and sometimes to friends. This lets out some of the pressure, but doesn't help conquer any real block such as: is this any good? will anyone want to buy it? That has to be conquered by reading one of the zillion books I own on creativity in general and writing in particular. (Phyllis Gebauer)

Of course, when it's not happening, I don't deal with it well. I will do anything to avoid sitting down at my desk—do the dishes, vacuum the floor, take the car in for a tune-up, pay my bills. I have become, by professional necessity, a disciplined writer, but it's still hard for me to work through things like writer's block, which tend to make me want to run. I do like to get up and pace around the house, talking to myself, trying to stumble upon the breakthrough idea that will get me back into a piece. But it's hard, and often, I'll just pick up a book and start to read, put off the writing for another day. (David L. Ulin)

When Chitra Banerjee Divakaruni is stuck, when either nothing is coming or what does come feels frankly "bad," it makes her unhappy, and generally, if it's her writing time, she'll try to sit there and think about it, rather than getting up and doing something else. She adds,

I try to give myself about three to four hours every weekday. If I'm at a scene and here's this character, and nothing's happening, then maybe I'll freewrite about the mental state of the character. Sometimes it works. I haven't found any foolproof method. It happens several days in a row not very often. Then I'll say, I'll just go ahead and write it, and if it's bad, I'll scrap it. And sometimes I'll write a really bad section and I'll get a few good sentences out of it.

Richard Jones speaks frankly here about the misery he often feels between flow states, though he understands such spells are a requisite part of his creative process:

> When I sit down to write, just because I'm sitting at my desk doesn't mean the flow is going to start. That can be very frustrating. I go through different periods as a writer, and that includes times when I'm not in any sort of mood to write, when I don't feel anything inside me, when there's nothing to say. I almost never talk about these long dry spells, those times when I might be going to my desk but I'm not being productive, neither generating material nor revising with any insight or wisdom. Revision is a part of flow—maybe the most important part. Revising well means marrying imaginative energy to technical skill, making judgment calls and reasoned determinations, trying to understand what the poem needs, trying to bring the poem to completion. But when I look at poems that need work, and I'm not in what we are calling "the flow," I just feel a sense of despair and alienation. Or, more accurately, I feel the despair and alienation that the poem is struggling to overcome. It's terrible, that sense of disconnection when the writing doesn't come. The half-written, scratched-through poems on my desk might as well be broken tablets of cracked stone covered with indecipherable hieroglyphics chiseled by some stranger. I don't know what to do with them.

The final and largest category is comprised of those writers who reframe the nonwriting periods they *do* have as simple interruptions in writing output, usually brief but sometimes more lengthy. (Remember, I'm speaking of those writers whom I interviewed; there may be a lot more writers at various levels and many would-be writers who never master this ability to manipulate how they think about nonwriting times.) For example, Marvin Bell describes what he thinks is happening when writers claim to be blocked, and what can be done about it:

> Writing blocks are just time in-between. When they seem an oppression or overlong it's because the writer is cooperating with the writing block. At least, that's been my experience. Anyone can break through a writing block by writing whatever it is he or she can manage at that time. It's the conscious mind, the schoolteacher mind, that creates writing blocks. Psychological B.S. I have them, but I don't believe in them. A student can't write a poem or a "theme" or whatever. Can't do it. Then the teacher says do it by tomorrow morning or I'll kill you. The student can do it. So much for so-called writing blocks. A free-verse poet says he can't write a sonnet, no way. She says, if you write ten sonnets by tomorrow night, I'll sleep with you. Poof: ten sonnets. And because he

wrote ten, "flow" began (if he is able yet to enter that state) and something pretty good emerged.

Sometimes you have to diverge from the routine, to change something in yourself or your environment in order to come back to your writing refreshed. Leave the work that's giving you trouble in order to stimulate yourself, perhaps working on something in another genre, another project in the same genre, or doing something diametrically opposed to what you're used to. Says Wanda Coleman: "I have no writing blocks. I have regenerative lapses when I require rest and stimulation. I read, go to movies, watch TV, write letters to friends and don't worry about writing." Or:

> I suppose that blocks arise from the fear of failure, or from feelings of staleness, but no amount of self-analysis or self-knowledge can make them go away. I fear one must accept periods of fallowness or exhaustion. When not moved to write poems I do something less imaginatively demanding. (Richard Wilbur)

> What keeps me out of flow is simply times when I do not respond as keenly to the world around me, when I need to read (or walk or think) and take in, rather than write and give out. I do not believe one can write all of the time, although I do not believe in what most people call writing blocks because I think they are either fancy excuses for not writing, or simply times when one needs to take in rather than give out. (Myra Cohn Livingston)

Not writing, but not blocked

Whether a nonwriting period lasts for hours, days, weeks or even months, nothing of great emotional import is necessarily going on. Perhaps you can't write due to practical obligations. Blocks can certainly be instigated by a lack of social supports and an uncongenial environment, as well as by your inner turmoil or sense of dryness. It's well known by now that environmental and familial intrusions have denied many women the solitude they craved in which to work effectively and thus achieve eminence in creative fields. But whether you're male or female, a writer's life is frequently conflicted.

Poet Frank X. Gaspar says that anxiety about something in the world is usually what keeps him out of flow, and that he "tends to obsess over personal difficulties, arguments, misunderstandings, things like that,

> **Q.** I usually start my writing day by editing, spell-checking, re-formatting my pages, rereading what I've already written, or anything that doesn't require creativity and thought. Usually, after a few minutes, the creative juices begin to flow and I'm fine. So, once I begin writing, I'm okay, but how can I get myself to sit down and begin?
>
> **A.** It sounds to me like you have already found one or two productive ways to begin: by setting out with something word-related, yet simple and rather mechanical, and by going back over what you've previously written. Editing, spell-checking, and reformatting serve as a kind of warm-up, keeping you from having to jump into the more creative stuff absolutely cold. Re-reading what you've written is a step up in complexity. It quickly puts you back into the same mindset in which you composed the material originally, and thus gets you ready to write some more. If you avoid sitting down to begin because you think of these techniques as somehow negative, change your attitude. They're very positive and psychologically sound ways to start the writing day. Plan for them and be glad they work so consistently for you.

and it's very, very difficult for me to write until I feel as though those are resolved." Others express similar sentiments, such as Phyllis Gebauer: "What keeps me out? Any pressing concern from my everyday life. Doctor's appointment. Phone calls I have to make to friends. Student manuscripts that have to be read. An appointment of any kind that imposes a time limit." Clearly, the context of a writer's life is relevant to understanding periods of both not writing and nonflow. Marvin Bell, a gregarious, fun-loving and playful poet, sometimes finds life's distractions more enticing than writing:

> I go weeks without writing a poem because my life doesn't permit it, or because I am unwilling to give up other things that are to be enjoyed if I don't stay up. What keeps me out of flow? Job, family, good students, a greediness for experience (Want to go to the movies? I'm ready. Coffee? Here I come. Let's take a walk. I think I'll call so-and-so. Watch the basketball game. I signed us up for Saturday's CPR class. We need a car so let's go look. E-mail? Snail mail? Who wants what? Party? Dancing? Do I play golf or tennis? Sure, give me a minute and I will. And who's that?).

Q. The way I work is I have to see the whole picture before I start writing. So I keep revising my dissertation outline again and again, but not much progress actually shows. This only matters because I go to a study group where we're supposed to bring in new material to discuss. The instructor says "just start writing," assuming I'm blocked somehow. I don't think I'm blocked, but it's hard to keep explaining myself.

A. It's hard enough to learn to respect your own learning and writing style, much less get others to understand how you work best. For some minds, the most efficient way to gain control over a huge project such as a dissertation or a book is to think long, hard and continuously about it. Once it's organized mentally and in the form of a thorough outline, the writing is almost easy. A nonfiction writer I know told me she was able to tackle a particularly troublesome article once she had the outline: "Writing the outline calmed me down about the project." Others prefer to compose an outline, then begin writing some part of the project, then go back to the outline.

Perhaps you might give yourself a deadline to accept your outline as "ready to work from," even if it doesn't feel perfect or fully detailed. The way you see "the whole picture" may, and often does, change continuously during the process of committing words to paper.

Why writing doesn't happen

What causes blocks—real anxiety-provoking blocks—in the first place? Sometimes there's a simple explanation for the high anxiety that signals a block, researchers have found. It may be that your writing skills, at least for this particular project, are not all they need to be. For flow to kick in, you need a high enough level of skill to satisfy the task at hand. You may need to learn something additional. That "something" might be how to write an effective flashback, or it might be that you need to learn more about, for instance, how children react to the death of a parent, or you may need to reflect further on your feelings about a betrayal you once experienced before you can proceed. (It may also be that your feelings won't become clear until you *do* write, but for that to happen, you may need to loosen up more thoroughly.)

The need for additional information, whether emotional or purely factual, can slow you down no matter what your genre. Lawrence Weschler, a staff writer for *The New Yorker* and a nonfiction Pulitzer-Prize finalist, describes his creative struggle: he takes notes in the field for many weeks, honing the *question* that his piece will be based around. He says the whole enterprise suddenly opens much like tumblers on a safe when he finds the right question. He fills fifteen notebooks, then indexes them for weeks, until he becomes utterly bored. At this point, he is blocked. "That dust ball is really interesting," he finds himself thinking. This period takes additional weeks, but he has learned to *endure* it. What he does is play with forms, making a cathedral of blocks, for instance, that somehow relates to the form of the article. He ponders the structure, puts stuff together for formal reasons, but finds that it helps make sense of the actual world. Then, suddenly, the writing goes very quickly: it only takes a week or 10 days to complete his article.

Studies of writer's block, while focused for the most part on students or academic writers, may offer some insights as to what's going on. It seems that one of the ways writers get blocked is by thinking negatively. Talking to yourself about how unpleasant writing is, becoming impatient, being perfectionistic, worrying about being evaluated and trying to follow rigid writing rules have all been implicated in not being able to write consistently. Writers who block have been found to make twice as many of these maladaptive thoughts and discouraging or delaying statements, and only one-seventh as many thoughts that encourage writing, compared to nonblocked writers.

Much of the difficulty less experienced writers have comes from feeling the obligation to satisfy a number of constraints at the same time. In addition to the overall structure of the text, you must consider paragraph, sentence and word structure. Ideas must connect smoothly. Going back and forth from the sense of the whole to the structure of the many parts is a complex series of acts. Until you can integrate those requirements in a second-nature kind of way, flow won't occur. Experienced writers, of course, usually have gotten this aspect under control.

Which doesn't mean it's ever *easy*—every major new project brings with it a series of questions and quandaries, and with those come opportunities to obsess, to doubt yourself and to feel blocked. As I near completion of this book, I have to admit that it's mainly the immanent deadline that keeps me facing the computer screen for many hours a day. This is the point at which every doubt I've ever had about my abilities—and the meaningfulness of my life, while I'm at it—are up for intense and skeptical reanalysis. Fortunately, I've been through this before. I recognize the normal signs of nearing the end of a lengthy and challenging endeavor, that point at which you can no longer say, "Oh, by the way, I've changed my mind, I don't want to do this after all." (Analogously, giving birth the second time was slightly less traumatic for me because I remembered I'd survived it the first time, and that it had absolutely been worth the effort.)

Once you've learned to finesse all the technical constraints, you can still find yourself with a major case of creative block if you're petrified of what your audience and the critics are going to say. One psychiatrist, in fact, suggests that one of the primary causes of blocks is the fact that society treats artists badly. He suggests a therapeutic approach that emphasizes helping the blocked writer feel less put upon by those negative voices. How? By limiting contact with negative people, even if it means developing a whole new set of friends, and by not reading negative reviews (which I suppose means having someone else screen your reviews for you, should you be lucky enough to get some).

Remember all those assigned papers you had to do in school? You can now learn something—finally—from that homework, particularly the way it made you feel and the way you dealt with it. Studies done on high-school students (chosen for their vulnerability to emotional fluctuations) working on assigned term papers found that nearly all the students experienced anxiety during the process of writing, some whenever they sat down to write. But then differences emerged between the students who were able to enter flow and those who were not. Once their research was completed, many students felt no sense of challenge or excitement about the task of writing. (Those students' papers were evaluated as being more uninteresting and plodding as a result.) The fact that some of the student writers managed to find something interesting in the task indicates that it's possible to get yourself motivated even when you're working on something that has been assigned by someone else. In fact, those students who managed to enter a state of flow in their writing used deliberate strategies to get there, such as taking control of their emotions, redirecting their attention to more interesting aspects of the subject, setting up daily work times and goals, and shortening the writing session when feeling overwhelmed. The young writers who flowed monitored their own internal states and energy levels, moderating them as required so as not to be exhausted, adjusting challenge to ability in order to stay in flow. Those who didn't pursue those strategies found themselves blocked.

The lesson here is that if you weren't motivated or mature or wise enough to learn these how-to-flow skills when you were in school, you surely are now. And the same theory applies: if you can add some challenge to any writing task, a challenge you yourself find engaging, it will make all the difference for you. No effort you expend on fulfilling a challenge is ever wasted, even if the results never get submitted anywhere because you decide to edit them out later.

Another study found that spontaneity and flexibility about rules are more conducive to a free flow of ideas. Low-blockers tend to tell themselves to just write a few words when they get stuck, rather than expecting the whole project to spill out at once. Nothing produces a stunning case of writer's block more dependably than a rigid set of attitudes. Again, the more open personalities have the edge here, but you can revamp your attitudes in a more open direction at any point.

Most blocks are in some way related to fear and anxiety. Peter Clothier tells what keeps him out of flow: "Fear. The worry that the work is not up to standard. The fear that no one will like what I'm writing, or want to read it. The fear of being foolish. Towards midpoint in a sustained writing project, the fear of not being able to finish it. The fear of dying before it's done. The fear of losing the rhythm I've begun to create. The fear that I've wasted my time."

Such a mood is the antithesis of confidence, the opposite of flow. If you do not feel that what you have written (your internal feedback) matches what you had in mind when you were composing (your internal ideal), you are bound to feel apprehensive and slip right out of flow. Apprehension caused by this nonmatching may be highly functional, since it allows you to go back and revise the substandard work. Or it may be dysfunctional, if it reflects a deep-seated perfectionism that eventually keeps you from working at all.

Learning to be a better writer

"Maybe writing really is like making an omelet, and greater knowledge of the processes involved in both cases will make it easier in the future," Alfred Corn wrote to me, adding, "It would be nice to believe it would."

Is it merely wishful thinking to believe that you can learn both to

Q. Sometimes I feel frightened at the thought of dropping down into the deep well of myself that I seem to be writing from when I'm in flow. How can I get over that hesitation to let go?

A. If you don't find it exhilarating to throw yourself down the well of your own creative sources, it's possible that you're anxious about getting in touch with the highly charged emotional material that's lurking there. Is there something in particular that you're avoiding writing about? Have you experienced a terrible loss that you aren't ready to write about yet? In order to write powerfully and genuinely about an event, you have to be willing to put yourself back in the emotional place you were in when you first experienced an event. If you haven't resolved your feelings about it, you may fear that writing the poem or story will force you to face all that painful stuff. And maybe there's something hiding there—something about yourself or your reactions?—you haven't even admitted to yourself. If certain of your ideas or feelings feel dangerous to you, you could be resisting writing.

A psychologist who is also a poet has suggested you try writing from another point of view (third person instead of first) or trying on another persona (speak from someone else's voice). If none of the loosening techniques and rituals described in this book make a difference, and if trying to get yourself on a regular writing schedule (useful for overcoming daily resistance) doesn't work either, you might want to consider seeing a psychotherapist to investigate what may be deeper issues for you.

write better and to enter flow more readily? I no longer have any doubt that it's possible to increase your fluency at getting into a flow state. And if you take seriously what a number of famous writers have admitted, it is also possible to learn to be a better writer, mainly by writing *a lot*. More flow equals more writing equals better writing over the long haul.

Consider Sue Grafton. She started writing seriously when she was eighteen, completing her first novel at twenty-two. But the first one she got published was the fourth she'd written. Numbers one, two, three, six and seven never made it into print. Or Michael Connelly, whose first published book was actually his third attempt. "I tried twice before," he says, "but didn't finish the books because these were not books I'd want to read. I abandoned them." Or Chitra Banerjee Divakaruni, who considers her early poetry writing part of her growth process. "I didn't start out writing very good poetry," she says. "I started writing some bad poetry. Slowly, it got better, little by little." And then there's John Nichols, who wrote *The Milagro Beanfield War* and *The Sterile Cuckoo*. He claims to have written about eighty books, though only fifteen have been published. "*Sterile Cuckoo* I think was about the eighth novel I'd written," he said in an interview. "I wrote a novel a year when I was in college. So I do an awful lot of writing that doesn't get recompensed or published."

Some of these "bad writing" confessions make me think of Anne Lamott's excellent advice, based on her father's words to her brother when he was struggling with a report on birds, "Write it bird by bird." That of course means "word by word," and you might actually gain confidence if you allow yourself to produce "turd by turd."

Another writer who wasn't born knowing how to construct Pulitzer Prize-winning stories is Robert Olen Butler. Butler was adamant that I note the following figures correctly so I could share them with aspiring writers: "I've got five unpublished ghastly novels, forty unpublished dreadful short stories and twelve godawful full-length plays. I wish I'd had *me* to talk to back then. I had to learn all this the hard way. Almost all of that stuff is bad because it was coming from my head." Although Butler believes that some of what he wrote back then is as good as material by others that *does* get published, apparently he needed years to learn to delve deeper, to access a more primary place, in order to achieve the results that have made him such a fine literary writer today.

The road to success for Faye Kellerman, whose many mystery novels have given so many readers a great deal of enjoyment, was neither a speedy nor an angst-free passage. She reports having spent a great deal of time watching her husband Jonathan write, deciding to write fiction herself only when she was seven months' pregnant. This was after she completed her dentistry studies and suddenly found her imagination had come back as though from a long hiatus. Still, it took her five years of trial and error to accomplish a publishable novel. When she showed a draft to Jonathan, she said, "Here, read this. You won't like it." But he did, and her career as a novelist began in earnest. Jonathan Kellerman himself admits that he wrote eight novels that never got published.

According to Margot Livesey, "A lot for me about writing is just tolerating my own mediocrity. My first drafts are typically a lot worse than most of my students', even sometimes than undergraduates'. In my first draft I just try to see things clearly and see what the overall shape of the work is going to be." It's always astonishing to hear a good writer—and Livesey's work is delightfully, carefully crafted—admitting that her work begins in such an ordinary way. It should give us all hope.

Even in an art we tend to think of as spontaneous—jazz—it takes a great deal of tedious practice to reach the wildly creative end-product we admire. A sociologist (a former studio musician) found that the good jazz musicians typically spend several hours daily for many years practicing a challenging piece. Much later, when we hear the inspired "improv" performance, we forget that it is due to the musician's lengthy practice sessions that now allow him or her to perform it in his or her own voice. Along these lines, more than one writer told me to share this sound advice to novices: prepare for a long apprenticeship.

Breaking your blocks

By now I assume you're convinced that it takes energy and patience to approach mastery of the art and craft of writing. But how do you learn to get past those inevitable thick brick walls of inertia, those frustrating slowdowns in your ability to write that make you wonder whether you've chosen the right line of work after all? Ultimately, it seems that those who have had an easy time of something often give the least usable advice, such as, "Just do it." I once asked my former husband how he knew how to do so many home repairs. "It's just common sense," he told me. But it certainly wasn't my kind of common sense.

For instance, how do you hang a picture on the wall? Simple, someone might tell you. "Hammer a nail or a picture hook into the wall at the height you want the picture." But it doesn't work that way. Maybe our brains are more like computer programs than we'd like to think. I have to be told *exactly* how to perform physical tasks that are new to me, until I know what I'm doing. What kind of hammer? What size nail or hook? When I tried it the first time, a chunk of plaster fell out of the wall. I later read that a little bit of tape on the wall might prevent loosening of the plaster. And if you don't mark the spot first, making allowance for the fact that the hook won't usually be quite at the top of the frame, the picture won't end up where you intended it to.

Maybe Jonathan Kellerman or Donald Hall can "just do it" by now. Just realize that it wasn't always that way, even for the best writers.

The best advice comes in a personalized form. I'd recommend you find a smooth-writing pen or pencil or clackety old typewriter or a word-processing program that seems to disappear when you use it (or practice on it until it does). If you're a morning person, get some writing done as early as possible, each time you possibly can. But if you're not, don't try to squeeze yourself into someone else's mold. If you crave variety, switch genres or projects freely rather than trying to finish each one before going on to the next. If you have a hard time finishing anything, stop and figure out what's happening, what your resistance is to the hard work of completing. Or, if starting is the main hitch in your productivity, tell yourself to think of yourself as a starter, a doer, and give yourself a new chance every day to succeed at starting.

Go back and try any of the techniques and tricks described in earlier chapters to get past a temporary block. If necessary, backtrack to chapters three and four on motivators and attitudes to discover whether you're sabotaging yourself in some deeper way, by thinking in a rigid manner, by having ridiculously high expectations of your first drafts or perhaps by forgetting why you want to write altogether.

Beyond those suggestions, I gathered a few favorite insights. For instance, when Diana Gabaldon is asked for her "secrets" of writing success, she offers what she calls "Gabaldon's three rules for writing." Here is their essence: 1) read lots so you'll learn to tell the difference between good and bad and why things work or don't work; 2) write— the only thing that matters is getting words on paper, and it's the only way you'll discover what works for you. It doesn't matter if you write the book in a straight line, backward, if you use an outline, if you write it in little pieces and glue them together; and 3) don't stop—the only way you can fail at writing is to give up.

Many of the writers I talked to attest to having gotten better at jumpstarting their writing sessions over the years, such as Suzanne Lummis, who said, "It happens when years of training suddenly hot-wire you to your best instincts," or Charles Harper Webb, who admitted that he wasn't very good at getting into flow when he first began writing, but "I would say the reason I'm good at it now is just because I've done it a long time."

Apparently they have learned how to make the Master Keys work for them regularly. Some think of it as having learned the various aspects of their craft, so that the decisions involved in creating their poems or stories have become more and more intuitive. For instance, a playwright, Willard Simms, told me he found that working on two pieces at once was the solution he learned to avoid blocks. Others have learned their own ways, through years and trial and error:

> What you are calling "flow state" seems to me to be the condition in which all skilled work is done—work one has learned how to do, so that the concrete aspects of it have become automatic—including muscular coordination and total familiarity with the medium (whether the medium be paint, or basket-withes, or a dancer's own body or, for a writer, word-sound, syntax, etc.). (Ursula K. Le Guin)

> I set myself up every day to write a scene. The process of getting into that scene becomes a regimen that's pretty standard, that involves a grey notepad, a .01 pen, and as short a distance as I can manage from sleep. I began to realize that that was effective for me, even for the stories, but it took a long time, because if I wrote a scene that happened to be very short, as many of mine are, I would feel like I hadn't worked today. And it had to do with my whole image, my whole of idea of what it meant to work. (Ellery Washington C.)

Or you may learn, over time, that it's part of your personal means of creating to have to stop and wait, and not to take those temporary blanknesses of mind as anything more than they are. As Ed Ochester explains, "I think after a while you get your own tricks of picking it up, you don't feel it has to go all at once, and I start to feel anyway it doesn't go all at once, as when I'm pretty well written out and I just have to rest a little bit."

It's also possible that the struggle to write and enter flow may not get easier for you, but you'll get used to it, so that it won't evoke such emotional trauma every time. "You do learn to trust your own instincts a little more. And I think that could pass for encouragement," suggests Diane Johnson.

It is possible to learn to deal with interruptions with less disruption to your creative process, by building up your confidence over time as to your ability to reenter flow after a short or longer break. "I can get back there really quickly," says David St. John. "And that's something I think has really happened over my writing life. I think I've really trained myself to be able to do that." Some literally trained themselves in whatever psychological techniques are indispensable for them to face the work with confidence, such as David Gerrold, who says, "Whatever it is, the break is an opportunity for a pat on the back so that every time that I stop, instead of acknowledging failure, which makes it harder to get back to the work, I'm acknowledging my success at moving forward. And so the fun of going back is you get to add more success."

Poet Elizabeth Macklin describes how she suddenly realized what it would take to manage her time and her life so she could write regularly:

> Last summer I had a house I rented where I had total solitude. One of the things I ended up thinking about, or being struck by, was the varieties of ways to get into writing. Each day contained various moments or times when I was writing, and each time seemed extremely different from the others as far as where I was sitting in the house, or what was going on. So that in a sense the whole month was a sporadic flow state. And there was no punishment for going out of it. It really made me understand once and for all the value of time.
>
> In my regular life, I work a nine-to-five job. There's that sense of "Oh, I shouldn't stop now." Which in fact stops you. But during that month it was perfectly all right to stop, even just to pick up a murder mystery and read fifty pages. There was always more time, and you *didn't* in fact stop. This was also duplicable: any workday evening could be like that, just by being home. My job is either leavable at the end of the workday, or I can brood about it. I found it was a matter of making an active decision not to brood about it: brooding does absolutely no good whatsoever, so blow it off and re-create the little pleasure dome.

People are sometimes amazed by what I've accomplished over the past couple of decades, when only I know how much struggle has been involved in fighting my own urge to get up and walk away from the work, again and again and again—and, the fact is, it's usually a losing battle: I *do* get up and walk away, but, and here's the key, I *return* just as often. "Keep on starting, and finishing will take care of itself," is one of the major tools offered by a psychologist in his book on overcoming procrastination. I seem to have stumbled on this method naturally. I have a strong sense of responsibility, and, as an article or book writer, I always have prior agreements with editors that I would dread breaking. With creative work like writing poetry and stories or novels, this is much less often the case. Of course, when I'm writing stories or poems, I'm so excited by the unexpected freedom of the process that avoidance rarely becomes an issue.

Go back to your motivation: why are you writing in the first place? If it's because you definitely want to, and no one is coercing you, then you need to learn not to think of yourself as forcing yourself. For some personalities, anything on the mental to-do list automatically becomes a task to rebel against, as though Mom, Dad or Boss were the ones giving the orders. If this sounds like your problem, think about the advice to "just keep starting," without giving any thought to an obligation to finish. Starting, working for small amounts at a time, allowing yourself to stop when you want to, but coming back again and again on some sort of regular basis—that's all it takes to succeed. Here's how Steve Reynolds, recently over a nonwriting period, describes this system working for him:

> I tried to alter my schedule to finish a short story for the party tonight and found that that did not work at all. The whole idea of trying to "finish" the story by a certain time runs exactly counter to the idea of "what can I get started?" and provides an excellent example of how well the "what can I get started?" idea works (at least for a type like me, since other things weren't already working).
>
> As soon as I switched over to "let me see if I can get this *done* by Sunday night," everything else started coming apart, meaning, other things around the apartment all of a sudden weren't getting done, bills aren't being paid and I wasn't getting any exercise. In short, it started a road to burnout (just the "road," but I've been to the lovely town of burnout enough times to know when I'm on that road). The "balance" achieved with the other schedule dissipated rapidly. Before, I was waking up each morning with an expectation of getting things done and looking forward to it. By yesterday afternoon, that had pretty much left (for the day, I mean, not overall) because I had reached a point in the "party" short story where I normally would switch to working on another story—that's what I do when I hit a spot that needs to "simmer" for a longer period of time in order to figure out how the story is going to go. But this time I tried to force my way through the block and I just rediscovered that it doesn't work at all to do that. So I have happily switched over to my other story this morning and I find things immediately pick up again and I have plenty of ideas. This means I will have ideas for the other story sometime later this week. Good. If you put something in a wine press, you will either get wine or something that is not wine, but crushed (well at least with my personality, your mileage may differ).

Diana Gabaldon admits to being a procrastinator (such a common confession among writers!), yet she manages to be remarkably productive overall. How? "You have to keep coming back to it," she says.

I will know there are certain things that need to be done or should be approached and I will sit down with the intention of doing them and half an hour later I'm still playing solitaire. Then, with luck, I will finally get around to doing it. Sometimes I don't. Sometimes the phone will ring. If you let interruptions stop you, they will. A lot of people I've talked to say they feel they have failed for the day and may as well give up. The next day isn't any better, and eventually they do quit.

A little trick that may help you get back to a project you don't feel like doing is to give yourself permission to write something else—anything you want. At least, you'll get some indication as to how motivated and committed you are to the original piece. Maybe you'll learn that it should wait in line until you're more ready for it.

The openness to experience that prevails in successful writers' personalities helps them manage intense affect and anxiety, and as we've discussed earlier, it's possible to work on becoming more of an open person yourself. Such an ability may be analogous to a form of courage, entering the fray regardless of your terror. Read how the following writers learned to put aside their fear and anxiety:

> When I had writer's block ages ago, and had taken off to write on unemployment, I couldn't write because it was too important. If it's too important, I can't do it. As I'd go to the same place and try to do it, it became more and more loathsome. Finally, I took the typewriter with an extension cord into the garden and I found a different place to type. The changed environment didn't have the negative associations that had built up around the other. (Stephen Perry)

> I'd say there is sometimes a kind of very low-level anxiety for me usually when I sit down. It's nothing like what it used to be. Occasionally I used to have a block that I had to have a hammer and chisel to work away at. I haven't had a block in a long time. I think, for one thing, just the practice of doing it day in and day out. It's like speaking another language maybe. Pretty soon you begin to become more or less fluent in it, and so almost in spite of your anxious self you feel fairly comfortable. (Stephen Yenser)

> There were times when depression, anxiety, whatever, might have [kept me out of flow], in my mid- to late-twenties. I still get depressed and anxious, but I just don't let it stop me. I've just learned to move it to one side if I want to work. (David St. John)

A nonfiction writer I know said that over time she has changed her routine with regard to flow. "I used to start and stop working on articles readily. Now I don't stop working on one until I must because I need further information to proceed. I stay in flow and run with it as far as I can. I think I used to stop because I was afraid."

Procrastination at the start of a day's work is one of the most common ways writer's block manifests itself. Yet, some forms of delay—thinking and worrying about the writing but not feeling ready or able actually to write—may not necessarily be writer's block and may be, in fact, part of good writing. A friend told me that every time she presents herself at her computer to begin work on her doctoral dissertation, she first permits herself to play three games of Hearts. Exactly three, and then she minimizes the game window so that it's no longer in her visual field. Individuals have their own writing patterns over time, some quite uneven. Realize that warming up, and the delays that go with that, are your way of preparing to write, so that, as authors Mack and Skjei put it, "you'll find that you've trained yourself to treat wandering around the office or house as a useful prelude to writing."

A graduate student at UCLA told me he figured out just what he needed to do to get over his inability to write productively on his thesis. Now he regularly takes a yellow pad to a coffee shop first thing in morning and jots down ideas and sentences. This doesn't feel as intimidating to him as tackling the whole thing. Once he gets going, he returns home to where his dissertation is waiting on the computer.

Only a few writers purposely set about to train themselves to deal with interruptions, blocks or other setbacks. In general, ability to enter flow does improve with years of practice. As you learn the craft, those "what is best for this piece of work" kinds of decisions become more intuitive and less disruptive of your flow state. Your focus on the writing is less often broken by having to stop and consciously think of what to do next.

In addition, over time, and sometimes serendipitously, some writers find ways to enter flow that mesh perfectly with their own idiosyncratic personalities. When the needs of parenting or employment intrude, you can learn to enter flow quickly and efficiently because it is the only option you have, short of not writing at all. I learned, for example, that by allowing myself to run the expensive air conditioner all summer, the physical discomfort of sitting for long periods would be minimized.

215

Q. I'm an editor working on turning a compendium of articles by other writers into a book for a client. I need to do a lot of rewriting of this material. Whenever I sit down to write, I ask myself, "Will it happen or won't it?" When "it" happens, I'm able to work without feeling distracted, and I actually enjoy myself. Later, when I read what I've done, it all hangs together just right. When I don't work from that great place, the resulting work reads like a mess. I wish I could enjoy whatever I'm doing, not just some of it.

A. You have more control over your creative process than you think. First, try to determine what the difference is between the projects (articles or book sections, in this case) that engage you and the ones that leave you totally uninspired. Then you need to find a way to make the less interesting sections work for you. That is, think of trying out a new way of leading into the chapter, just for the fun and challenge of it. How about imagining that you will use this piece of work as a sample of what you can do for a future client, and thus add some flair to it? Ask yourself, "What is there in this piece of writing that *does* or *might* interest me if I changed it just a bit?" Find and focus extra attention on some tiny part of each section that is more engaging (or less boring!) than the rest. Some people seem naturally capable of enjoying anything they do. The rest of us can learn how.

This small increment of comfort actually made a difference in my writing fluency.

A friend, Patti Couch, who has struggled with lack of confidence in herself over the years has nonetheless managed to complete some quite stunning poetry. Yet only recently has she written regularly. I asked her to what she attributed this flood of creativity lately. Her E-mailed response:

Ummm . . . aaa . . . well—that's the scary part. I'm not sure, so I'm constantly petrified it will just STOP. If I had to guess, though, I might say it is partly due to widening my myopic view of available subject matter. I used to write about my mother, my mother, and my screwed-up mother. And screwed-up relationships, which generally reflected my relationship with my screwed-up mother. I've lately figured out there is a wealth of other subject matter available to me. AND I've found that most of the times I sit down to write, if I give myself the proper amount of time to push through the drivel, I usually hook into something—and it doesn't take that long, either. Maybe I used to give up too soon, like five minutes into it or something. Or, maybe I am just hooking in faster these days. Obviously, the kids becoming more independent has made time more available to me, but really, I'm comparing now to before I had kids, when I used to write about four good poems a year—maybe. I had LOTS of time on my hands then—I guess I was too busy acting out my dysfunctional behavior to write about it. Maybe it does have to do with being a little bit more centered—better relationship and quality of life. I'll have to give this more thought . . . Hey, I know! It's [my husband] Don's influence on me! I'm more organized and disciplined now. I've got a job to do, so I is doin' it!! There.

Simply knowing that flow exists can be beneficial. In addition, learning to recognize that you *have* experienced flow, regardless of activity, enhances your possibility of entering flow in another activity. By recognizing the signs of your own entry into flow, you can then analyze, formally or more intuitively, the keys you used to get there. And then your task is to find a way to replicate those keys in the new activity.

It seems to me that even those writers who insist that will is not involved are willing themselves to enter the physical place and mental space that allows the work to begin. You take a step toward the possibility of creative work while you are still mired in ordinary reality. It is that more-or-less conscious decision, which eventually becomes habitual, that seems so often to lead to flow and a positive outcome.

Researchers who have specifically studied writer's block, usually in educational settings, have come up with some techniques that have also proven helpful to poets and novelists. For example, we've already mentioned not thinking about your audience until late in the revision process, breaking the writing into smaller tasks and writing something (*anything*) in spite of your anxiety. Additionally, learn to monitor your internal states as well as your environment, so that you can enter and leave the writing situation when you need to. If, say, you're on the verge of exhaustion, take a break. Or if you suddenly realize a lot of noise is seeping into your consciousness, find a better place to work or figure out whether your awareness of the noise is due to your tiredness and inability to focus any longer without rest.

This next is my least favorite recommendation, but I'll mention it because it has been shown to help a few writers get past a writing block. A group of writers in one experiment allowed themselves to be motivated by external contingencies: they agreed that they would donate money to organizations they hated if they did not meet their writing goals. At the same time, they learned to set small, reasonable, steady goals, rather than to pursue their previous habit of writing in large bursts, if at all. In this situation it sounds as if the typical effusions of flow were actively discouraged, and only output was rewarded, that being what these writers most wanted. Perhaps surprisingly, however, the unblocked writers rated their work as being creative. Embarking on regular writing habits provided the best conditions for the writers who participated in this experiment. Since they were writing regularly, their writing improved, and it became less of a struggle and thus more enjoyable.

Individual differences count a great deal. Unfortunately, the self-help literature for blocked writers, based on anecdotal evidence, generally takes little account of personal variance. If you're genuinely blocked, not merely engaging in a little time-honored writerly procrastination, time-management skills and eliminating distractions may have little impact on your problem. You might benefit from forcing yourself to write whatever comes to mind. The recommendation to put a first draft away for a few days can be deadly to a serious blocker, or it can be a lifesaver if the self-lacerating voices attached to the draft then have time to wither and die. Finally, Dorothea Brande, the author of a classic work of writers' advice, insisted on two exercises: getting up earlier than usual to write, in order to tap into the unconscious, and setting oneself a strict fifteen-minute writing appointment every day, to be kept precisely. The key is to remind yourself that you're training yourself to write regularly, and that good quality at this stage is absolutely unimportant. "If you fail repeatedly at this exercise, give up writing," she wrote. Good advice? Generally, though it's not the only way. For me, as for some others, the emotional pull of the material got me hooked on writing—or doing writing-related tasks—regularly.

Know yourself. If you'd increase your success rate of entering flow, you would do well to work at understanding the underlying processes— the Master Keys—rather than attempting to imitate the specific methods used by other writers. That is, think deeply about what it takes to bring out your confidence, how you best deal with fear and anxiety, what keeps you motivated persistently in spite of difficulties. Then, with an interesting writing project in mind, experiment with some of the methods others have found to enhance the loosening up and focus-ing in processes. Give yourself time to learn to balance among the predominantly subconscious opposites: when to be in control and when to let go, when to think and when to intuit, when to try harder and when to relax.

It may be much easier than you think to make changes in your writing habits if another set of practices promises to be more effective. Stephen, in order to give himself more than one chance at success per day, experimented with writing at other times than immediately upon awakening, a regimen he had kept to for years. Instead of feeling as though he's missed his sole opportunity if he doesn't write, or write well, in the morning, he now feels he has all day to make up for it.

Along those lines, reflect on your own internal condition *at the moment*, taking account of your mental, physical and emotional states. You may be better able to enter flow if your emotional state is positive, so this may be a good time to tackle new projects, draft something for the first time or take on a tough revision. If you don't have the emo-tional stamina to delve into your subconscious, but physically and men-tally you feel fine, this may be a better time to take care of the more energy-consuming detail tasks that are part of every kind of work, whether research, copyediting your writing or marketing-related activi-ties. No matter how you feel, unless you're utterly physically and men-tally exhausted and clinically depressed (and there are exceptions to this as well), you should be able to do *something* that will help you achieve the goals you've set for yourself. Learn to respect your moods without using them as a total excuse for giving up all effort. Unless, of course, you realize you need time for recharging. Time off is also time well spent.

I'd like to share the following E-mail exchange with you, to make the point one more time that the difficult process of creative writing can evolve over time, becoming at least a little less angst-ridden and more flow-filled and satisfying. First, here's Steve Reynolds:

> I needed to go out to my Dad's this morning to help out for a while because he's having some foot surgery done today, so it turns out I got up around 5:30 just so I could get more work done on my story. There's no way I would have done that if I hadn't been writing so much every day, but the habit just made me feel I *wanted* to get something done, even if it was minor, before I left. And the entire day took much longer than expected, meaning I left this morning around 8:15 and didn't get

home until 7:30 this evening. And what did I do when I got home? Immediately sat down and kept going on my story where I left off this morning. Whoa . . . this is getting kind of spooky.

Stephen responded as follows (the ellipses are his):

I know what you mean. The habit stuff is pretty habit-forming. Also, I find myself writing more and more as I write more and more. Flow is addictive. Plus, I've been going more into my writing sessions with the feeling of looking forward to it. Maybe, it's partly the result of hitting gold fairly frequently, but I'm suspecting more because I'm more and more just trying to entertain myself . . . with stuff like, "What can I do that's weirder than anything I've done before . . . or "Let's see what happens if . . ." or "How can I make this fun . . ." The key is to just keep doing it . . . and then everything starts to conspire with the process . . . maybe because we're hungry for it then . . . I think it's been about six weeks now that I've written whenever I can . . . almost every day . . . and I feel that I'm getting back to that first sustained period of mine where I went for several years on this plan . . . only I have a suspicion I'm enjoying it more now . . . it's a real high, isn't it? it makes me feel really alive . . . and also if nothing happens I don't worry about it, but just shrug and look forward to the next day . . . I guess behaviorists would say this is intermittent reinforcement . . . it's hard to tease the web apart, but it's holding . . . *Great* to hear that you seem to be past the event horizon yourself.

Final thoughts

What I've shared with you in this book are ways to think and act that should allow you to mine your own deepest sources of creativity. Such internal sources do exist, even if what often turns up on the page in the morning is nowhere near what you dreamed in the night. Getting closer—in daylight—to that loosened, halfway dreamy place is one of the most important parts of learning to flow. Assuming you want to and believe you can, then all you have to do is open yourself up to the vastness of your options, and surrender and focus and balance the paradoxes that are integral to the art of writing. It makes no difference, finally, whether all these come easily to you or you have to draw up a list and work hard to learn them one by one.

When I started this project, I assumed that by focusing on the transition into flow, I was choosing a simple topic. Of course, it's not that at all. Flow, as part of the creative process, is as multifaceted, changeable and individual as each one of us is. By now you ought to be convinced that it's in your power to enhance your own creativity. You also now have some valuable tools—the Five Master Keys and more— to help make your writing life a more gratifying, lasting and meaningful one. My advice is to write as much and as often as you can, allow yourself to try new techniques and attitudes, give yourself a great deal of freedom to fail and fail again on the way to ultimate success. That's the best way to ensure that you'll eventually create works of which you can feel proud, as you search for your unique place in the lengthy chain of imaginative writers past, present and future.

Appendix | *The Art of Studying the Writer's Art*

THIS BOOK EVOLVED FROM MY doctoral dissertation for which I studied 62 creative writers. Subsequently I eliminated a couple of participants and interviewed 16 additional novelists and poets. I also integrated a great deal of information gathered from reading about, listening to and questioning experienced writers at various venues.

For the 29 written interviews, I sent 118 personalized request letters with questionnaires to a convenience sample (one not selected in any scientifically systematic manner or intended to be representative, but rather one that contains willing and able participants who represent the characteristics the researcher wants to study) of people who were listed in A *Directory of American Poets and Fiction Writers* (1995-1996 Edition), which contains some 7,000 contemporary writers. Of the 47 in-depth face-to-face, telephone or E-mail (two instances) interviews, I was previously acquainted with about half a dozen of the writers. The rest are novelists and poets with whose work I or my husband Stephen were familiar or whom I'd met briefly at public readings. Most of them were listed in the aforementioned directory, and all are eligible for inclusion (except for the non-American). To be listed, a writer must have published either twelve poems, three short stories, a book of poetry, a chapbook or a novel or story collection.

The writers' ages range from 32 to 88, with those in their forties, fifties and sixties predominating. The number of years they have been writing ranges from 16 years to "since childhood" or "all my life" (64 years is the highest specific number anyone offered), with 20 to 40 years being the predominant length of time. Here's the breakdown of contacts and responses:

Contacts attempted: 174	118 questionnaires, 56 requests for interviews 100 male, 74 female; 76 poets, 98 fiction writers
Total participants in book: 76	43 male; 33 female; 36 poets, 40 fiction writers
Personal interviews: 47	17 poets [13 male, 4 female]; 30 fiction writers [14 male, 16 female]
Questionnaires completed: 29	19 poets [13 male, 6 female]; 10 fiction writers [3 male, 7 female]
Respondents I wrote to who specifically declined: 38	13 poets, 25 fiction writers; 16 male, 22 female

Questions and more questions

I began my investigations with the question, "Have you ever had a fiction or poetry writing experience in which you've lost track of time? Think about the most recent time you entered this state—which I'll call flow—and describe your experience of what led up to that shift in consciousness." This was followed by the following list of probe questions, which I referred to as "idea-sparkers" in the written interviews:

- Did you use any pre-writing rituals?
- What were you doing or what was happening immediately before you entered flow?
- What were your thought processes before sitting down to work? After sitting down to work but prior to flow?
- At what point in the writing process did flow begin (such as, a half-hour into the writing session or during editing)?
- Did you notice any physiological changes as you entered flow?

- At what stage did you think of your audience, if at all?
- Did you enter flow more than once during this writing session?
- Did you feel more in control or out of control as you entered flow?
- Did you use a computer?
- Was this a typical writing experience for you? If not, why not?
- What are your personal patterns of flow? Daily? Weekly?
- What keeps you out of flow? How do you deal with writing blocks, both productively and non-productively?

Though interviewing writers personally (including by phone) provided me with a more complete picture of flow, a writer's main means of communication with the world is to write. Writers often like to ponder their responses and prefer not answering questions aloud without an opportunity to edit. Therefore, by also obtaining written responses by means of questionnaires, I improved the likelihood of getting at a more generalizable writer's truth. Additionally, I allowed those interviewees who requested it an opportunity to read a draft in order to confirm that what they had told me—and the way I'd interpreted it—was what they *meant* to say.

Are these writers representative?

It's impossible to know how representative my sample is of creative writers in general. For one thing, some, though eligible to be listed in the *Directory*, have not applied. Perhaps those who take the trouble to get themselves listed, as well as those who take the time to respond to questionnaires, are a specialized sample who then would have a particular set of work habits and flow experiences. I also scrutinized the responses of those who kindly took the time to tell me *why* they did not wish to discuss their writing process. It's understandable that some of those who are household names are inundated with multiple requests from the public and might refuse all such requests. Personalities differ, too: some writers can't help but be polite and responsive and generous to one and all, while others are more single-minded. I won't deny the relevance of personal connection, in that no one turned down an interview when asked by me personally or by phone (though a couple of those did not, finally, come through).

The questionnaire itself, certainly, is not the best way to reach strangers. If I'd spoken, instead of written, to everyone who refused a mail request, I would have been able to explain my study more clearly and possibly gotten their cooperation.

Some writers indicated that my asking about their creative process made them uncomfortable. Alison Lurie, for example, wrote, "For me, the process of writing is mysterious, and I feel it would be a mistake for me to attempt to analyze it closely and scientifically." Wrote Anne Tyler: "I'm convinced that even mentioning the 'flow state' would scare off the elf who brings it on, so I'll regretfully decline your invitation to contribute to your dissertation." Poet C. K. Williams explained his reluctance this way:

> What you're calling "flow" (which isn't a word I'd use) is something that's possibly too private, too fragile, or, most likely, too complicated to take the time to consider. . . . Somehow the creative process, at least for me, doesn't have anything to do any longer with the mechanics of it, but with its themes, forms, and necessities of content, which drive consciousness to take the risk of meditating on itself. The attention that's implied seems to be dissipated if you're looking at the attention at the same time . . . even for a moment, somehow.

Some experienced my questions as a kind of invasion of their fundamental privacy, such as this one who scribbled on a postcard, "But it would be tantamount to offering you our orgasms for study. Their quality shows in the writing. Analyze that." Others wrote that they didn't know how to answer my questions, such as Donald Justice, who wrote, "Look, I *am* sorry, but these terms are just not terms I think in with writing in mind—or if they come close at times I still cannot give answers, certainly not answers of any interest or value."

Charles Wright shared that, for him, time doesn't stop any more in the midst of writing than it does in any other totally absorbing task. But he adds that "it does 'disappear' at the moments of highest concentration and escalation. As for 'before,' you itch and scratch, itch and scratch—you need good fingernails, not too long, not too short, not too sharp, not too dull." As you can see, what Wright has described *does* fit into the definition of flow. Marianne Boruch indicated that making poems is such a private experience that "I can't think of a way to step outside it in the light (too bright a light) of your questions. I'm sorry." And then she generously sent me one of her books, referring me to an essay about being outside time.

What may be the most meaningful category for research purposes includes those writers who indicated they do not experience the phenomenon I asked them about, that of sensing that time has stopped while they write. For instance, Charles Simic responded, "Your questionnaire has nothing to do with how poems get written—mine, at least." John Irving's assistant Lewis Robinson wrote to say that "he doesn't feel he can participate in your 'flow state' study because (I quote) 'nothing flows in my writing process—my job is to make it flow for the reader, and that is a very deliberate, very slow, very unflowing process.' " J.D. McClatchy expressed similar thoughts: "The project sounds, I guess, like an interesting one, but I must confess that I don't know what you're talking about. Don't know, that is, from my own experience. I'm *always* aware of time while I write—and whether the teapot is on, and has the lawn been mowed, and what time the news is on. Whatever the opposite of 'flow' may be, I'm it."

There's no way to know how many of those who didn't respond at all do or do not experience flow. It seems to me, finally, that those who did agree to be interviewed are not the only creative writers who experience flow, nor are they likely to be the only ones who experience it in the ways I have described in this book. What mainly distinguishes this group of writers may be their willingness to look deeply into and to share with strangers such an intimate and mysterious process as flow.

Talking about flow

The least skittish writers, and those who have the knack of entering flow easily and often, were not disturbed by being asked to become aware of their own process. It's possible that talking about flow, becoming aware for the first time of how you enter that state, may slow you down a moment the next time you write. Yet you can also learn to relax and continue. Think of those television screens with a tiny window in the corner so you can keep track of what's happening on another channel, or a Windows computer program in which you temporarily open a small window to quickly perform another application. Similarly, it's not unusual to be able to safely open up a bit of consciousness in order to notice the rest of yourself begin to lose yourself in flow. In a wholly positive vein, talking about flow—like discussing other desirable experiences—may motivate you to want to have the experience more often.

The writers sometimes could not answer my main question directly, as to how they enter flow, but roughly a half hour or so into the interview they would suddenly tell me something that *did* answer the question. At first, I would ask writers to describe the most recent incident of having lost track of time while writing. Nearly all indicated that this had happened to them, either rarely, occasionally, frequently or each time they write. Yet only a few were able to comply with my request and describe the most recent particular incident. Most preferred to describe a typical writing experience, or all typical writing experiences. It became apparent to me that these writers had worked so long and so "routinely," that one incident of flow in writing no longer stood out in memory, not to mention the difficulty of remembering a specific instance of time stopping and of losing consciousness of self.

Though I am reluctant to use the word "efficient" when talking about either sex or creativity, when I first got married, for example, I could, at any time of any day, recall the last time or two of making love. Each single event stood out as particular and unusual. As time went by, I began not to be able to distinguish one session from another in memory. Each was still enjoyable and much looked-forward to, but less and less easily remembered after a few days of intervening experiences. It seems to me that something like that occurs with writing in flow. As you get into a routine, you begin to lose recall of any particular writing session, except for the peak experiences, the ones undertaken in a new place or inspired by something unusual. As with sleep, too, who remembers how they fell asleep last Tuesday? But you might recall the high school graduation night you stayed up to watch the sunrise, or the time you slept on your friend's couch, or speaking of myself, the time, more than 30 years ago, that I slept on the damp ground in a park with my boyfriend in Israel, because I'd missed curfew and had been locked out of the youth hostel. And so on.

As for the written interviews, I found that I did not necessarily get *different* responses from them, but rather answers that in some cases corresponded with the earlier stages of responses I received in my personal interviews.

During this project, I attended a public poetry reading of one of my written respondents, Billy Collins. He read a poem in which he described the importance of his favorite writing chair and of smoking while writing. He mentioned neither in response to my questionnaire, despite a probe about rituals and routines (and I don't know if the poem is true). In one sense, then, this *might* be construed as a benefit of a questionnaire, in that the respondent answers what's most immediately salient to him. While more detail may be elicited in an interview with probing questions, it's also possible the respondent is then giving me what I'm asking for and not what's most pivotal to him.

At a reading by Ursula Le Guin, I saw another side of the question. Say you ask, as one of the members of the audience did at this particular event, "How do you work?" The expected response may be what I've taken to calling "a cat answer." (Le Guin said something like, "I work, then I stop to pet the cat, then I work some more, then I pet the cat.") In her written answer to the same question for this book, she was not specific, stressing the importance of keeping the mystery in the process. Both aspects of the writer's process offer enlightenment.

Analyzing the data

I didn't seek to capture external reality so much as to understand subjective experience, and I asked my respondents two main things: not only "What do you *do?*"—which can be construed as correlative but not necessarily causative—and, "What is your experience? How do you feel and think about this phenomenon?" As I analyzed what I'd discovered, I felt responsible for representing social science to a group of artists I admire. I didn't want them to feel I had in any way diminished their art by examining it with a scientific lens.

To ensure reliability, I did what any credible qualitative researcher does: I kept a journal, took field notes and recorded my passing insights, prejudices, moods and reactions as I collected data. This way I was able to best assess how I might be affecting the data and how I could use this knowledge to amplify the study.

For the doctoral study, I put all my data, including complete transcripts of all personal interviews (typed myself from the tape recordings), scanned copies of the written responses, and memos from my journal, into one large (265 single-spaced pages) computer file (WordPerfect 7.0 for Windows '95). I used the database program FileMaker Pro 3.0 to create computer note cards for sentences or paragraphs that related to one or more variables. I coded for seventy key concepts: from "activity" (i.e., the activity itself precipitates flow), through "importance" (i.e., the writer spoke about how important writing is), to "when" (relating to time of day the writer usually writes or gets into flow). In the book you're holding, when I say *many* writers tend to do such-and-such, I mean that such an activity came up again and again, as often as or more often than in half the interviews.

As I was struggling with the arrangement of these chapters, I was reminded of those multifaceted balls that hang and twinkle from the ceilings of grand ballrooms. I imagined that the whole truth of the complex phenomenon of flow was hidden within one of these balls. If you were to lower one and look at it up close, what you see would depend on which prism you looked at, as well as the angle of your vision. Add to that the fact that such sparkling balls are in reality made up of dozens of tiny mirrors, and you realize that what you see may be mostly yourself reflected back at you: your own unique way of perceiving. Flow does seem to be sometimes a particle and sometimes a wave, shape-shifting before our clipboard-carrying selves. And living, creative human beings rarely hold still long enough to become hard facts.

As to the specifics of analysis, I found little difference attributable to gender. Extent of writing experience and personality seemed to account for most of the individual differences that came to my attention. Poets and fiction writers do differ, of course, here and there, and I mentioned such divergences in the relevant sections. Yet they don't seem to differ very much in their experience of flow entry.

It's true that if you ask the same writer the same question on two separate occasions, you will probably get revised answers. As a novelist pointed out to me in her feedback, "Remember that fiction writers are liars by nature—embellishers—who invent their stories, and often themselves, too as they go!" A poet wrote, "The work is fascinating and unusual because the poets appear to have told the truth."

Another issue is change over time. For instance, I just read that Octavia E. Butler now rises daily at five and takes a walk, and that her most recent book is the first to be written on a computer. Such changes are inevitable. Yet the responses I obtained—and the patterns and themes underlying the specific details—were so consistent among all the writers, including those I talked to more than once, that they reflect a healthy level of accuracy about the writing-in-flow experience.

Writers who participated

This book is based on my interviews with seventy-six novelists and poets. The following biographies will point you toward their own creative work:

Ralph Angel's first poetry collection was *Anxious Latitudes*. His second, *Neither World*, received the James Laughlin Award of The Academy of American Poets.

Madison Smartt Bell's novels include *The Washington Square Ensemble*; *Waiting for the End of the World*; *Straight Cut*; *The Year of Silence*; *Soldier's Joy*; *Doctor Sleep*; *Save Me, Joe Louis*; *All Souls' Rising* and *Ten Indians*. He has also published the short-story collections *Zero db* and *Barking Man and Other Stories*, and a textbook, *Narrative Design*.

Marvin Bell's books include *Things We Dreamt We Died For*; *A Probable Volume of Dreams*; *The Escape Into You*; *Residue of Song*; *Stars Which See, Stars Which Do Not See*; *These Green-Going-to-Yellow*; *Old Snow Just Melting: Essays and Interviews*; *Segues: A Correspondence in Poetry (with William Stafford)*; *Drawn by Stones, by Earth, by Things That Have Been in the Fire*; *New and Selected Poems*; *Iris of Creation*; *A Marvin Bell Reader: Selected Poetry and Prose*; *The Book of the Dead Man*; *Ardor: Vol. 2 of The Book of the Dead Man*; *Poetry for a Midsummer's Night*; and *Wednesday, an Irish selected poems*.

T. Coraghessan Boyle's novels include *The Road to Wellville*; *East Is East*; *World's End*; *Budding Prospects*; *Water Music*; *The Tortilla Curtain* and *Riven Rock*, a *Los Angeles Times*-best-seller. He has also authored several collections of short stories, including *Without a Hero*; *If the River Was Whiskey*; *Greasy Lake and Other Stories*; *Descent of Man* and *T. C. Boyle Stories*.

Andrea Hollander Budy is the author of two poetry collections, *House Without a Dreamer*, which won the Nicholas Roerich Poetry Prize and was named one of the Best Poetry Books of the Year by *Writer's Digest* magazine, and *The Other Life*. Her chapbooks are *Living on the Cusp*; *Happily Ever After* and *What the Other Eye Sees*.

Octavia E. Butler's novels include *Patternmaster*; *Mind of My Mind*; *Survivor*; *Kindred*; *Wild Seed*; *Clay's Ark*; *Dawn*; *Adulthood Rites*; *Imago*; *Parable of the Sower* and *Parable of the Talents*. *Bloodchild* is her collection of short stories. Butler has won both Nebula and Hugo Awards, as well as a MacArthur Foundation Fellowship ("genius award").

Robert Olen Butler is the author of eight novels: *The Alleys of Eden; Sun Dogs; Countrymen of Bones; On Distant Ground; Wabash; The Deuce; They Whisper* and *The Deep Green Sea.* His two volumes of short stories include *A Good Scent from a Strange Mountain,* which won the Pulitzer Prize, and *Tabloid Dreams.*

Ethan Canin's first short-story collection, *Emperor of the Air,* was a *New York Times* best-seller. His second volume of short stories was *The Palace Thief.* He also wrote the novels *Blue River* and *For Kings and Planets.*

Susan Taylor Chehak is the author of several novels, including *The Story of Annie D.,* which was a *New York Times* Notable Book of the Year and an Edgar Award Nominee, *Harmony; Dancing on Glass; Smithereens* (a Hammett Award Nominee) and *Rampage.* She also authored a play, *Last Chance Café,* and three dramatic series pilots for television.

Peter Clothier has authored two novels, *Chiaroscuro* and *Dirty-Down.* He also wrote two books of poems, *Aspley Guise* and *Parapoems;* a critical biography, *David Hockney;* and a memoir, *While I Am Not Afraid: Secrets of a Man's Heart.*

Wanda Coleman has written several books of poems and stories, including *Imagoes; Heavy Daughter Blues; A War of Eyes and Other Stories; African Sleeping Sickness; Dicksboro Hotel; Hand Dance* and *Bathwater Wine.* She has also published a collection of her occasional journalism, *Native in a Strange Land: Trials and Tremors.*

Billy Collins is the author of six books of poetry: *Pokerface; Video Poems; The Apple That Astonished Paris; Questions About Angels,* which was selected for the National Poetry Series; *The Art of Drowning;* and *Picnic, Lightning.*

Phoebe Conn has written more than two dozen contemporary, historical and futuristic romance novels and has seven million copies of books in print under her own name and that of her pseudonym, Cinnamon Burke. Among these are *Love's Ellusive Flame; Savage Fire;* the *New York Times*-bestseller *Captive Heart; Loving Fury; Arizona Angel; No Sweeter Ecstasy; Love Me 'Til Dawn; Tangled Hearts; Swept Away; Paradise; Beloved Legacy; A Touch of Love; Forbidden Legacy* and *Wild Legacy.*

Michael Connelly's first Harry Bosch police procedural novel, *The Black Echo,* won an Edgar Award. Among his other novels are *The Black Ice; The Concrete Blonde; The Last Coyote; Trunk Music; The Poet; Blood Work* and *Angels Flight,* several of which have been national best-sellers.

Bernard Cooper is the author of two collection of memoirs, *Maps to Anywhere* and *Truth Serum,* and the novel *A Year of Rhymes.* He received a PEN/Ernest Hemingway Award and an O. Henry Prize.

Alfred Corn's collections of poetry include *All Roads at Once; A Call in the Midst of the Crowd; The Various Light; Notes From a Child of Paradise; The West Door;*

Autobiographies and *Present*. He has also written a novel, *Part of His Story*, a collection of critical essays, *The Metamorphoses of Metaphor*, and a textbook, *The Poem's Heartbeat: A Manual of Prosody*. He edited *Incarnation: Contemporary Writers on the New Testament*.

Peter Davison's first collection of poetry, *Breaking of the Day*, won the Yale Series of Younger Poets Award. His other volumes include *The City and the Island; Pretending to Be Asleep; Dark Houses; Walking the Boundaries: Poems, 1957-1974; Praying Wrong: New and Selected Poems, 1957-1984; The Great Ledge* and *The Poems of Peter Davison: 1957-1995*. He has also written two books of prose: *One of the Dangerous Trades: Essays on the Work and Workings of Poetry* and *The Fading Smile: Poets in Boston, from Robert Lowell to Sylvia Plath*, as well as a memoir, *Half Remembered: A Personal History*. Davison is the poetry editor of *The Atlantic Monthly*.

Gerald DiPego has written five novels, including *With a Vengeance; Forest Things; Shadow of the Beast; Keeper of the City* and *Cheevey*. He has also written the screenplays for twenty films, including *Born Innocent; The Four Feathers; Sharky's Machine; Keeper of the City; One More Mountain; Nothing Lasts Forever; Phenomenon; Message in a Bottle* and *Instinct*.

Chitra Banerjee Divakaruni's short-story collection, *Arranged Marriage*, won an American Book Award. She is the author of the novels *The Mistress of Spices* (chosen by *Los Angeles Times* as one of their Best Books of 1997) and *Sister of My Heart*, as well as several poetry volumes, including *Leaving Yuba City: Poems*.

Harriet Doerr's first novel, *Stones for Ibarra*, won an American Book Award. She also authored the novel *Consider This, Señora* and a compilation of essays, *The Tiger in the Grass*.

Stephen Dunn's many volumes of poetry include *Looking for Holes in the Ceiling; Full of Lust and Good Usage; Circus of Needs; Work and Love; Not Dancing; Local Time; Between Angels; Landscape at the End of the Century; New and Selected Poems 1974-1994* and *Loosestrife*, a National Book Critics Circle finalist. He has also written two prose collections, *Walking Light: Essays and Memoirs* and *Riffs and Reciprocities*.

Judith Freeman, a Guggenheim fellowship recipient, has authored three novels, *The Chinchilla Farm; Set for Life* and *A Desert of Pure Feeling*, as well as a collection of short stories, *Family Attractions*.

Diana Gabaldon is a *New York Times*-best-selling author of a series of "historical fantasias," a blend of historical fiction, time travel and adventure. Her Outlander series includes *Outlander; Dragonfly in Amber; Voyager* and *Drums of Autumn*, with two more novels to come. She also wrote *The Outlandish Companion*.

Frank X. Gaspar's first poetry collection, *The Holyoke*, won the Samuel French Morse Prize, and his second, *Mass for the Grace of a Happy Death*, won the Anhinga Prize for Poetry. His forthcoming novel is titled *Leaving Pico*.

Phyllis Gebauer is the author of a novel, *The Pagan Blessing*. Her short stories have appeared in *Modern Maturity* and the Santa Barbara City College Literary Magazine, and she is on the staff of the Santa Barbara Writers' Conference.

Merrill Joan Gerber's novels include *An Antique Man; Now Molly Knows; The Lady with the Moving Parts; King of the World*, which won the Pushcart Editors' Book Award, and *The Kingdom of Brooklyn*. Her books of short stories are *Stop Here, My Friend; Honeymoon; Chattering Man: Stories and a Novella; This Old Heart of Mine: The Best of Merrill Joan Gerber's Redbook Stories* and *Anna in Chains*. She has also published a personal memoir, *Old Mother, Little Cat: A Writer's Reflections on Her Kitten, Her Aged Mother . . . and Life*, as well as nine novels for young adults.

David Gerrold's novels include *When Harlie Was One; Yesterday's Children; The Man Who Folded Himself; Moonstar Odyssey; Deathbeast; Voyage of the Star Wolf; Under the Eye of God; A Covenant of Justice*, four volumes in the series *War Against the Chtorr* (*A Matter for Men; A Day for Damnation; A Rage for Revenge* and *A Season for Slaughter*) and *The Middle of Nowhere*. His short stories have appeared in *Galaxy; If; Amazing; Twilight Zone; The Magazine of Fantasy and Science Fiction*, among others, as well as in several collected volumes. Gerrold has also written for television, including episodes for the *Star Trek* series. He published a nonfiction account of writing for television, *The Trouble With Tribbles*. Gerrold is a nine-time Hugo and Nebula award nominee, and he won both awards in 1995 for his semiautobiographical novelette, "The Martian Child."

Sue Grafton is the author of the best-selling and award-winning mystery novel series that includes *"A" Is for Alibi; "B" Is for Burglar; "C" Is for Corpse; "D" Is for Deadbeat; "E" Is for Evidence* and so on through the alphabet, with her most recent being *"N" Is for Noose*.

Donald Hall's poetry collections include *Exiles and Marriages; The Dark Houses; A Roof of Tiger Lilies; The Alligator Bride; The Yellow Room: Love Poems; Kicking the Leaves; The Happy Man; The One Day; Old and New Poems; The Museum of Clear Ideas; The Old Life* and *Without*. His volumes of prose include *String Too Short to Be Saved; Seasons at Eagle Pond; Life Work* and *Their Ancient Glittering Eyes*. He has also written several children's books, including *Old Home Day; When Willard Met Babe Ruth; Lucy's Summer; Lucy's Christmas; The Man Who Lived Alone* and *Ox-Cart Man*, which won the Caldecott Medal.

Sam Hamill is the author of more than thirty books including *Destination Zero: Poems 1970- 1995*; essays collected in *A Poet's Work*; recent poems, *Gratitude*; and among many volumes of translations, *The Essential Basho* and *The Essential Chuang Tzu*. He edited *The Erotic Spirit*, a poetry anthology, and *The Gift of Tongues*, and is founding editor at Copper Canyon Press.

Lola Haskins's books include *Planting the Children; Castings; Across Her Broad Lap Something Wonderful; Forty-Four Ambitions for the Piano; Hunger* (which won the Edwin Ford Piper Award, formerly the Iowa Poetry Prize), *Visions of Florida* (Introductory essay—prose poem—to photographs by Woody Walters) and *Extranjera*.

Anthony Hecht's second poetry collection, *Hard Hours*, won the Pulitzer Prize. His other volumes of poetry include *A Summoning of Stones; Millions of Strange Shadows; The Venetian Vespers; Collected Earlier Poems; The Transparent Man* and

Flight Among the Tombs. He has also published critical essays (*Obbligati*; *On the Laws of the Poetic Arts*), a study of Auden (*The Hidden Law*), light verse and translation.

Brenda Hillman, recipient of a Guggenheim fellowship, the Delmore Schwartz Memorial Award for Poetry and the Poetry Society of America Norma Farber First Book Prize, has authored collections of poetry including *Coffee, 3 A.M.*; *White Dress*; *Fortress*; *Death Tractates*; *Bright Existence* and *Loose Sugar*.

Jane Hirshfield's books of poems include *The October Palace*; *Alaya*; *Of Gravity and Angels*; and *The Lives of the Heart*. She also authored a book of essays, *Nine Gates: Entering the Mind of Poetry*, and edited and cotranslated *Women in Praise of the Sacred: 43 Centuries of Spiritual Poetry by Women* and *The Ink Dark Moon: Love Poems by Ono No Komachi and Izumi Shikibu of the Ancient Court of Japan*.

Marnell Jameson is the author of *California Palms*, a collection of short stories. She has completed the manuscript for a novel, *Where the Sun Beats*, and writes regularly for the *Los Angeles Times*.

Diane Johnson is the author of the *Los Angeles Times* best-selling novel, *Le Divorce*, as well as *Fair Game*; *Burning*; *Loving Hands at Home*; *The Shadow Knows*; *Lying Low*; *Persian Nights* and *Health and Happiness*. She has also written biographies, essays, short stories and screenplay adaptations.

Richard Jones is the author of several books of poetry, including *Country of Air*; *At Last We Enter Paradise* and *A Perfect Time*. His selected poems, *Rough Grace*, will be published in the spring of 2000. He edited the critical anthologies *Poetry and Politics* and *Of Solitude and Silence: Writings on Robert Bly*. Jones is the founder and editor of the literary journal *Poetry East*.

Nora Okja Keller's first novel, *Comfort Woman*, about the Korean sex slaves of the Japanese, won an American Book Award.

Faye Kellerman's first novel, *The Ritual Bath*, won the Macavity Award for Best First Novel from the Mystery Readers of America. There are more than five million copies of her novels in print, including *Sacred and Profane*; *Milk and Honey*; *Day of Atonement*; *False Prophet*; *Grievous Sin*; *Sanctuary*; *Justice*; *Prayers for the Dead*; *Serpent's Tooth* and *Moon Music*. She is also the author of the historical novel of intrigue, *The Quality of Mercy*. Her short stories and reviews have been anthologized in several collections, including two volumes of the *Sisters in Crime* series, Sara Paretsky's *A Woman's Eye*; *The First Annual Year's Finest Crime and Mystery Stories* and others.

Jonathan Kellerman's first novel, *When the Bough Breaks*, became a national bestseller, won Edgar and Anthony awards, and was adapted as a television movie. His other best-selling mysteries include *Blood Test*; *Over the Edge*; *The Butcher's Theater*; *Silent Partner*; *Time Bomb*; *Private Eyes*; *Devil's Waltz*; *Bad Love*; *Self-Defense*; *The Clinic*; *The Web* and *Survival of the Fittest*. His first non-Alex Delaware novel in a decade is *Billy Straight*. There are currently over twenty-five million copies of his books in print. He is the author of two volumes for children, *Daddy,*

Daddy, Can You Touch the Sky? and *Jonathan Kellerman's ABC of Weird Creatures*, and three psychology books, including the latest, *Savage Spawn: Reflections on Violent Children.*

Nancy Kress is the author of three fantasy novels: *The Prince of Morning Bells*; *The Golden Grove* and *The White Pipes*, as well as six science-fiction novels: *An Alien Light*; *Brain Rose*; *Beggars in Spain*; *Beggars and Choosers*; *Beggars Ride* and *Maximum Light*. Her recent thrillers are *Oaths and Miracles* and *Stinger*. *Beggars in Spain* was based on her novella of the same name which won both Nebula and Hugo awards. She has also written three collections of short stories, *Trinity and Other Stories*; *The Aliens of Earth* and *Beaker's Dozen*, plus two books on writing fiction, *Beginnings, Middles & Ends* and *Dynamic Characters*. Kress is the monthly "Fiction" columnist for *Writer's Digest.*

Ursula K. Le Guin's many science-fiction novels include *The Earthsea* tetralogy; *The Left Hand of Darkness*; *The Dispossessed*; *The Lathe of Heaven* and *Always Coming Home*. Her short-story collections include *Unlocking the Air and Other Stories*; *Four Ways to Forgiveness* and *Searoad: The Chronicles of Klatsand*. There are three million copies of her books in print. She has won five Nebula Awards, five Hugo Awards, the National Book Award, the World Fantasy Award and many others. She has also written eleven books for children, collections of essays, poetry and criticism, as well as *Tao Te Ching: A Book About the Way and the Power of the Way*, Le Guin's rendering into English of the words of Lao Tzu, the founder of Taoism.

Philip Levine's many books of poetry include *The Simple Truth*, which won the Pulitzer Prize for poetry, as well as *On the Edge*; *Not This Pig*; *Red Dust*; *Pili's Wall*; *They Feed The Lion*; *1933*; *The Names of the Lost*; *Seven Years from Somewhere*; *Ashes*; *One for the Rose*; *Selected Poems*; *Sweet Will*; *A Walk with Tom Jefferson*; *New Selected Poems* and *What Work Is*. He also published two books of translations from Spanish; a collection of interviews, *Don't Ask*; essays on poetry, *So Ask*; and *The Bread of Time: Toward an Autobiography*. *Ashes* and *What Work Is* both won the National Book Award in poetry, and *What Work Is* won the *Los Angeles Times* Book Award in poetry.

Aimee Liu is the author of two novels, *Cloud Mountain* and *Face*, as well as *Solitaire*, an autobiographical narrative. She also coauthored several nonfiction books, including *The Codependency Conspiracy*, *Success Trap* and *False Love and Other Romantic Illusions*, all with Dr. Stan J. Katz.

Margot Livesey is the author of two novels, *Homework* and *Criminals*, as well as a collection of stories, *Learning by Heart*. Her thus-far untitled new novel is forthcoming in 1999.

Myra Cohn Livingston wrote or edited more than eighty-three books of her own poetry, poetry anthologies for young people, and books concerning poetry and young people. A sampling includes *Whispers and Other Poems*; *Poem-Making: Ways to Begin Writing Poetry*; *Let Freedom Ring: A Ballad of Martin Luther King, Jr.*; *A Time to Talk: Poems of Friendship*; *Flights of Fancy and Other Poems* and *Call Down* *the Moon: Poems of Music*. She wrote two books on children and creative writing, *The Child As Poet: Myth or Reality?* and *When You Are Alone/It Keeps You Capone*. She also authored an award-winning filmstrip series, *The Writing of Poetry*. (Livingston died August 23, 1996).

Suzanne Lummis has authored three books of poetry, *Idiosyncrasies*, *Falling Short of Heaven* and, most recently, *In Danger*. She also edited, with Charles Harper Webb, *Grand Passion: The Poets of Los Angeles and Beyond*. Her two plays, *October 22, 4004 B.C.*, *Saturday* and *Night Owls*, produced in Los Angeles and elsewhere, earned Drama-Logue awards for playwriting.

Elizabeth Macklin is the author of a book of poetry, *A Woman Kneeling in the Big City*, and has had poems in *The New Yorker*; *Paris Review*; *The Threepenny Review*; *Southwest Review*; *Yale Review*; *The Nation*; *The New York Times* and *The New Republic*, among others.

Bill Mohr's poems have appeared in *Sonora Review*; *Santa Monica Review*; *Antioch Review*; *ZYZZYVA*; *Wormwood Review*; *Pearl*; *Blue Mesa Review*; *Asylum Annual*; *ONTHEBUS*; *Caffeine*; *Rain City Review*; *Blue Satellite* and *Hummingbird*, as well as such anthologies as *Grand Passion* and *Stand-Up Poetry*. He is the author of *Hidden Proofs*, a poetry collection, and *Vehemence*, a collection of poems on compact disc.

Faye Moskowitz authored two collections of essays, *A Leak in the Heart* and *And the Bridge Is Love*, as well as a collection of short stories, *Whoever Finds This: I Love You*. She also edited *Her Face in the Mirror: Jewish Women on Mothers and Daughters*. More than sixty of her essays have appeared in publications such as *The Washington Post* and *The New York Times*. Her work has been anthologized in *Mixed Voices: Contemporary Poems About Music*; *The Sound of Writing II* and *Hot Flashes: Women Writers on the Change of Life*.

Carol Muske (a.k.a. Carol Muske Dukes) writes both poetry and novels, as well as books of criticism. Her poetry books include *Camouflage*; *Skylight*; *Wyndmere*; *Applause*; *Red Trousseau* and *An Octave Above Thunder: New and Selected Poems*. Her novels are *Dear Digby*; *Saving St. Germ* and *Two Secrets*. She also wrote *Women and Poetry: Truth, Autobiography and the Shape of the Self*.

Cees Nooteboom has published novels, short stories, ten books of poetry, and travel books. Among his novels that have been translated into English are *Rituals*, winner of the Pegasus Prize for Literature and the Bordewijk Prize; *A Song of Truth and Semblance*; *Philip and the Others*; *The Knight Has Died*; *Mokusei*; *The Following Story*, which won the European Literary Prize for Best Novel and was named a *New York Times* Notable Book of the Year; and *In the Dutch Mountains*. *The Roads to Santiago* is his collection of essays about his passion for Spain.

Ed Ochester has published nine volumes of poetry, including *Allegheny*; *Miracle Mile* and *Changing the Name to Ochester*. He has completed a new poetry manuscript, *The Land of Cockaigne*. He was, for the past twenty years, director of the Writing Program at the University of Pittsburgh, where he continues to head the Pitt Poetry Series.

Stephen Perry has poems published or forthcoming in *The New Yorker*; *Sewanee Review*; *Virginia Quarterly Review*; *Kenyon Review*; *Yale Review*; *North American Review*; *Antioch Review*; *Denver Quarterly*; *Wisconsin Review*; *Midwest Quarterly*; *Nimrod*, *Cimarron Review*; *Beloit Poetry Journal*; *Poetry East*; *The Journal*; *Night Sun*; *Jacaranda Review* (UCLA); *Sycamore Review*; *5AM*; Colorado North Review; *Tar River Poetry* and many others. His poems have been included in Milkweed Editions' *Mixed Voices: Contemporary Poems About Music*; *The Bedford Introduction to Literature* and *Poetry: An Introduction*. His poetry manuscript, *Homecoming*, was a finalist for the Pitt Poetry Prize.

Samuel H. Pillsbury is the author of a novel, *Conviction* and *The Invasion of Planet Wampetter*, a book for children. His most recent book is nonfiction: *Judging Evil: Rethinking the Law of Murder and Manslaughter*. A former newspaper reporter and federal prosecutor, he is now a professor of law at Loyola Law School in Los Angeles.

Robert Pinsky, the current Poet Laureate of the United States, has written five books of poetry: *Sadness and Happiness*; *An Explanation of America*; *History of My Heart*; *The Want Bone* and *The Figured Wheel: New and Collected Poems 1966-1996*. He has also published three books of prose, *Landor's Poetry*; *The Situation of Poetry* and *Poetry and the World*. Pinsky's translation of *The Inferno of Dante* won the *Los Angeles Times* Book Prize. He is Poetry Editor of *Slate*.

Wyatt Prunty's six books of poetry include *Domestic of the Outer Banks*; *The Times Between*; *What Women Know, What Men Believe*; *Balance as Belief*; *The Run of the House* and *Since the Mail Stopped*. He also wrote a critical work on contemporary poetry, *Fallen From the Symboled World*. A volume of his *New* and *Selected* poems is forthcoming. He founded and directs the Sewanee Writers' Conference and is editor of the Sewanee Writers' Series.

James Ragan's poetry collections include *In the Talking Hours*; *Womb-Weary*; *The Hunger Wall*; *Lusions* and *The World Shouldering I*. He also co-edited *Collected Poems 1952-1990: Yevgeny Yevtushenko*, and he wrote the plays "Saints" and "Commedia." Ragan is a Fulbright Professor and the director of the Graduate Professional Writing Program at the University of Southern California.

Donald Revell has written six books of poetry: *From the Abandoned Cities* (National Poetry Series Winner); *The Gaza of Winter*; *New Dark Ages* (PEN Center USA West Award); *Erasures*; *Beautiful Shirt*; and *There Are Three*.

Steve Reynolds has humorous short stories published or forthcoming in *Pinehurst Journal*; *Checking It Out* and *The MacGuffin*, as well as essays in a variety of publications.

Mark Salzman's first book was *Iron and Silk*, an account of two years he spent in China, and it was a Pulitzer Prize nonfiction finalist. He also wrote the screenplay and starred in the film of the same name. His novels include *The Laughing Sutra* and *The Soloist*, and his memoir is *Lost in Place*.

Lynne Sharon Schwartz has published five novels, including *Rough Strife*; *Balancing Acts*; *Disturbances in the Field*; *Leaving Brooklyn* and *The Fatigue Artist*. She also wrote two collections of short stories, *Acquainted With the Night and Other Stories* and *The Melting Pot and Other Subversive Stories*, as well as a book for children, *The Four Questions*; a nonfiction book, *We Are Talking About Homes: A Great University Against Its Neighbors*; and a memoir, *Ruined by Reading: A Life in Books*. Her work has been anthologized in *The Best American Short Stories*; *The O. Henry Prize Stories*; *The Pushcart Prize* and other volumes.

Carolyn See has published six novels: *The Rest Is Done with Mirrors*; *Mothers, Daughters*; *Rhine Maidens*; *Golden Days*; *Making History* and *The Handyman*. She also authored three novels as one-third of "Monica Highland" (with Lisa See and John Espey). Her nonfiction includes *Blue Money* and the family memoir, *Dreaming: Hard Luck and Good Times in America*.

Maurya Simon's collections of poetry include *The Enchanted Room*; *Days of Awe*; *Speaking in Tongues*; *The Golden Labyrinth* and *Weavers*. Her poems have been included in such anthologies as *The Erotic Spirit*; *Dog Music*; *What Will Suffice*; *Articulations*; *Atomic Ghost: Poets Respond to the Nuclear Age*; *Marriage: An Anthology*; *In My Mother's Garden*; *Changing Light*; *Blood to Remember: American Poets on the Holocaust* and *Anthology of Magazine Verse and Yearbook of American Poetry*.

Jane Smiley's fiction includes *Barn Blind*; *At Paradise Gate*; *Duplicate Keys*; *The Age of Grief*; *The Greenlanders*; *Ordinary Love and Good Will*; *A Thousand Acres* (which won the Pulitzer Prize and other major awards), *Moo* and *The All-True Travels and Adventures of Lidie Newton*.

David St. John poetry collections include *Hush*; *The Short*; *No Heaven*; *Terrace of Rain: An Italian Sketchbook*; *Study for the World's Body: New and Selected Poems*; *In the Pines: Lost Poems 1972-1997* and *The Red Leaves of Night*. He also authored *Where the Angels Come Toward Us: Selected Essays, Reviews, and Interviews*. St. John is Editor-at-Large of *The Antioch Review*, as well as Director of Creative Writing at The University of Southern California.

Mark Strand, a former Poet Laureate of the United States and MacArthur Fellowship winner, has published poetry collections that include *Sleeping With One Eye Open*; *Reasons for Moving*; *Darker*; *The Story of Our Lives*; *The Late Hour*; *Selected Poems*; *The Continuous Life*; *Dark Harbor* and *Blizzard of One*. He has also written a book of short stories, *Mr. and Mrs. Baby and Other Stories*, and a comic meditation on literary immortality, *The Monument*. In addition to several poetry translations, three poetry anthologies and a number of books and articles on art, Strand has authored three children's books: *The Planet of Lost Things*, *The Night Book* and *Rembrandt Takes a Walk*.

Henry Taylor is the author of several poetry collections, including *The Flying Change*, which won the Pulitzer Prize. Others are *The Horse Show at Midnight*; *An Afternoon of Pocket Billiards* and *Understanding Fiction: Poems 1986-1996*. He has also written a textbook, *Poetry: Points of Departure*, and a book of essays, *Compulsory Figures: Essays on Recent American Poets*. He is co-director of the MFA program in Creative Writing at the American University, in Washington, D.C.

David L. Ulin is the author of a book of poems, *Cape Cod Blues*. His fiction and poetry have appeared in *Vignette; Exquisite Corpse; Bakunin; The Brooklyn Review; Sensitive Skin; B City; Caffeine; New Observations; Rampike* and the anthology *Unbearables*. He has had essays and criticism published in *The Nation; Village Voice; GQ; Newsday; The Chicago Tribune; San Francisco Chronicle; Los Angeles Times* and *L.A. Weekly*. He is a contributing editor to *The Bloomsbury Review*. His book of cultural criticism entitled *Kerouac's Ghost* is forthcoming.

Michael Ventura's novels include *Shadow Dancing in the USA, Night Time Losing Time, The Zoo Where You're Fed to God,* and *The Death of Frank Sinatra*. He also wrote the screenplays for *Roadie* and *Echo Park,* and he has published essays and nonfiction books, including *We've Had a Hundred Years of Psychotherapy and the World's Getting Worse* (with James Hillman, 1992) and *Letters at 3 AM*.

Ellery Washington C. has had short fiction published or forthcoming in *Puerto del Sol* and *The Berkeley Fiction Review*. An excerpt from his first novel, *Scenes of Substance and Other Still Lifes Wasted,* is forthcoming in *Griots Beneath the Baobab: Tales from Los Angeles,* an anthology of African American writers.

Weatherly (a.k.a. Thomas Elias Weatherly) is a poet whose collections include *Maumau American Cantos* and *Thumbprint*. He also co-edited an anthology, *Natural Process: New Black Poets*. His poetry has most recently appeared in *The Garden Thrives: Twentieth Century African American Poetry* and *American Poetry Since 1970: Up Late, 2nd Edition*.

Charles Harper Webb was awarded the Samuel French Morse Poetry Prize and the Kate Tufts Discovery Award for his collection, *Reading the Water*. His other poetry collections include *Zinjanthropus Disease; Everyday Outrages; A Weeb for All Seasons* and *Dr. Invisible and Mr. Hide*. He edited *Stand Up Poetry: The Anthology* and co-edited *Grand Passion: The Poets of Los Angeles and Beyond*. He is also the author of a novel, *The Wilderness Effect,* and a book of poetry and psychology, *Poetry That Heals*.

Richard Wilbur, a former Poet Laureate of the United States, has been awarded the Pulitzer Prize for both *Things of This World* and for *New and Collected Poems*. His other poetry collections are *The Beautiful Changes and Other Poems; Ceremony and Other Poems; Advice to a Prophet and Other Poems; Walking to Sleep: New Poems and Translations* and *The Mind-Reader*. He has also written several books for children, including *Opposites; More Opposites; A Game of Catch* and *The Disappearing Alphabet,* as well as two collections of literary essays, *Responses: Prose Pieces 1953-1976* and *The Catbird's Song*.

Hilma Wolitzer's novels include *Ending; In the Flesh; Hearts; In the Palomar Arms; Silver* and *Tunnel of Love*. She has also written several novels for young readers.

Stephen Yenser has published a volume of poetry, *The Fire in All Things,* as well as books of criticism: *The Consuming Myth: The Work of James Merrill; Circle to Circle: The Poetry of Robert Lowell* and the forthcoming *A Boundless Field: American Poetry at the Century's Turning*. Yenser directs the Creative Writing Program in the English Major at UCLA.

Notes

Introduction

relatively new term. Flow is similar to White's notion of competence (1959), deCharms' concept of personal causation (1968), Bandura's effectance motivation (1977), Deci & Ryan's autonomy (1985) and Amabile's intrinsic motivation (1983, 1985). Also, Maslow's descriptions of self-actualization (1968) and peak experiences (1970) relate to flow, as does transcendence (1971), in which one loses self-consciousness, self-awareness and the normal sense of time.

Flow is not exactly the same as peak experience, though there are many parallels. Maslow suggested that many people are capable of temporary states of self-actualizing creativeness, or peak experiences, which occur when an individual becomes a "spontaneous, coordinated, efficient organism, functioning like an animal without conflict or split, without hesitation or doubt, in a great flow of power that is so peculiarly effortless, that it may become like play, masterful, virtuoso-like" (Maslow, 1970, p. 164).

Privette & Bundrick (1989, 1991) differentiated among peak experience, peak performance and flow. Peak experience relates to intense joy or a moment of the greatest happiness, while the definition of peak performance is optimal functioning. A study of the peak experiences of artists (Yeagle, Privette, & Dunham, 1989) found that the majority of their peak experiences, those moments that elicited the greatest joy, were triggered by activities involving beauty or creativity, contemplation of nature and sexual love. While the qualities of absorption, meaning and creativity in the Yeagle et al. study overlap common aspects of flow, the triggering events for peak experiences were not necessarily the ones that trigger flow. It is possible for a flow experience to be characterized by neither optimal performance nor intensity of feeling. Rather, more typically, "Flow is fun" (Privette & Bundrick, 1991, p. 171).

essential and universal human experience. Flow is experienced similarly across age, gender and cultural lines (Massimini, Csikszentmihalyi, & Fave, 1988). [Csikszentmihalyi is pronounced "chick-sent-me-high."]

one researcher has found. Bruner (1979) writes that he asked about a dozen of his "most creative and productive friends whether they knew what I meant as far as their own work was concerned," regarding entering into a state of full absorption when they are most creative. "All of them replied with one or another form of sheepishness, most of them commenting that one did not talk about this kind of personal thing" (p. 25).

Novelist Howard Norman said at a meeting of a book group (September 23, 1998) in Brentwood, California, when asked about his creative process, "When I get together with other writers, we don't talk about this sort of thing."

doctoral dissertation. Perry (1996).

Chapter one

following requirements. What it takes, generally, to enter flow in any activity, including creative endeavors, has been reported by Csikszentmihalyi (1996, 1993, 1990, 1988, 1975).

athletic activities. Jackson (1996) and Jackson and Csikszentmihalyi (1999) have examined flow in elite athletes. De Koven (1978) writes in particular about the pleasures of cooperative games.

computer games. Turkle (1984). Spending time on-line can also lead to flow, according to research by Vanderbilt University marketing professors Donna Hoffman and Thomas Novak, discussed in a *Los Angeles Times* Cybernews column by Geirland, J. and Sonesh-Kedar, E. (1998).

pleasure reading. Nell (1988).

live life more fully. Being in a state of flow has a number of consequences: it makes people happier, leads to creativity, enhances peak performance, is conducive to talent development for students, increases worker productivity, raises self-esteem, reduces stress and may lead to clinical healing through improving the quality of life (Csikszentmihalyi, 1993). Flow may confer a survival advantage to the human species as well, since it encourages exploration, risk-taking and skill development. "It is likely that . . . meeting of difficult challenges became genetically linked with a form of pleasure," writes Csikszentmihalyi (1985, p. 496). When individuals are bored or frustrated, they are moved to take action, make changes and develop in more complex ways (Csikszentmihalyi & Rathunde, 1993).

we make it happen when our mind. The physiological components of flow are less well-known than the purely subjective, except that it appears that the monitoring of time is mostly a left-hemisphere activity. "We know from EEG recordings that left-hemisphere activity becomes reduced, so it's not surprising that its time-monitoring capabilities are inhibited," said exercise researcher Brad Hatfield (quoted in Dorfman, 1985, p. 26). In addition, according to Princeton Biofeedback Center Director Lester Fehmi, during flow, the brain's right and left hemispheres produce brain waves more in synchrony than usual ("Go with the Flow," 1995).

decided to use the word *flow*. Csikszentmihalyi noted this in *Beyond Boredom and Anxiety* (1975).

He and his colleagues. Csikszentmihalyi (1990), p. 74.

David Crosby, a musician. Quoted in Boyd (1992), p. 81.

British singer Graham Bell. Quoted in Boyd (1992), p. 161.

a rock-climber. This quote is from Csikszentmihalyi (1975), p. 92.

Anna Karenina. This excerpt is from Tolstoy, L. (1993), p. 286-289.

no single point at which sleep appears. See Adler (1993).

shift to sexual arousal. See Davis (1983).

creators do not learn to increase. The theory that the more artistic or scientific works you produce over a lifetime, the more great works you may produce, comes from Dean Simonton's extensively detailed empirical studies of eminent creators over time (clarified in a personal conversation, July 1, 1996). For a popular account of this research, see Simonton (1994).

psychologists have studied. Blakeslee, S. (1998) discusses the work of psychologists who posit the existence of a "clock" in the human brain, powered by dopamine. They found that when one is busily involved in a task, one tends to estimate that three minutes have gone by when, in reality, *more* time has gone by (and the older you get, the more time goes by before you *feel* as though three minutes have passed). During an accident when dopamine and similar-acting chemicals flood the brain, it seems as though time is standing still or moving very slowly (and dopamine levels naturally fall as we age). It has also been expressed that "when one is interested in a book or movie, prospective time seems to collapse" (Zakay, D., and Block, R.A., 1997, p. 16). It is probably best for a writer to put all such complexities aside (does time slow, stop, collapse, stretch out?) and enjoy the undisputed alteration of *how time feels* that is a hallmark of flow and that all those who experience it say is one of flow's greatest pleasures.

"Everything is." Schuster, 1986, p. 699.

"longing for the moment." Nowotny, 1994, p. 132.

Barbara Kingsolver. Beattie (1996), p. 154.

Chapter two

such a desirable state. As to the desirability of total absorption in an activity, see, for example, Csikszentmihalyi's body of work and that of Amabile (1983, 1996). Additionally, to arrive at the conclusion that more writers value full absorption than manage to achieve it, I read more than two-hundred interviews, profiles and essays related to eminent writers (e.g., Beattie, 1996; Bell, 1994; Boruch, 1995; Brown, 1995; Calvino, 1988; Cherry, 1995; Cooper, 1996; Els, 1994; Heffron, 1994, 1995; Oates, 1983; Pack and Parini, 1991; Pearlman, 1990, 1993; Plimpton, 1976, 1981, 1984, 1986, 1988, 1992); Richter, 1988; Shelnutt,

1991, 1992; Sternburg, 1980, 1991; among many others), and interviewed or spoke with more than one-hundred writers.

stages of the creative process. These stages have been described by Wallas (1976) and accepted (or varied) by numerous other theorists and researchers (several are cited in a review by Arieti, 1976).

For a writer, this means. The complex process of creative writing has most often been studied by researchers in school and laboratory settings, where subjects have typically been students or academics who are required to publish (see, e.g., Rose, 1985). One outside-the-lab study of poets found that after a stage of preparation, "it is generally a mood which is incubated . . . [and] that the *incubated idea or mood recurs from time to time* during the incubation period" (Patrick, 1935, p. 31-32). The same study learned that the incubation period varied from person to person and from time to time within the same individual. Illumination followed incubation, and with most poets, this was when the poem was actually composed. Though most poets were in an emotional state while composing their poems, a fifth of them asserted they were not in such a state. The verification stage entailed revising, with many poets revising only minimally and a few not at all.

overlapping, and repeating parts. See, e.g., Bailin (1994) for a fine discussion of the creative process.

one researcher's description. This quote is from Shaw (1994), p. 6, who is discussing the creative process of a group of scientists.

Esther M. Friesner. Sargent (1997), p. 59-60.

John Fowles. Fowles (1969) p. 163.

Mario Vargas Llosa. Setti (1992), p. 264.

John Irving. Irving shared this at a public talk at UCLA on February 23, 1997.

Virginia Woolf's. Woolf (1927), p. 237-238.

recognized the phenomenon. It may be impossible to know, much less to express, the *precise moment* flow is entered, particularly since flow appears to occur on a continuum. "Since cognition and control—and hence consciousness—is distributed around in the brain, no moment can count as the precise moment at which each conscious event happens" (Dennett, 1991, p. 169).

Peter Davison. Davison (1991), p. 179.

Elizabeth Hand. Sargent (1997), p. 272.

not directly translatable into English. Here's another way to express why metaphor works when more direct language does not: "Metaphor reveals in subtle ways that skirt around the fringes of reality, surrounding an idea rather than pointing a finger straight at one particular aspect of interest" (Olds, 1992, pp. 39-40).

In addition, flow itself is a metaphor and thus evinces other metaphors in response, once the word has come up in discussion. A few writers told me they were in flow when they spoke or wrote their responses to my questions. Since flow is a connective sort of process, metaphors naturally occurred in their responses. Also, flow, paradoxically, although it is entered into by writers when writing, is a nonverbal psychological process. Because it is imagistic, metaphor is needed to paint a holistic picture of it for someone else. Just as one of my respondents described the difficulty of translating the movies in her mind onto the page—in effect, translating a four-dimensional scene where everything is present and is happening at once into words, imparting the desired import to each factor so that the reader can then translate them back into a four-dimensional scene that approximately matches what the writer had in mind—metaphor is a convenient way to translate a felt phenomenon into words so someone else can reconstruct it.

a professor of religion. This was said by Robert Forman, quoted in Blakeslee (1996).

brain chemistry of flow. A study (reported in a popular article by Hotz, 1998) in which the brains of Buddhist monks were scanned while they were meditating—not a wholly reliable measure—indicated that mental activity diminished in the frontal and parietal lobes, which are parts of the brain we use, among other tasks, to orient ourselves in regards to space and timing. Perhaps the same thing happens in flow when we lose touch of time and place.

erotic shift analogy. Davis (1983), p. 75.

how one becomes sexually aroused. Sex researchers (Meshorer & Meshorer, 1986) found that women who are easily and consistently orgasmic have in common the following three principles: they accept themselves, including the particular way their bodies are made to feel good; they make a conscious decision to "let it be," that is, they decide to allow themselves to be receptive to pleasure; and they surrender to nature, meaning they give up doubt and anxiety and focus on the building sensations.

flow, wrote one researcher. Keyes (1995), p. 190. One can't help but speculate as to why sex and flow are so often compared throughout these discussions. I'll suggest three possible reasons: both processes are basic and universal, both have important biological aspects and both involve a shift in consciousness to an altered state. Since sex is, in some ways, the more concrete of the two and the more well known, it's used as a metaphor for flow more often than the other way around.

Tom Robbins. Robbins said this originally in an interview published March 1988 and later reprinted in "How I Write," *Writer's Digest*, December 1995, p. 33.

Chapter three
Michael Crichton. Crichton shared this at the Los Angeles Times/UCLA Festival of Books at UCLA on April 19, 1997.

John Rechy. Rechy said this at the Los Angeles Times/UCLA Festival of Books on April 20, 1997, during a panel on "The Craft of Fiction."

Susan Straight. Straight shared this insight at the Los Angeles Times/UCLA Festival of Books April 20, 1997, during a panel on "The Craft of Fiction."

Andrew Vachs. Mehren (1998), p. E2.

Amy Tan. Tan (1996), p. 9.

Behaviorist psychology. Skinner (1971).

Less mechanistic theories. For more on nonbehaviorist theories of motivation, see, e.g., Deci (1975, 1995); Kelly (1958); Seligman (1975/1992); Bandura (1997).

Kelly. Kelly (1958), p. 47.

to feel and act helplessly. Seligman's (1975/1992) theory of learned helplessness states that some individuals quickly learn to give up hope when there seems to them to be no way they can work their way out of a dilemma—even when the initial conditions have changed and, by effort, they might now extricate themselves. Yet, "actual controllability and actual uncontrollability can produce identical expectations" (Seligman, 1975/1992, p. 49).

not focused on your ego. Hennessey & Amabile (1988).

researchers Csikszentmihalyi and Rathunde. Csikszentmihalyi & Rathunde (1993), p. 76.

challenge of the work itself. Hennessey & Amabile (1988); Russ (1993).

safety from external evaluation. Hennessey & Amabile (1988).

Karin Mack and Eric Skjei. Mack & Skjei (1979).

Frank McCourt. McCourt made this comment at the Los Angeles Times/UCLA Festival of Books at UCLA on April 20, 1997.

Terry Gilliam. Quoted in O'Neill (1995), p. 12.

Jean Cocteau. Fifield (1982), p. 75.

Elmore Leonard. Quoted in Levine (1998), p. E4.

Kelly Cherry. Cherry (1995), p. xxi.

Ray Bradbury. Bradbury (1989), p. 40.

James Lee Burke. Sipchen (1996), p. E6.

Ayala Pines. A. Pines (personal communication, August 15, 1994).

Anne Lamott. Lamott talked about her writing process on April 13, 1997, at the Mark Taper Auditorium of the Los Angeles Public Library, as part of the "Racing Toward the Millennium: Voice from the American West" series of readings.

Jonathan Kent. Quoted in Lyman (1997), p. B2.

need to beat boredom. Hamilton's (1981) study of individual differences in physiological habituation found that those who get bored easily have to find ways to continually challenge themselves if they wish to keep entering and staying in flow.

Alice McDermott. McDermott spoke to a book group at Dutton's Brentwood Books in Brentwood, California, on February 24, 1998.

Harriet Doerr. Doerr said this during her keynote address at the Pasadena Writers' Forum at Pasadena City College on March 8, 1997.

John Irving. Hansen (1988) p. 417.

Thomas Wolfe. Wolfe (1952), p. 193.

Isabel Allende. Epel (1993), p. 8.

Ursula Hegi. Hegi is quoted in McLellan (1996).

may be undermined. Hill & Amabile (1993).

reduce your inner urge. Deci (1975); Ryan (1993).

One psychologist. This quote is from Sternberg & Lubart (1995), p. 236.

as if from the outside. Deci (1975); Ryan (1993).

reduces the likelihood of entering flow. As to whether holding out a reward undermines intrinsic interest in a task and reduces the odds of entering flow, studies have come up with conflicting results, depending on how creativity was defined and the salience of the reward involved. But many such studies do find a decrease in creativity or interest following extrinsic rewards (see, e.g., Eisenberger & Selbst, 1994; Condry, 1977; Hennessey & Amabile, 1988). "It appears that the perception of a task as the means to an end is the crucial element for creativity decrements in task engagement" (Hennessey & Amabile, 1988, p. 22). Degree of task engagement directly relates to the likelihood of entering flow.

control by someone else. Hennessey & Amabile (1988).

mini-deadlines. Setting oneself explicit proximal goals that lead to larger future ones has been found to be behaviorally motivating (Bandura & Schunk, 1981, p. 587).

some theorists. Weisberg (1993); Eysenck (1995).

the conclusion that. Amabile (1983, 1996).

It's possible that. Hennessey & Amabile (1988).

negative effects of extrinsic rewards. Once you're experienced and sophisticated in a domain, you may be able to counteract any potentially negative effects of being offered a reward for doing what you like to do anyway, whereas it's possible that young people studied in most lab research have not yet learned this.

feel constrained to do them. Sansone, Weir, Harpster, & Morgan (1992).

distinction between extrinsic and intrinsic motivation. As to the complexities of when extrinsic and intrinsic motivators can be additive, see, e.g., Amabile (1996); Hennessey & Amabile (1988); Calder & Staw (1975); Harackiewicz & Elliot (1993); and Elliot & Harackiewicz (1994). Negative feedback can increase motivation, for example, if it is seen as a challenge or as purely informational by an intrinsically motivated person. "Intrinsic and extrinsic motivational orientations are also best understood as two unipolar constructs . . . Some highly autonomous individuals, while retaining high levels of intrinsic motivation toward their work, might also be highly motivated to achieve compensation for that work" (Amabile, Hill, Hennessey, & Tighe, 1994, pp. 959-965).

Jack Kerouac. Berrigan (1976), p. 383.

Christopher Isherwood. Scobie (1976), p. 239.

Donald Hall. (1993), p.4.

Hall. Hall (1993), pp. 25-26.

Martin J. Smith. McLellan (1997), p. E4.

Chapter four

Attitudes, in fact, are most. Psychologist Robert J. Sternberg is a strong proponent of the view that attitudes are of crucial importance in producing creative work, which he reiterated at the American Psychological Association Convention in San Francisco on August 15, 1998, in response to my question.

all the worldly acclaim you'd like. Regarding the complexities of how creative products are judged by society, see the work of Csikszentmihalyi (1996), Barron (1995) and Amabile (1996). If you're *too* creative, in fact, your work may not be acclaimed at all. Robert J. Sternberg (personal communication, September 9, 1998) has written an article speculating on the fact that the most creative, boundary-breaking works are less accepted by various domains than work that merely makes small leaps into originality.

creative people to be introverted. MacKinnon's (1978) study of architects found that those who are most creative hold some inner artistic standard of excellence, in addition to possessing traits of individuality, introversion, limited social engagement, self-sufficiency and initiative. That inner artistic standard of excellence fulfills the requirement for clear feedback in order to enter and remain in flow (something writers also have to provide themselves internally). In a follow-up study of those same architects twenty-five years later, using Rorschach tests, Stephanie Duduk (discussed at the American Psychological Association Convention in San Francisco on August 16, 1998) found them to have a great deal of openness, the capacity to get animated and high access to fantasy and affect.

another found them immensely demanding. Howard Gardner's (1988, 1993, 1994) studies of eminent creators from disparate realms of accomplishment revealed that individuals are not creative or noncreative in general, but are "at promise" in specific domains. Creative individuals are characterized by "a tension, or lack of fit, between the elements involved in creative work," or "fruitful asynchrony" (1994, p. 146), that motivates the person to strike out in a new direction or produce a creative product. Gardner also determined that the most highly creative individuals are very energetic, extremely demanding of themselves and others, and are prepared to use others.

found them to possess strong egos. In Frank Barron's (1988) study of fifty-six creative writers, the more creative (measured by scores on a common personality test, the MMPI) scored high on ego strength, personal effectiveness, psychological-mindedness and the ability to achieve through independent effort. It was concluded that creativity comes from a personal style that includes a tolerance for ambiguity, a willingness to resist group pressure and to form independent judgments, a preference for complexity coupled with a drive to find an underlying order, and a willingness to take risks and seize opportunities.

don't have great mood swings. Brand (1989) researched the affective side of writing by studying twenty-four actively publishing writers, eleven of whom primarily wrote poetry, six of whom wrote fiction.

found writers to be especially intuitive. Barron discusses the intuitive tendencies of creators in his Introduction to Barron, Montuori, & Barron (1997).

summing up decades of research. Barron (1997), and personal telephone conversation with Barron on September 8, 1998.

Gardner's study of eminent creators. Gardner (1993).

Frank Barron puts it. Barron (1995), p. 333.

it's a combination of being curious. McCrae (1987), p. 1258.

When researchers looked at. King, Walker, & Broyles (1996).

a blurring of the expected boundaries. Gardner (1993) found a similar phenomenon in the eminent creators he studied.

Jim Harrison. Harrison is quoted as saying this in "Jim Harrison," by Jim Fergus, *The Art of Fiction CIV*, based on an interview done in 1986.

Ursula Le Guin emphasizes. Le Guin (1989), p. 197.

Jon Kabat-Zinn. Kabat-Zinn (1994), pp. 44-45.

Charles T. Tart. C. Tart (personal communication, August 21, 1998).

playwright Sam Shepard. Joyner (1998).

it's possible to become more open. Although I usually dislike puzzles and role-playing, my husband and I have spent countless presleep minutes puzzling out the intractable game scenarios of computer adventure games, much in the way a novelist lets her presleep brain grapple with plot movement. Among my favorite games is *The Beast Within: A Gabriel Knight Mystery* (Sierra) and all the now-classic Infocom text-only games.

Anne Rice. Gilmore (1995), p. 94.

Whit Stillman, who wrote and directed. Marano (1998), p. 28.

desire for control is higher than average. Desire for control is a fairly stable and measurable personality facet, according to Burger (1992).

You are fully absorbed when. Absorption has been defined as "a disposition for having episodes of 'total' attention that fully engage one's representational . . . resources" (Tellegen & Atkinson, 1974, p. 268).

it's also been argued. Tellegen (1981).

interesting connections have been shown. For more on how absorption, openness to experience and hypnotizability may relate to one another, see Tellegen & Atkinson (1974); Glisky, Tataryn, Tobias, Kihlstrom, & McConkey (1991). In fact, absorption may be "central to an understanding of the nature of subjective experience" (Roche & McConkey, 1990, p. 91).

absorption and fantasy-proneness may also be related. Researchers who found this relationship are cited by Roche & McConkey (1990): "The findings are consistent with the notion that absorption involves a desire and readiness for affective engagement" (p. 96).

a high-absorption type. The difference between high- and low-absorption subjects is in their ability to selectively inhibit a modality-irrelevant area (Davidson, Schwartz, & Rothman, 1976).

successes of a tenacious striver. Albert Bandura discussed self-efficacy in similar terms at a session of the American Psychological Association Convention, August 16, 1998.

Ron Wallace. This information and quote are from an essay by Wallace (1997), p. 28.

time spent creating isn't always. Per Schuldberg (1994), there are some disturbing aspects of the creative process, including loss of boundaries (the experience of fluidity in conceptual or perceptual boundaries), loss of guideposts, fear of madness and fear of a failed product.

Michael Crichton. Crichton shared this with a large audience at the Los Angeles Times/UCLA Festival of Books on April 19, 1997.

advice from a sports psychologist. Sports psychologist Bob Rotella was quoted in Brubach (1997), p. 48.

that a link exists between genius. See Eysenck (1994), among others.

researchers who have scoured. Several of the studies I mention are cited by Eysenck (1994).

yet a fourth. Ludwig (1992) studied 1,005 individuals whose biographies were reviewed in *The New York Times Book Review* over a thirty-year period.

final study I'll mention. Ludwig (1994) did a study of 59 female writers and 59 members of a matched comparison group.

give them personality questionnaires. Eysenck (1994), p. 212.

When you look at the evidence. Russ (1993, 1995). Individuals can be high, medium or low on a variety of personality dimensions that contribute to creativity, and "the profile of the manic-depressive would be high on a number of these dimensions, especially during the hypomanic phase. By being high on dimensions such as divergent thinking and access to affective states, the odds of their coming up with a creative product would be increased" (1995, p. 307).

There has been some controversy over the quality of what manic-depressives create during their manic phases. You have to measure quality as well as quantity, and the latter is not simple. For a brief rundown of the issues, with additional references, see Repp (1996) and Weisberg (1996).

Chapter five

Eysenck, a noted researcher. Eysenck (1994), p. 224.

into the problem-solving process. Eysenck (1994) p. 231.

Carl Jung, comparing James Joyce. Ellman, R. (1983), p. 679. A footnote says this quote comes from a 1953 interview with Dr. Carl G. Jung.

Author Joan Didion. Didion (1980), p. 20.

personality at the looser end. Ornstein (1993), p. 71, suggests a division of the personality along a continuum of "deliberation-liberation," in which the links and mental boundaries are looser in what he calls the more liberated person, or what I'd call the person who is more loose.

looser-than-usual connection. Restak (1993).

bacteria that inhabit the human mouth. Find out more than you might want to know about such bacteria in Glausiusz (1997).

should be respected, not trivialized. How the brain works—what goes on in which half and how the halves communicate, particularly during creative activity— is an ongoing controversy among neuroscientists and psychologists. Colin Martindale, at the APA Convention, San Francisco, August 15, 1998, cited studies finding that creative people seem able to move back and forth more readily between primary and secondary process states, which relates to a continuum of arousal rather than to particular places in the brain. Primary process is the state in which ideas are randomly bumping up against each other and in which the brain shows lower cortical arousal. As attention is less focused, you can think about more than one thing at once, which can result in leaps of insight, intuition or inspiration (also see Noppe, 1996). This corresponds to my Key Three, loosening up. Martindale explained that when EEGs are used to measure arousal, their frequency decreases as arousal decreases, adding that anything that increases cortical arousal, say having your foot placed in cold water, perceiving a threat or being offered a reward, makes your responses to paper and pencil creativity tests less good, as well as affecting recall. The problem with EEGs, though, is that they can only tell us something useful if performed with an appropriate control state and activation procedure, and even something unrecognized, like being worried about what your spouse's headache means, can affect the readings.

More relevant to creative writers, individuals who are more creative have shown a lower baseline level of cortical arousal when they are asked to think of a story. Lower arousal means that, measured by EEG, electrical charges are moving through clusters of neurons in the brain's cells at a slower rate; in delta, for instance, which occurs during sleep, the rate is approximately 1-4 cycles per second, or hertz [Hz]. Theta is a little faster, though still deeply relaxed, and then comes alpha, at about 7-13Hz. Beta, normal waking consciousness, can range all the way from 12 Hz to a hyper 35 Hz. Flow may be a particular state of relaxed concentration (thus, my advice to "loosen up and focus in").

A recent reevaluation of split-brain studies indicates that, contrary to what was believed earlier, the left brain is the inventive and meaning-making half (though it does its work outside of conscious awareness), while the right is more literal and truthful (Gazzaniga, 1998a). Nevertheless, another point made by neuroscientist Gazzaniga is that 98 percent of what goes on in the brain is outside of our conscious awareness (1998b). Finally, you need both halves to be creative:

> The microsystem in the left hemisphere is certainly capable of creativity and leaps of insight. A point-to-point analysis allows us to check the world closely and to manipulate it with precision. So part of the final difference is that the distinction is not language versus non-language, perception versus nonperception, or different senses connected to each side. Rather, it's an understanding of meaning, the small meaning of events and the overall meaning of a situation (Ornstein, 1998, p. 158).

extraordinarily playful. Flow can even inspire *giddiness*, "the emotional acceleration and pleasure involved in the playful, excited or driven phases of creative work" (Schuldberg, 1994, p. 88).

interview with actor Jim Carrey. Kronke (1998), p. 32.

self-help books for writers. See, i.e., N. Goldberg (1986); Cook (1992); B. Goldberg (1996).

Lillian Hoban . . . her obituary quoted her. Saxon (1998), p. 26.

Bill Watterson. I discovered this tidbit of information in "Walter Scott's Personality Parade," in the September 7, 1997, issue of *Parade*, on page 2.

choose several apparently unrelated items. This exercise was suggested by Thomas Lynch in "Notes on 'A note on the rapture to his true love,' " in a special issue of *Poetry East*, No. 43, Fall 1996, called "Origins: Poets on the Composition Process."

Chapter six

Typically, if your attention. Wicklund (1979).

a journalist interviewed. Shainberg (1989), p. 35.

A researcher found that those who performed well. Hamilton (1981), p. 282. It's also been noted that differences in attentional capacity may explain creativity differences among individuals. The more the person's attentional capacity, the more likely he is able to make combinational, creative leaps. According to Martindale (1995), attention must be narrowly focused during the preparation phase of the creative process. During incubation, the creative person's mind will keep working at the problem, and when a relevant node is activated, attention will be brought to it, resulting in inspiration. Attention is again focused during the verification stage. Flow entry can occur at any segment of the process during which focus is intense.

give yourself an assignment. This exercise is suggested in Elbow (1998), where Elbow credits Kenneth Koch with originating the idea. I've changed it somewhat here.

psychologist Ellen J. Langer. Langer (1997), p. 23.

paying attention in those situations. Langer (1997), p. 39.

Lawrence Block. Block (1997), p. 29.

Letty Cottin Pogrebin. Pogrebin (1996), p. 33.

Milton Erickson. Erickson (1969/1990), pp. 60-61.

Erickson concluded that. Erickson (1969/1990), p. 86.

your field of focus must. A contracted frame of reference seems to be integral to entry into trance states (Shor, 1969/1990), similar to the narrowed field of flow entry.

good hypnotic subject. Shor (1969/1990), p. 284. Several studies cited by Spanos (1996) indicate, though, that hypnosis does not actually produce a trance state that is a unique form of consciousness, and that it is much more ordinary than it initially appears. It is possible, then, that trance and flow are actually more alike than previously supposed.

forms of altered consciousness. "To be moved, captivated, spellbound, signify to be possessed by something; and without such a fascination and the emotional tension associated with it, no concentration, no lasting interest, no creative process are possible. Every possession can justifiably be interpreted either as a one-sided narrowing or as in intensification and deepening" (Neumann, 1959, pp. 177-78).

Thomas B. Morgan. Morgan (1983).

Janet Burroway. Burroway (1980), p. 187.

William Maxwell. Seabrook & Plimpton (1986), p. 53.

Henry Miller. Quoted in "Miller's Tales" in "The Talk of the Town" in *The New Yorker* issue for April 11, 1994, p. 35.

Neil Simon. Mitchell (1995), p. 7.

Stephen Spender. Stitt (1984), p. 72.

Conrad Richter. Richter (1988), p. 82.

Amy Tan. Epel (1993), p. 284.

slice the salami. This was one of the more pertinent ideas that came up when I got together with a small group of writers for what we called a "Time Symposium" (August 5, 1998). We sipped iced tea and ate peanuts on a balcony overlooking the hills of Silverlake (until it got so hot we had to adjourn to the shady lower level of the garden), while discussing how best to tackle time management. Indeed, Rosenberg & Lah (1982) determined that writing behavior increased when the goal was presented as something to be reached through chaining of smaller, more manageable tasks.

other writers have called this. Mack and Skjei (1979), p. 56.

make an outline. Rosenberg & Lah (1982).

Chapter seven
Mario Vargas Llosa. Setti (1992), p. 265.

able to adapt and shift position. As Gruber (1986) suggested, in order to fill out our theories of creativity, we need to understand how the writer or other creator shuttles between "*surrendering* himself or herself to the requirements of the task and *mobilizing* every personal resource to surmount its difficulties" (p. 259). This back-and-forth movement of the writer between letting go and resuming critical analysis of what the less conscious mind has proffered is what entering and leaving flow is all about.

one researcher found that. Brand (1989), p. 15.

Howard Norman. At a book group meeting at Dutton's Brentwood Books on September 23, 1998.

Toni Morrison. Morrison said this at Holman United Methodist Church in Los Angeles, at a reading sponsored by Esowon Books, on July 24, 1998.

learned helplessness. Seligman (1975/1992).

an alternate kind. The psychoanalyst Ernst Kris (1976), describing essentially the same phenomenon as flow, wrote that during a creative act the individual moved from what he called secondary process (logical, analytical, reality-oriented) cognition to primary process (analogical, free-associative) cognition. The latter took over during the initial inspirational phase, Kris believed, followed by a stage of elaboration during which secondary process thought returned.

dominance in spatial tasks. See, e.g, Perkins (1981).

brain studies. Cited by Restak (1993).

left brain to right brain shift. See, e.g., Edwards (1979/1989).

other writers' manuals. See, e.g., Goldberg (1986); Heard (1995).

work best in a mix. See, e.g., Perkins (1981); Ehrenwald (1986).

the process of creating. Bailin (1994), p. 67.

Rollo May said it well. May (1975), p. 49.

Edward Hirsch. Hirsch (1995), p. 174.

few artists, in fact, would insist. In his study of the place of creativity in a market-driven society, Hyde (1979), p. 144, discusses this sense of the work arriving to the artist as a gift, which then the artist feels compelled to pass along to others.

free flow of ideas be inhibited. To experience a "free flow of ideas" is a subjective phenomenon, not necessarily related to the rating an outside critic would give your finished work. A study of university freshmen by Roen & Willey (1988) concluded that attending to audience can be effective for improving the overall quality of writing, but that this strategy is less effective in the drafting stage than in the revision stage.

to focus on the eventual audience. I came across an amusing "letter to the editor" by Robert Neuwirth in *Harper's Magazine* (December 1996, vol. 293, no. 1759, p. 78) on this topic: "Kurt Vonnegut argues [Letters, July] that writing is therapy. Then David Foster Wallace [Letters, September] replies that Vonnegut is 'full of shit': authors must think about their audience. So the guy who writes slim, readable books is saying that he writes only for himself, while the guy whose latest book contains more than one thousand pages of pyrotechnics is arguing that writers must consider their readers. What the hell is going on here?"

Obviously, what's going on is that this particular reader's belief in the preferences of Wallace's audience contradicts Wallace's opinion. Each creative writer envisions a distinct audience. Some readers delight in delving into one thousand pages of pyrotechnics and appreciate that Wallace has thought of them. Those who don't are not the audience Wallace has considered.

Once again proving that (almost) all generalizations are wrong, here's a quote by W.P. Kinsella, author of *Shoeless Joe*, from which the movie *Field of Dreams* was made: "I always aim for the largest possible market; anyone who doesn't is a fool" (Thorndike, 1994, p. 1).

Chitra Banerjee Divakaruni once said in an interview. On April 9, 1998, in "A Woman's Places: A Conversation With Chitra B. Divakaruni," on the Web site of *Atlantic Unbound.*

Desmond Morris worked with a chimp. Morris is quoted in Boxer (1997), p. A15.

Hall described his process. Blue (1995), p. 1.

I asked Melanie Lee Johnston. Johnston (1999).

Chapter eight
following passage by a novelist. Stevenson (1995), pp. 5-6.

family pressures . . . impinge on a creative life. See the classic essays by Tillie Olsen (1978) and Virginia Woolf (1929), as well as a recent set of interviews with writers about balancing motherhood with work in Rosenberg (1996).

Playing Smart. Perry (1990).

immediacy of feedback. M. Csikszentmihalyi (personal communication, January 10, 1996).

Martha Soukup. *Nebula Awards 30* (1996), pp. 222-223.

one researcher who has studied ways. Boice (1994).

Chapter nine
Maurice Sendak. Epel (1993), p. 231.

has ever worked as well. The process of effective self-regulation and changing persistent habits is complicated and goes beyond the scope of this study (see Baumeister, Heatherton, & Tice, 1994, for an enlightening discussion of self-control theory).

Gore Vidal. Clarke (1981), p. 311.

all it takes is starting to work. In the Massimini et al. study (1988) of the onset of flow, 40 percent of the respondents' answers related to "the activity itself."

James Lee Burke. Sipchen (1996), p. E6.

Margaret Atwood. Gibson (1992), p. 4. Atwood also has an assistant who screens interview requests, thus protecting her from the temptation to stray from her focus on writing.

regulate your internal state. According to Goleman (1988), one of the neurophysiological aspects of flow is finely tuned cortical specificity, allowing skilled flexibility in meeting the demands of the environment. "The person who is chronically anxious, or habitually locked into *any* given configuration of arousal, is likely to confront more situations where his internal state is inappropriate for optimal fit with environmental demands—that is, non-flow" (p. 182).

Madison Smartt Bell. Bell (1996), p. 14.

help you focus attention. Goleman (1988).

Joyce Carol Oates. Oates described her writing process for a book group discussion at Dutton's Brentwood Books on October 28, 1997.

Michael Crichton. Dutka (1993), p. 74.

Annie Dillard. Dillard (1989), pp. 49-50.

silencing the internal critic. Goodwin (1988).

James Lee Burke. Steinberg (1995), p. 35.

Malcolm Cowley. Young (1986), p. 11.

Hemingway is well known for. Phillips (1984), p. 43.

Malcolm Cowley. McCall & Plimpton (1986), p. 12.

John Irving. Gussow (1998), p. B1-6.

A vast catalog of. A variety of odd rituals are detailed in an essay by Diane Ackerman (1989), which was adapted from her book (1990).

Chapter ten

popular advice books for writers. See, for example, Keyes (1995); Friedman (1993); Lamott, (1994); Bolker (1997); Simon (1997).

sexual dysfunction can be divided. Weeks (1987).

a lack of social supports. Bloom (1985) categorized the contexts of writing blocks this way: intellectual factors (knowledge of subject, writing skills), artistic factors (whether the artist is creative, independent, insightful, risk-taking, rule-breaking), temperamental factors (motivation), biological factors (health, energy), emotional factors (fears) and external contexts.

intrusions have denied many women. Ochse (1991).

writer's life is frequently conflicted. See the conversations on women's conflicts compiled by Chamberlain (1988).

researchers have found. Selfe (1985).

Lawrence Weschler. At a book group meeting at Dutton's Brentwood Books on June 2, 1998.

studies of writer's block. Boice (1985); Bruce, Collins, Rubins, & Guentner (1982); Roen & Willey (1988); Larson (1988); Rose (1984); Daly (1985); Bloom (1985).

have all been implicated. Boice (1985).

writers who block have been found. Boice (1985).

Much of the difficulty. Bruce, Collins, Rubins, & Guentner (1982).

one psychiatrist. Kantor (1995). One of Kantor's *less* constructive suggestions is for blocked writers to understand that the reason audiences and critics "mistreat" artists is because they are jealous. It seems to me more realistic to realize that critics are paid to use their own idiosyncratic perceptions and standards when they write reviews, and that audiences are generally fickle. The writer who finds a way to hold fast to his or her *own* ideals, whether writing entertainment or highly artistic prose or poetry, is on a smoother track toward avoiding frequent or long-lasting blocks.

Studies done on high school students. Larson (1988).

Another study. Rose (1984).

bound to feel apprehensive. Daly (1985).

psychologist who is also a poet. Kolodny (1997).

more writing equals better writing. Far from being spontaneous and mysterious, creativity is often the result of countless hours of preparation, education and practice in a particular domain. Any artist has to master the domain before becoming capable of making a genuinely creative contribution. When you listen, for instance, to a musician play for an hour, you aren't seeing "the over 10,000 hours of deliberate practice that preceded the performance . . . Given that the extended prior preparation is not visible or even known to some of the members of the audience, the virtuoso performance is perceived as truly exceptional and so far removed from the level attainable by amateur musicians that nothing less than innate talents seems to be able to explain it" (Ericsson, 1998, p. 95).

John Nichols. Benke (1997), p. 8.

Anne Lamott. Lamott (1994).

Faye Kellerman. Kellerman discussed her origins as a writer at a session of the American Psychology Association's 106th Annual Convention in San Francisco, on August 14, 1998.

a sociologist. Sociologist Robert Faulker's research is described in a popular article by Cohen (1998).

offered by a psychologist in his book. Fiore (1989), p. 109.

a form of courage. Keyes (1995).

Procrastination at the start. See, for example, Mack & Skjei (1979); Cook (1992); Selfe (1985); Keyes (1995).

Mack and Skjei. Mack & Skjei (1979), p. 59.

researchers who have specifically studied. See, especially, Daly (1985); Salovey & Harr (1990); and Boice (1994).

group of writers in one experiment. Boice (1983).

rated their work as being creative. "Clients who were forced to write by powerful external contingencies not only produced more writing, but they also conjured more novel and useful ideas than did clients who wrote when they felt like it" (Boice, 1983, p. 205). Of course, self-reports of creativity may not be the most accurate indicators. As is to be expected, when the external contingencies were removed, output lessened dramatically.

Later, Boice (1994) compiled in some detail the six steps to writing fluency that he found effective for a sample of 52 writers who had taken his course, half of whom were nonacademic writers. Boice's recommended program takes as long as a year to produce optimal results. His guidelines for writers who would "journey to comfort and fluency" are explicit, though, as he admitted in his introduction, occasionally contradictory. For instance, Rule #1 is "Wait," by which he meant to ready oneself sufficiently for the writing, while Rule #2 is "Begin before feeling fully ready. Motivation comes most reliably in the wake of regular involvement" (p. 236). Other rules include being patient, writing regularly, stopping before becoming fatigued, spending as much time prewriting as writing, not writing in large, undisrupted blocks of time, using external pressures to keep yourself writing, using rational self-talk instead of oughts and shoulds, constraining hypomania by planning and prewriting, and getting exterior feedback early in the writing process.

benefit from forcing yourself. Daly (1985).

the recommendation to put a. See, e.g., Mack & Skjei (1979). "For the blockers in my studies, the longer away from a project, the greater the likelihood of re-blocking" (Boice, 1985, p. 211).

Dorothea Brande. Brande (1934), recently reissued.

give up writing. Brande (1934), p. 79.

References

Ackerman, D. (1989, November 12). O muse! you do make things difficult! *The New York Times Book Review.*

Ackerman, D. (1990). *A natural history of the senses.* New York: Random House.

Adler, T. (1993, September). Scientists have clearer view of body's descent into sleep. *American Psychological Association Monitor,* p. 21.

Amabile, T. M. (1983). *The social psychology of creativity.* New York: Springer Verlag.

Amabile, T.M. (1985). Motivation and creativity: Effects of motivational orientation on creative writers. *Journal of Personality and Social Psychology, 48,* 393-399.

Amabile, T.M. (1996). *Creativity in context (Update to The social psychology of creativity).* Boulder, CO: Westview Press.

Amabile, T.M., Hill, K.G., Hennessey, B.A., & Tighe, E.M. (1994). The work preference inventory: Assessing intrinsic and extrinsic motivational orientations. *Journal of Personality and Social Psychology, 66,* 5, 950-967.

Arieti, S. (1976). *Creativity: The magic synthesis.* New York: Basic Books.

Bailin, S. (1994). *Achieving extraordinary ends: An essay on creativity.* Norwood, NJ: Ablex.

Bandura, A. (1977). Self-efficacy: Toward a unifying theory of behavioral change. *Psychological Review, 84,* 191-215.

Bandura, A. (1997). *Self-Efficacy: The exercise of control.* New York. Freeman.

Bandura, A., & Schunk, D.H. (1981). Cultivating competence, self-efficacy, and intrinsic interest through proximal self-motivation. *Journal of Personality and Social Psychology, 41,* 586-598.

Barron, F. (1988). Putting creativity to work. In R.J. Sternberg, (Ed.), *The nature of creativity: Contemporary psychological perspectives* (pp. 76-98). Cambridge, England: Cambridge University Press.

Barron, F. (1995). *No rootless flower: An ecology of creativity.* Cresskill, NJ.: Hampton Press.

Barron, F., Montuori, A., & Barron, A. (Eds.) (1997). *Creators on creating.* New York: Tarcher/Putnam.

Baumeister, R.F., Heatherton, T.F., & Tice, D.M. (1994). *Losing control: How and why people fail at self-regulation.* San Diego, CA: Academic Press.

Beattie, L.E. (Ed.). (1996). *Conversations with Kentucky writers.* Lexington, KY: The University Press of Kentucky.

Bell, M. (1994). *A Marvin Bell reader: Selected poetry and prose*. Hanover, NH.: Middlebury College Press.

Bell, M.S. (1996, May/Summer). Unconscious mind: The art & soul of fiction, in *AWP Chronicle, 28,* 6, 1-14.

Benke, R. (1997, September 15). Pursuing prose in valleys and high plateaus of a writing life. *The Orange County Register,* Accent section, p. 8.

Berrigan, T. (1976). Jack Kerouac. In G. Plimpton (Ed.), *Writers at work: The Paris Review interviews, Fourth Series* (pp. 361-395). New York: Penguin.

Blakeslee, S. (1996, April 16). The conscious mind is still baffling to experts of all stripes. *The New York Times,* p. B9. [All page numbers for *The New York Times* refer to the Los Angeles area edition.]

Blakeslee, S. (1998, March 24). Running late? Researchers blame aging brain. *The New York Times,* p. B13.

Block, L. (1997, March 9). The bumpy road to inspiration. *The New York Times,* Travel section, p. 29.

Bloom, L.Z. (1985). Anxious writers in context: Graduate school and beyond. In M. Rose (Ed.), *When a writer can't write: Studies in writer's block and other composing-process problems* (pp. 119-133). New York: Guilford Press.

Blue, M. (1995, May/Summer). A conversation with Donald Hall & Jane Kenyon. *AWP Chronicle, 27,* No. 6, pp. 1-8.

Boice, R. (1983). Experimental and clinical treatments of writing blocks. *Journal of Consulting and Clinical Psychology, 51,* 183-191.

Boice, R. (1985). Cognitive components of blocking. *Written Communication, 2,* 91-104.

Boice, R. (1994). *How writers journey to comfort and fluency: A psychological adventure*. Westport, CT: Praeger.

Bolker, J. (Ed.). (1997). *The writer's home companion: an anthology of the world's best writing advice, from Keats to Kunitz.* New York: Henry Holt and Company.

Boruch, M. (1995). *Poetry's old air*. Ann Arbor, MI: The University of Michigan Press.

Boxer, S. (1997, November 8). It seems art is indeed monkey business. *The New York Times,* p. A15.

Boyd, J., with George-Warren, H. (1992). *Musicians in tune: Seventy-five contemporary musicians discuss the creative process*. New York: Fireside.

Bradbury, R. (1989). *Zen in the art of writing: Essays on creativity*. Santa Barbara, CA: Capra Press.

Brand, A.G. (1989). *The psychology of writing: The affective experience*. New York: Greenwood Press.

Brande, D. (1934). *Becoming a writer*. New York: G. P. Putnam's Sons.

Brown, K. (Ed.). (1995). *Writing it down for James: Writers on life and craft*. Boston: Beacon Press.

Brubach, H. (1997, November 2). Doc Rotella's cure for the thinking athlete. *The New York Times Magazine,* pp. 46-49.

Bruce, B., Collins, A., Rubins, A.D., & Gentner, D. (1982). Three perspectives on writing. *Educational Psychologist, 17,* 131-145.

Bruner, J. (1979). *On knowing: Essays for the left hand* (expanded ed.). Cambridge, MA: Harvard University Press.

Burger, J. M. (1992). *Desire for control.* New York: Plenum Press.

Burroway, J. (1980). Opening nights: The opening days. In J. Sternburg (Ed.), *The writer on her work* (pp. 187-215). New York: W.W. Norton.

Calder, B., & Staw, B. (1975). Self-perception of intrinsic and extrinsic motivation. *Journal of Personality and Social Psychology, 31,* 599-605.

Calvino, I. (1988). *Six memos for the next millennium.* Cambridge, MA: Harvard University Press.

Cherry, K. (1995). *Writing the world.* Columbia, MO: University of Missouri Press.

Clarke, G. (1981). Gore Vidal. In G. Plimpton (Ed.), *Writers at work: The Paris Review interviews, Fifth Series* (pp. 283-311). New York: Penguin.

Cohen, P. (1998, August 29). Sociologists with a gig off the beat. *The New York Times,* p. A13.

Condry, J. (1977). Enemies of exploration: Self-initiated versus other-initiated learning. *Journal of Personality and Social Psychology, 35,* 459-477.

Cook, M. (1992). *Freeing your creativity: A writer's guide.* Cincinnati, OH: Writer's Digest Books.

Cooper, S. (1996). *Dreams and wishes: Essays on writing for children.* New York: Margaret K. McElderberry Books.

Csikszentmihalyi, M. (1975). *Beyond boredom and anxiety.* San Francisco: Jossey-Bass.

Csikszentmihalyi, M. (1985). Reflections on enjoyment. *Perspectives in Biology and Medicine, 28,* 469-97.

Csikszentmihalyi, M. (1988). Motivation and creativity: Toward a synthesis of structural and energistic approaches to cognition. *New Ideas in Psychology, 6,* 159-176.

Csikszentmihalyi, M. (1990). *Flow: The psychology of optimal experience.* New York: HarperCollins.

Csikszentmihalyi, M. (1993). *The evolving self: A psychology for the third millennium.* New York: HarperCollins.

Csikszentmihalyi, M. (1996). *Creativity: Flow and the psychology of discovery and invention.* New York: HarperCollins.

Csikszentmihalyi, M., & Larson, R. (1987). Validity and reliability of the Experience-Sampling Method. *Journal of Nervous and Mental Disease, 175,* 526-536.

Csikszentmihalyi, M., & Rathunde, K. (1993). The measurement of flow in everyday life: Toward a theory of emergent motivation, in J. E. Jacobs, (Ed.), *Developmental perspectives on motivation.* Lincoln, NE: University of Nebraska Press.

Daly, J.A. (1985). Writing apprehension. In M. Rose (Ed.), *When a writer can't write: Studies in writer's block and other composing-process problems* (pp. 43-82). New York: Guilford Press.

Davidson, R.J., Schwartz, G.E., & Rothman, L.P. (1976). Attentional style and the self-regulation of mode-specific attention: An electroencephalographic study. *Journal of Abnormal Psychology, 85,* 611-621.

Davis, M.S. (1983). *Smut: Erotic reality/obscene ideology*. Chicago: The University of Chicago Press.

Davison, P. (1991). *One of the dangerous trades*. Ann Arbor: The University of Michigan Press.

deCharms, R. (1968). *Personal causation: The internal affective determinants of behavior*. New York: Academic Press.

Deci, E.L. (1975). *Intrinsic motivation*. New York: Plenum Press.

Deci, E.L., & Ryan, R.M. (1985). *Intrinsic motivation and self-determination in human behavior*. New York: Plenum Press.

De Koven, B. (1978). *The well-played game: A player's philosophy*. Garden City, NY: Anchor Press/Doubleday.

Dennett, D.C. (1991). *Consciousness explained*. Boston: Little, Brown and Company.

Didion, J. (1980). Why I write. In Sternburg, J. (Ed.). *The writer on her work* (pp. 17-25). New York: W. W. Norton.

Dillard, A. (1989). *The writing life*. New York: Harper & Row.

A *Directory of American poets and fiction writers* (1995-1996 ed.). (1995). New York: Poets & Writers.

Dorfman, A. (1985, June). Racing the brain. *Science Digest*, p. 26.

Dutka, E. (1993, May 16). With the player, you get a brain. *Los Angeles Times Calendar* section, pp. 3, 74, 76.

Edwards, B. (1979/1989). *Drawing on the right side of the brain*. Los Angeles: J.P. Tarcher.

Ehrenwald, J. (1986). *Anatomy of genius: Split brains and global minds*. New York: Human Sciences Press.

Eisenberger, R., & Selbst, M. (1994). Does reward increase or decrease creativity? *Journal of Personality and Social Psychology*, 66, 1116-1127.

Elbow, P. (1998). *Writing with power: Techniques for mastering the writing process*, Second Edition. New York: Oxford University Press.

Elliot, A.J., & Harackiewicz, J.M. (1994). Goal setting, achievement orientation, and intrinsic motivation: A mediational analysis. *Journal of Personality and Social Psychology*, 66, 5, 968- 980.

Ellman, R. (1983). *James Joyce*. Oxford: Oxford University Press.

Els, S.M. (1994). *Into the deep: A writer's look at creativity*. Portsmouth, NH: Heinemann.

Epel, N. (1993). *Writers dreaming*. New York: Carol Southern Books.

Erickson, M.H. (1969/1990). A special inquiry with Aldous Huxley into the nature and character of various states of consciousness. In C.T. Tart (Ed.), *Altered states of consciousness*, Revised edition (pp. 58-90). San Francisco: HarperSanFrancisco.

Ericsson, K.A. (1998). The scientific study of expert levels of performance: general implications for optimal learning and creativity. *High Ability Studies*, 9 (1), pp. 75-100.

Eysenck, H.J. (1994). The measurement of creativity. In M.A. Boden (Ed.), *Dimensions of creativity*. (pp. 200-242). Cambridge, MA: The MIT Press.

Eysenck, H.J. (1995). *Genius: The natural history of creativity*. Cambridge, England: Cambridge University Press.

Fifield, W. (1982). *In search of genius*. New York: William Morrow & Co.

Fiore, N. (1989). *The Now habit: A Strategic program for overcoming procrastination and enjoying guilt-free play*. Los Angeles: Tarcher.

Fowles, J. (1969). Notes on an unfinished novel. In T. McCormack (Ed.), *Afterwords: Novelists on their novels* (pp. 161-175). New York: St. Martin's Press.

Friedman, B. (1993). *Writing past dark: Envy, fear, distractions, and other dilemmas in the writer's life*. New York: HarperPerennial.

Gardner, H. (1988). Creative lives and creative works: A synthetic scientific approach, in R.J. Sternberg (Ed.), *The nature of creativity: Contemporary psychological perspectives* (pp. 298- 321). Cambridge, England: Cambridge University Press.

Gardner, H. (1993). *Creating minds*. New York: Basic Books.

Gardner, H. (1994). The creators' patterns. In M. A. Boden (Ed.), *Dimensions of creativity* (pp. 143-158). Cambridge, MA: The MIT Press.

Gazzaniga, M. S. (1998a, July). The Split brain revisited. *Scientific American, 279* (1), pp. 51-55.

Gazzaniga, M S. (1998b). *The mind's past*. Berkeley: University of California Press.

Geirland, J. and Sonesh-Kedar, E. (July 6, 1998). What is this thing called flow? Think Nirvana on the web. *Los Angeles Times* (p. D3).

Gibson, G. (1992). Dissecting the way a writer works, in E.G. Ingersoll, (Ed.), *Margaret Atwood: Conversations* (pp. 3-19). London: Virago Press.

Gilmore, M. (1995, July 13-27). The Devil and Anne Rice. *Rolling Stone*, Issue 712-713, p. 92- 98.

Glausiusz, J. (1997, October). The good bugs on our tongues. *Discover*, pp. 32-33.

Glisky, M.L., Tataryn, D.J., Tobias, B. A., Kihlstrom, J.F., & McConkey, K.M. (1991). Absorption, openness to experience, and hypnotizability. *Journal of Personality and Social Psychology, 60*, 263-272.

Go with the flow. (1995, September). *Good Housekeeping*, p. 135.

Goldberg, B. (1996). *Room to write: Daily invitations to a writer's life*. New York: Tarcher/G.P. Putnam.

Goldberg, N. (1986). *Writing down the bones: Freeing the writer within*. Boston: Shambhala.

Goleman, D. (1988). *The meditative mind: The varieties of meditative experience*. New York: Tarcher/Perigee.

Goodwin, D. W. (1988). *Alcohol and the writer*. Kansas City, MO: Andrews and McMeel.

Gruber, H. E. (1986). The self-construction of the extraordinary. In R.J. Sternberg & J. E. Davidson (Eds.), *Conceptions of giftedness* (247-263). Cambridge, England: Cambridge University Press.

Gussow, M. (1998, April 28). A Novelist builds out from fact to reach the truth. *The New York Times*, p. B1-6.

Hall, D. (1993). *Life work*. Boston: Beacon Press.

Hamilton, J.A. (1981). Attention, personality, and the self-regulation of mood:

Absorbing interest and boredom. In B.A. Maher (Ed.), *Progress in Experimental Personality Research, 10*, 281-315.

Hansen, R. (1988). John Irving. In G. Plimpton (Ed.), *Writers at work: The Paris Review interviews, Eighth Series* (pp. 415-441). New York: Penguin.

Harackiewicz, J.M., & Elliot, A.J. (1993). Achievement goals and intrinsic motivation. *Journal of Personality and Social Psychology, 65*, 5, 904-915.

Heard, G. (1995). *Writing toward home*. Portsmouth, NH: Heinemann.

Heffron, J. (Ed.) (1994). *The best writing on writing*. Cincinnati, OH: Story Press.

Heffron, J. (Ed.) (1995). *The best writing on writing, Volume Two*. Cincinnati, OH: Story Press.

Hennessey, B.A., & Amabile, T.M. (1988). The conditions of creativity. In R.J. Sternberg (Ed.), *The nature of creativity: contemporary psychological perspectives* (pp. 11-38). Cambridge, England: Cambridge University Press.

Hill, K.G., & Amabile, T.M. (1993). A social psychological perspective on creativity: Intrinsic motivation and creativity in the classroom and workplace. In S.G. Isaksen, M.C. Murdock, R.L. Firestien, & D.J. Treffinger (Eds.), *Understanding and recognizing creativity: The emergence of a discipline* (pp. 400-432). Norwood, NJ: Ablex.

Hirsch, E. (1995). Following what you lead: The mystery of writing poetry. In K. Brown (Ed.), *Writing it down for James: Writers on life and craft* (pp.165-176). Boston: Beacon Press.

Hotz, R. L. (1998, April 26) Divining the brain's role in spirituality. *Los Angeles Times*, pp. A1, A30.

Hyde, L. (1979). *The gift: Imagination and the erotic life of property*. New York: Vintage Books.

Jackson, S.A. (1996). Toward a conceptual understanding of the flow experience in elite athletes. *Research Quarterly for Exercise and Sport, 67* (1), pp. 76-90.

Jackson, S.A. and Csikszentmihalyi, M. (1999). *Flow in sports: The keys to optional experiences and performances*. Champaign, IL: Human Kinetics.

Johnston, M.L. (1999). *Getting in the Hollywood writing game: How television's leading writers wrote their way to the top*. Scottsdale, Arizona: Burkett-Street Press.

Joyner, W. (1998, July 8). Television review: Sam Shepard, beyond the writing and acting. *The New York Times*, p. B6.

Kabat-Zinn, J. and M. (1994). *Everyday blessings: The inner work of mindful parenting*. New York: Hyperion.

Kantor, M. (1995). *Understanding writer's block: A therapist's guide to diagnosis and treatment*. Westport, CT: Praeger.

Kelly, G.A. (1958). Man's construction of his alternatives. In G. Lindzey (Ed.), *Assessment of human motives* (pp. 33-64). Westport, CT: Greenwood Press.

Keyes, R. (1995). *The courage to write: How writers transcend fear*. New York: Henry Holt.

King, L.A., Walker, L.M., & Broyles, S.J. (1996). Creativity and the Five-Factor Model. *Journal of Research in Personality, 30*, 189-203.

Kolodny, S. (1997, March/April). Writing and the psyche's assessment of danger. *AWP Chronicle, 29*, 21-25.

Kris, E. (1976). On preconscious mental processes. In A. Rothenberg, & C.R. Hausman (Eds.). *The creativity question.* (pp. 135-143). Durham, NC: Duke University Press.

Kronke, D. (1998, May 31). The (Not so) odd couple. *Los Angeles Times Calendar,* pp. 3-32.

Lamott, A. (1994). *Bird by bird: Some instructions on writing and life.* New York: Pantheon.

Larson, R. (1988). Flow and writing. In M. Csikszentmihalyi & I.S. Csikszentmihalyi (Eds.), *Optimal experience: Psychological studies of flow in consciousness* (pp. 150-171). New York: Cambridge University Press.

Le Guin, U.K. (1989). *The language of the night: Essays on fantasy and science fiction.* New York: HarperCollins.

Levine, B. (1998, January 26). Sparring partners. *Los Angeles Times,* pp. E1-4.

Ludwig, A.M. (1992). Creative achievement and psychopathology: Comparison among professions. *American Journal of Psychotherapy, 46*, 330-356.

Ludwig, A.M. (1994). Mental illness and creative activity in female writers. *American Journal of Psychiatry, 151,* (11), 1650-1656.

Lyman, R. (1997, December 4). A plucky little theater in London has big ambitions. *The New York Times,* p. B2.

Mack, K., & Skjei, E. (1979). *Overcoming writing blocks.* Los Angeles: J.P. Tarcher.

MacKinnon, D. W. (1978). *In search of human effectiveness.* New York: Creative Education Foundation.

Marano, H.E. (1998, May/June). The soul of Whit Stillman. *Psychology Today,* pp. 28-65.

Martindale, C. (1995). Creativity and connectionism. In S.M. Smith, T.B. Ward, & R.A. Finke (Eds.). *The creative cognition approach* (pp. 249-268). Cambridge, MA: MIT Press.

Maslow, A.H. (1968). *Toward a psychology of being.* New York: Van Nostrand Reinhold Company.

Maslow, A.H. (1970). *Motivation and personality,* Revised third edition. New York: HarperCollins.

Maslow, A.H. (1971). *The farther reaches of human nature.* New York: Penguin.

Massimini, F., Csikszentmihalyi, M., & Fave, A.D. (1988). Flow and biocultural evolution. In M. Csikszentmihalyi & I.S. Csikszentmihalyi (Eds.), *Optimal experience: Psychological studies of flow in consciousness,* (pp. 60-81). New York: Cambridge University Press.

May, R. (1975). *The courage to create.* New York: Bantam.

McCall, J., & Plimpton, G. (1986). Malcolm Cowley. In G. Plimpton (Ed.), *Writers at work: The Paris Review interviews, Seventh Series* (pp. 3-22). New York: Penguin.

McLellan, D. (1996, March 20). Out of silence come the writer's great works. *Los Angeles Times,* p. E4.

McLellan, D. (1997, April 6). Proving that fear isn't a tamper-resistant emotion. *Los Angeles Times*, p. E4.

McCrae, R.R. (1987). Creativity, divergent thinking, and openness to experience. *Journal of Personality and Social Psychology, 52*, 1258-1265.

Mehren, E. (1998, May 19). Brutal truths. *Los Angeles Times*, May 19, 1998, p. E2.

Meshorer, M., and Meshorer, J. (1986). *Ultimate pleasure: The secrets of easily orgasmic women*. New York: St. Martin's Press.

Mitchell, S. (1995, April 30). Neil Simon's chapter three. *Los Angeles Times*, p. 7.

Morgan, T.B. (1983, January). The power of the trance: One man's experience with self-hypnosis suggests there's something in it for everyone. *Esquire*, pp. 74-81.

Nebula Awards 30 (1996). New York: Harcourt Brace & Company, pp. 222-223.

Nell, V. (1988). *Lost in a book: The psychology of reading for pleasure*. New Haven, CT: Yale University Press.

Neumann, E. (1959). *Art and the creative unconscious*. Princeton, NJ: Princeton University Press.

Noppe, L.D. (1996). Progression in the service of the ego, cognitive styles, and creative thinking. *Creativity Research Journal*, 9, (4), 369-383.

Nowotny, H. (1994). *Time: The modern and postmodern experience*. Cambridge, England: Polity Press.

Oates, J.C. (1983). (Ed.), *First person singular: Writers on their craft*. Princeton, NJ: Ontario Review Press.

Ochse, R. (1991). Why there were relatively few eminent women creators. *The Journal of Creative Behavior, 25*, 334-344.

Olds, L.E. (1992). *Metaphors of interrelatedness: Toward a systems theory of psychology*. Albany: State University of New York Press.

Olsen, T. (1978). *Silences: Classic essays on the art of creating*. New York: Delta/ Dell.

O'Neill, S. (1995, December 29-January 4, 1996). Image isn't everything. *Los Angeles View*, pp. 11-16.

Ornstein, R. (1993). *The roots of the self*. New York: HarperCollins.

Ornstein, R. (1998). *The right mind*. San Diego: Harcourt Brace & Company.

Pack, R., & Parini, J. (Eds.). (1991). *Writers on writing: A Bread Loaf anthology*. Hanover, NH: University Press of New England.

Patrick, C. (1935). Creative thought in poets. *Archives of Psychology, 178*.

Pearlman, M. (1990). *Inter/View: Talks with America's writing women*. Lexington: University Press of Kentucky.

Pearlman, M. (1993). *Listen to their voices: 20 interviews with women who write*. Boston: Houghton Mifflin.

Perkins, D.N. (1981). *The mind's best work*. Cambridge, MA: Harvard University Press.

Perry, S.K. (1990). *Playing smart: A parent's guide to enriching, offbeat learning activities for ages 4-14*. Minneapolis, MN: Free Spirit Publishing.

Perry, S.K. (1996). *When time stops: How creative writers experience entry into the flow state.* Dissertation Abstracts International, 58(08), 4484. (Order from Dissertation Express at UMI: 800-521-3042, Order #9805789, [http://www.umi.com]). Doctoral dissertation, The Fielding Institute.

Phillips, L.W. (Ed.). (1984). *Ernest Hemingway on writing.* New York: Charles Scribner's Sons.

Plimpton, G. (Ed.). (1976). *Writers at work: The Paris Review interviews,* fourth series. New York: Penguin.

Plimpton, G. (Ed.). (1981). *Writers at work: The Paris Review interviews,* fifth series. New York: Penguin.

Plimpton, G. (Ed.). (1984). *Writers at work: The Paris Review interviews,* sixth series. New York: Penguin.

Plimpton, G. (Ed.). (1986). *Writers at work: The Paris Review interviews,* seventh series. New York: Penguin.

Plimpton, G. (Ed.). (1988). *Writers at work: The Paris Review interviews,* eighth series. New York: Penguin.

Plimpton, G. (Ed.). (1992). *Writers at work: The Paris Review interviews,* ninth series. New York: Penguin.

Pogrebin, L.C. (1996, April 21). And miles to go. *The New York Times,* Travel section, p. 33.

Privette, G., & Bundrick, C.M. (1989). Effects of triggering activity on construct events: Peak performance, peak experience, flow, average events, misery, and failure. *Journal of Social Behavior and Personality, 4,* 299-306.

Privette, G., & Bundrick, C.M. (1991). Peak experience, peak performance, and flow: Correspondence of personal descriptions and theoretical constructs. *Journal of Social Behavior and Personality, 6,* 169-88.

Repp, B.H. (1996, March). The difficulty of measuring musical quality (and quantity): Commentary on Weisberg. *Psychological Science, 7* (2), p. 121-122.

Restak, R. (1993). The creative brain. In J. Brockman, (Ed.). *Creativity* (pp.164-175). New York: Simon & Schuster.

Richter, H. (1988). *Writing to survive: The private notebooks of Conrad Richter.* Albuquerque, NM: University of New Mexico Press.

Roche, S.M., & McConkey, K.M. (1990). Absorption: Nature, assessment, and correlates. *Journal of Personality and Social Psychology, 59,* 91-101.

Roen, D.H., & Willey, R.L. (1988). The effects of audience awareness in drafting and revising. *Research in the Teaching of English, 22,* 75-88.

Rose, M. (1984). *Writer's block: The cognitive dimension.* Carbondale, IL: Southern Illinois University Press.

Rose, M. (Ed.). (1985). *When a writer can't write: Studies in writer's block and other composing-process problems.* New York: Guilford Press.

Rosenberg, H., & Lah, M.I. (1982). A comprehensive behavioral-cognitive treatment of writer's block. *Behavioral Psychotherapy, 10,* 356-363.

Rosenberg, J.P. (1996). *A question of balance: Artists and writers on motherhood.* Watsonville, CA: Papier-Mache.

Russ, S.W. (1993). *Affect and creativity: The role of affect and play in the creative process.* Hillsdale, NJ: Lawrence Erlbaum.

Russ, S.W. (1995). Poetry and science—An exceptional blend: On Jamison's *Touched with Fire: Manic-Depressive Illness and the Artistic Temperament. Creativity Research Journal,* 8, 307-310.

Ryan, R.M. (1993). Agency and organization: Intrinsic motivation, autonomy, and the self in psychological development. In J.E. Jacobs (Ed.), *Developmental perspectives on motivation* (pp. 2-56). Lincoln, NE: University of Nebraska Press.

Sansone, C., Weir, C., Harpster, L., & Morgan, C. (1992). Once a boring task always a boring task? Interest as a self-regulatory mechanism. *Journal of Personality and Social Psychology,* 63 (3), 379-390.

Sargent, P., Ed. (1997). *Nebula Awards 31.* San Diego, CA: Harvest/Harcourt Brace.

Saxon, W. (1998, August 2). *The New York Times,* p. 26.

Schuldberg, D. (1994). Giddiness and horror in the creative process. In M.P. Shaw & M.A. Runco (Eds.), *Creativity and affect* (pp. 87-101). Norwood, NJ: Ablex.

Schuster, M.M. (1986). Is the flow of time subjective? *The Review of Metaphysics,* 39, 695- 714.

Scobie, W.I. (1976). Christopher Isherwood. In G. Plimpton (Ed.), *Writers at work: The Paris Review interviews, Fourth Series* (pp. 211-242). New York: Penguin.

Seabrook, J., & Plimpton, G. (1986). William Maxwell. In G. Plimpton (Ed.), *Writers at work: The Paris Review interviews, seventh series* (pp. 41-70). New York: Penguin.

Selfe, C.L. (1985). An apprehensive writer composes. In M. Rose (Ed.), *When a writer can't write: Studies in writer's block and other composing-process problems* (pp. 83-118). New York: Guilford Press.

Seligman, M.E.P. (1975/1992). *Helplessness: On development, depression and death.* New York: W.H. Freeman and Company.

Setti, R.A. (1992). Mario Vargas Llosa. In G. Plimpton (Ed.), *Writers at work: The Paris Review interviews, ninth series* (pp. 255-276). New York: Penguin.

Shainberg, L. (1989, April 9). Finding the zone. *The New York Times Magazine,* pp. 35-39.

Shaw, M.P. (1994). Affective components of scientific creativity. In M.P. Shaw & M.A. Runco (Eds.), *Creativity and affect* (p. 3-43). Norwood, NJ: Ablex.

Shekerjian, D. (1990). *Uncommon genius: How great ideas are born.* New York: Penguin.

Shelnutt, E. (Ed.). (1991). *The confidence woman: 26 women writers at work.* Atlanta, GA: Longstreet Press.

Shelnutt, E. (Ed.). (1992). *My poor elephant: 27 male writers at work.* Atlanta, GA: Longstreet Press.

Shor, R.E. (1969/1990). Hypnosis and the concept of the generalized reality-orientation. In C. T. Tart (Ed.), *Altered states of consciousness,* Revised edition (pp. 282-314). San Francisco: HarperSanFrancisco.

Simon, R. (1997). *The writer's survival guide*. Cincinnati, Ohio: Story Press.

Simonton, D. (1994). *Greatness: Who makes history and why*. New York: The Guildford Press.

Sipchen, B. (1996, August 13). A bond with the bayou. *Los Angeles Times*. p. E6.

Skinner, B.F. (1971). *Beyond freedom and dignity*. New York: Knopf.

Spanos, N.P. (1996). *Multiple identities and false memories*. Washington, D.C.: American Psychological Association.

Steinberg, S. (Ed.). (1995). *Writing for your life #2*. Wainscott, New York: Pushcart.

Sternberg, R.J., & Lubart, T.I. (1995). *Defying the crowd: Cultivating creativity in a culture of conformity*. New York: The Free Press.

Sternburg, J. (Ed.). (1980). *The writer on her work*. New York: W. W. Norton.

Sternburg, J. (Ed.). (1991). *The writer on her work: Volume II*. New York: W.W. Norton.

Stevenson, M. (1995, May). How I write: A personal exploration of the creative writing process. *Inside English*, 5-8.

Stitt, P. (1984). Stephen Spender. In G. Plimpton (Ed.), *Writers at work: the Paris Review interviews, sixth series* (pp. 39-73). New York: Penguin.

Strickland, B. (Ed.). (1989) *On being a writer*. Cincinnati, OH: Writer's Digest Books.

Tan, A. (Fall, 1996). Required reading and other dangerous subjects. *The Threepenny Review*, 5-9.

Tellegen, A. (1981). Practicing the two disciplines for relaxation and enlightenment. *Journal of Experimental Psychology: General, 110*, 217-226.

Tellegen, A., & Atkinson, G. (1974). Openness to absorbing and self-altering experiences ("Absorption"), a trait related to hypnotic susceptibility. *Journal of Abnormal Psychology, 83*, 268-277.

Thorndike, J. (1994, December). An Interview with W.P. Kinsella. *AWP Chronicle*, Vol. 27, No. 3, p. 1.

Tolstoy, L. (1993). *Anna Karenina*. Edited and introduced by Leonard J. Kent and Nina Berberova, Constance Garnett translation revised by the editors. Modern Library Edition, NY: Random House.

Turkle, S. (1984). *The second self: Computers and the human spirit*. New York: Simon & Schuster.

Wallace, R. (1997, September). He is mad which makes two: a sonnet project. *AWP Chronicle, 30* (1), pp. 28-31.

Wallas, G. (1976). Stages in the creative process. In A. Rothenberg, and C. Hausman, (Eds.). *The creativity question*. (pp. 69-73). Durham, NC: Duke University Press.

Weeks, G.R. (1987). Systematic treatment of inhibited sexual desire. In G.R. Weeks & L. Hof (Eds.), *Integrating sex and marital therapy* (pp. 183-201). New York: Brunner/Mazel.

Weisberg, R.W. (1993). *Creativity: Beyond the myth of genius*. New York: W. H. Freeman and Co.

Weisberg, R.W. (1996, March). Causality, quality, and creativity: A Reply to Repp. *Psychological Science*, 7 (2), pp. 123-124.

White, R.W. (1959). Motivation reconsidered: The concept of competence. *Psychological Review*, 66, 297-333.

Wicklund, R.A. (1979). The influence of self-awareness on human behavior. *American Scientist*, 67, 182-193.

Wolfe, T. (1952). The story of a novel. In B. Ghiselin (Ed.), *The creative process* (pp. 186-199). New York: Mentor/New American Library.

Woolf, V. (1927). *To the lighthouse*. New York: Harcourt, Brace, & World.

Woolf, V. (1929). *A room of one's own*. San Diego, CA: Harcourt Brace Jovanovich.

Yeagle, E.H., Privette, G., & Dunham, F.Y. (1989). Highest happiness: An analysis of artists' peak experience. *Psychological Reports*, 65, 523-530.

Young, T.D. (Ed.) (1986). *Conversations with Malcolm Cowley*, Jackson: University Press of Mississippi.

Zakay, D., and Block, R.A. (1997). Temporal cognition. *Current Directions in Psychological Science*, Vol. 6, No. 1, February 1997 (pp. 12-16).

Index